RACE
FOR THE
WORLD

RACE
FOR THE
WORLD

STRATEGIES TO BUILD A
GREAT GLOBAL FIRM

LOWELL BRYAN
JANE FRASER
JEREMY OPPENHEIM
WILHELM RALL

HARVARD BUSINESS SCHOOL PRESS
BOSTON, MASSACHUSETTS

Printed in the United States of America
03 02 01 00 99   5 4 3 2

Library of Congress Cataloging-in-Publication Data

Race for the world : strategies to build a great global firm / Lowell
   Bryan, . . . [et al.].
      p.   cm.
   Includes index.
   ISBN 0-87584-846-X (alk. paper)
   1. International business enterprises—Management.
   2. International economic integration.   I. Bryan, Lowell L.
858'.049–dc21   99-18401
                                                 CIP

*The paper used in this publication meets the requirements of the
American National Standard for Permanence of Paper for Printed
Library Materials Z39.49-1984.*

CONTENTS

PREFACE

THIS BOOK is not about classic multinational management issues such as international expansion, what to do with expatriates, and managing foreign affiliates. Instead it offers a new and useful way of thinking about strategy in a world economy that is rapidly integrating.

As everyone who reads the headlines knows, the world's economy is increasingly interconnected in surprising and often inscrutable ways. Three years ago we set out to learn what we could about these new connections—between industries, companies, customers, and countries. Our research led us to conclude that the pace of economic transformation will continue to accelerate over the next several decades. In the next thirty years we will see radical economic restructuring in every industry and in every national economy. From the perspective of a historian, this transformation is happening at an incredible pace. From the perspective of a manager, it looks different. While thirty years is the blink of an eye in human history, it represents the entire career of nearly everyone reading this book. And it may seem to be too distant a time horizon

For most companies—even large multinationals—"global strategy" has been limited to modest aspirations to gain market share outside "home" countries. But that is going to change, even in industries that are local today. Our objective is to help managers think clearly about how to take on the challenges of operating in a transition economy whose pace of integration will at times seem very slow and then remarkably fast—an economy that will be confusing and uncertain.

We take a close look at several industries that are at different stages in the process of becoming global, where what economists call the "law of one price" prevails. The process of globalization, not the end state, is the focus of our inquiry. We try to show how changes in industry structures will be caused by active economic agents (i.e., aggressive companies) and the enormous opportunities to raise market capitalizations that will result. Critical to success will be pace and timing—knowing not just what to do but when to do it. The answers will come as much from action as from analysis.

We are far from alone in thinking about these issues. We have drawn widely on the research of others, including economists, historians, and management researchers and theorists. Several books in particular inspired us. Jared Diamond's Pulitzer prize–winning *Guns, Germs, and Steel: The Fates of Human Societies*[1] encouraged us to ponder the profound influence of geography on human history and, in turn, to imagine what might happen in a world in which geographic constraints were rapidly removed. In his book *The New Organizational Wealth: Managing and Measuring Knowledge Based Assets,*[2] Karl Sveiby helped us understand the potential power of intangible capital in today's economy. Peter Bernstein's book *Against the Gods: The Remarkable Story of Risk*[3] brought home to us the potential to use risk management techniques to help companies shape their own destinies. Julian Simon, in *Ultimate Resource 2*,[4] the 1996 update of his 1981 classic that stresses the importance of human creativity in overcoming limits to growth, helped contribute to our thinking about the potential to earn "increasing returns" as the forces at work in the world economy relax those limits. From a different vantage point, we found W. Brian Arthur's article "Increasing Returns and the New World of Business" in the *Harvard Business Review*[5] particularly illuminating. Out of the rich history of books on managing global enterprises, we found C. K. Prahalad and Yves L. Doz's *The Multinational Mission: Balancing Local Demands and Global Vision*,[6] C. Bartlett and S. Ghoshal's *Managing Across Borders: The Transnational Solution*,[7] and G. Hamel and C. K. Prahalad's *Competing for the Future*[8] to be particularly relevant.

One of the most important sources of research was the McKinsey Global Institute, which continues to produce a series of reports on the competitiveness of various countries. Each of these reports examined the effects of macroeconomic policy on the productivity of several industries and other measures such as job creation.

One of the Institute's leaders, Bill Lewis, urged us to consider what the differences in industry productivity, some unbelievably large, represented in terms of opportunities to individual companies. With the help of McKinsey's practice leaders in electronics, automotive, telecommunication, banking, and other sectors, we took his advice. At about the same time, another practice group in McKinsey, led by Ted Hall, finished its research on the economic and political forces, such as deregulation, that were driving globalization. This group examined the impact of changing computing and communications technology on interaction costs by drawing on proprietary McKinsey data to assess how large these costs are today and how fast they might decrease.

We would also like to mention our appreciation to Michael Patsalos-Fox, David Meen, and Jonathan Day, coleaders of a research effort investigating the "Corporation of the Future," whose work on parallel issues resulted in much common thinking and many fruitful exchanges around the forces of disaggregation and the power of intangible assets. The usual caveats apply. This book represents the views of its authors and not McKinsey. Having said that, we owe much to many.

Our editors Saul Rosenberg, Bill Matassoni, and Janet Coleman helped us shape the material through a long gestation and development process into its final form. Without the patient backstopping of our assistants Lore McKenna, Susan Bergel, Andrea Giust, and Peggy Forrest, the project could not have been brought to so successful a conclusion. And insofar as the exhibits in the book *look* good, much credit goes to Gene Zelazny, who has been making McKinsey presentations visually attractive for over thirty years.

On the content side, a number of experts enriched the book's research and helped enlighten us in areas outside our own core competencies. We would like in particular to thank Glenn Mercer (automotive), Bill Lewis and Martin Baily (McKinsey Global Institute), Diana Farrell (capital markets), and Michael Silber and Katherine Bach (medical devices). Our research team—Mike Thompson, Rajesh Sah, Tony Simone, Marc Ricks, James Kwak, Erki Viirand, and Amanda Pustilnik—labored long and hard on all aspects of the material that went into the book. And McKinsey's larger global opportunities team—Dominique Turcq, Tim Lyons, Pete Sidebottom, Jim Rosenthal, Bradley Fried, Jennifer Sturman, Josh Leibowitz, Rob Samek, Doug Beck, Jon Firester, Joel Schwartz, Orly Mishan, Erik Caspersen, David Katz, Kristin Johnsen, and Vargha Moayed—provided an intelligent, challenging audience for the material as it evolved. Their questions and responses have significantly enriched the book. Mention is also due to Jim Rosenthal, Brad Fried, and Tim Lyons for their work on "Corporate Strategy for a Globalizing World: The Market Capital Imperative," an article published in the *McKinsey Quarterly* in September 1998, which was important in the development of Chapter 4 of this book.

Others contributed in less formal ways. Ted Hall, John Stuckey, and Tsun-yan Hsieh were thought-provoking foils for us again and again. Asheet Mehta, Vijay D'Silva, Bill Fallon, James Manyika, and Byron Auguste also left their mark on the book; the first three developed the idea of a "strategic control map" that continues to be a primary tool for communicating to our clients the market challenges globalization brings. Also—and with apologies—we would like to thank those colleagues who contributed in one or another form to the final product, but whom we may inadvertently not have mentioned here by name.

Finally, insofar as we have succeeded in our goal of setting forth a powerful reading of the forces tending toward a global transformation of the world economy that is prescriptive as well as descriptive, we have to acknowledge the help received from Rajat Gupta, our managing director, who provided unfailing support through thick and thin.

Any errors and shortcomings in the manuscript, are, of course, the authors' own.

Lowell Bryan
Jane Fraser
Jeremy Oppenheim
Wilhelm Rall
January 1999

INTRODUCTION

OR THE LAST DECADE, the world's national economies
have been integrating at an unprecedented rate. The increasing mobility of capital, deregulation, and new communications and computing technologies have eliminated most
of the barriers that formerly kept these economies distinct.

Some observers have labeled these developments the "new
economy," meaning one in which consumer incomes, corporate
earnings, and stock market valuations always rise, inflation never
does, and all emerging nations grow rapidly. By the mid-1990s
investors everywhere came to believe in the glittering possibilities of this new economy, thereby creating bull markets not just
for equities but also for high-risk bonds.

But in the late summer of 1998, fear returned. The financial
crisis that began in Asia spread to most of the world outside
the United States and Europe. Nation after nation experienced

banking and currency crises, which led in turn to broader political and economic crises. Even in the United States many began to wonder if being tied closely to a global economy was such a good idea. Some political leaders called for measures to protect workers and consumers and predicted dire consequences if these measures were not taken.

Which vision of the future is to be believed? Do we face the best of times or the worst of times?

Three years ago, we launched a research effort with the objective of helping our clients manage in a "globalizing" economy. Our initial idea was straightforward: we would have discussions with twenty of our largest clients, all of which had average market capitalizations over $15 billion and extensive international operations. We would interview people at all levels of these organizations, gathering information from both the head office and the field. Then we would compile a list of best practices.

We discovered that there were few, if any, best practices. Each company's approach and situation were idiosyncratic. Most of the participants in our study found competing in multiple countries to be incredibly challenging. Many thought it easier to "stick to their knitting," playing games of inches in spite of the widely shared view that much more should be possible. Some were, in truth, properly worried about the risks.

When we reviewed our findings with executives, they all said they found the exercise worthwhile. Maybe they found it comforting to know others were struggling too. We, on the other hand, were frustrated. Our work left us with more questions than answers. We had learned how a few industries had come to be dominated by a handful of multinationals, but we saw no patterns of globalization that extended across industries and no basic principles that could be used to think about different kinds of global strategies.

Gradually we realized that, like the companies with which we had been working, we were trapped in a mindset. We had grown up in a world in which economic activity has been largely organized by geography, a world in which it is meaningful to speak of the U.S. telecommunications industry, the French banking industry, the Japanese auto industry. Consciously or unconsciously, we had been working with a *straight-line projection* of what had been taking place historically—assuming, that is, that large companies with the resources, will, and desire would continue their steady march across borders until they were doing business in every corner of the planet. The world would be one—but not really. Interactions between nations—made ever easier by political change and technological innovation—would increase, but the basic local and national industry and market structures would remain intact.

We had failed to appreciate how the world's collective economy was moving on to a new phase of integration that involved far more than simply expanding the geographic reach of individual companies across borders. Supply and demand were aggregating across larger and larger markets and fundamentally transforming how the world's economy works. We had not discovered generalizable approaches to managing in a global economy because we framed the problem as understanding the impact of adding emerging markets to the economies of developed countries. But in fact economic integration *within* Europe and *within* North America has been much of what has been driving the new economy.

It became clear that we needed to change our focus. We had to think as much about what is happening in banking in the United States and telecoms in Europe as computer components in Indonesia or electronics in Asia. So we undertook research to better understand the microeconomics of arena expansion and the interplay between access to new markets, scale, and specialization. In particular, we looked at how the structures of industry value chains were evolving as companies learned to overcome geographic and other market constraints. And we began to see how old and new industry players were not just waiting for opportunities, but accelerating the *pace* of economic integration.

We asked ourselves what it would take to win (and what "winning" is) in industries whose structures had begun to change.

Because we couldn't discuss the activities of McKinsey's clients or the confidential interviews we conducted in our early research, we studied the histories of twenty-five companies that seemed to be driving restructuring in their industries. We managed to get several of McKinsey's industry practice leaders to contribute their personal time and resources to this analysis.

From this work we concluded that the rules for developing strategy and building organizations were fundamentally different from those that applied in the postwar era. It was no longer about adding two countries a year, achieving earnings growth of 10 percent, and earning 15 percent on your capital. It became clear to us that the ability to derive competitive advantage from privileged access to markets was diminishing, as was the need to own all parts of the business system and be an insider everywhere. Increasingly, it was the economy itself, rather than the company, that was accomplishing the integration of economic activity. Now the challenge was learning how to operate across integrating economies.

The key to growth, we concluded, was more about building unassailable value propositions than gaining access to markets and "being there." As economic integration accelerates, competitive advantage comes from being the best in the world in a specific part of the economy rather than being merely good across a spectrum of activities in your local market. And being best now usually means owning superior intangibles—intellectual property, talent, brands, networks. This ability to be the best through intangibles was being driven by the freedom to specialize, which in turn was the result of several developments that make it easier for companies to find customers regardless of geographic location. In fact, customers were finding the best suppliers in the world on their own and providing these suppliers with a "free ride" on past investment.

As a result, all companies, even newcomers, could upset the relationship between assets owned and value captured, often without taking extraordinary risks! Intangible strengths were allowing them to concentrate and capture value in small slices of the business, be it a component or a highly refined skill. The goal of globalization had changed from capturing countries and markets to capturing value.

Think of an industry as a picture puzzle with each piece representing a part of the chain of suppliers, manufacturers, and service providers that currently make up its structure. On the back of each piece is a number representing its value. Now take the puzzle apart and change the shape of the pieces—cut them in half, attach them to others, discard a few, and create new ones. Then assign new values to each piece, but use a much broader and higher range of numbers. Winning in economies that are integrating will be about shaping and owning the right pieces at the right time and putting them together in new ways.

The process of economic integration is not new. It has been under way, at a slow pace, for thousands of years. What is new is the pace and the scale. After decades of slow acceleration, integration of economic activity across ever bigger territory is quickening in one industry after another.

Our industry analyses made it clear, however, that things were not going to change overnight, that in some industries "globalization" would take decades. Indeed what we realized is that the key is to focus on the pace and process of the integration. Because we do not, and will not, live in fully global markets, companies can capture extraordinary profits through cross-geographic arbitrage, taking advantage of differences in the cost of production arising from the historical separation of markets and industry structures. The real challenge will be predicting how long local price umbrellas will last, and the answer will vary for different industries and in different parts of the world.

Nevertheless, companies must begin to act now and not become complacent with their arbitraged profits. As they lose privileged access to customers, labor, capital, and technology, many of the historic determinants of cost and value advantages will disappear. The biggest returns will go to those who have world-class skills in a specialized business. As companies do more business in their specialty, they will learn more, attract more talent, and find other specialists to acquire or partner with. They will also choose which risks to take and which to shed. If they can use their specialty to reshape the value chain and structure of their industry, they will win a new, truly global competition for which they have created the rules.

So the race is a matter of building momentum and capability, not winning the world with one fateful dash to victory. The winners of the race will not necessarily be those who can sprint the fastest. Companies designed to succeed in the transition to a global economy will build flexibility into their strategic decisions, often making them later rather than sooner as more information becomes available and uncertainty on key issues dissipates.

In most industries there will be time to play midgame strategies and thereby put yourself in position to win. But reaching the high ground will be a must. We have entered into an era of rough capitalism in which the capital markets reward the strong and punish the weak. If you are not moving toward a position of strength, you will be moving away from it. The only question is how fast, and in general the answer will be faster than last year. At stake is control of your destiny.

But we are beginning to get ahead of ourselves. Let's start by focusing on the transition economy.

Lowell Bryan
January 1999

I

THE RACE

1

THE TRANSITION
ECONOMY

TODAY, ALMOST 20 PERCENT of world output—about
$6 trillion of the $28 trillion world gross domestic product
(GDP)—is produced and consumed in global markets.[1]
In these markets all the world's consumers have access to *all*
products because industry structures exist to deliver output everywhere.[2] Most consumers, then, have limited access to 80 percent
of world output because products are being delivered primarily
through local or national industry structures. But this will change.

Within thirty years we estimate at least 80 percent of world
output will be in global markets. By then, worldwide GDP will
be $91 trillion,[3] so the globally accessible arena could be $73
trillion—a twelvefold increase in thirty years (Exhibit 1-1).
Thirty years may seem a long time, but it is not if you consider
that far more economic integration will occur, if our prediction

comes true, than was achieved in the previous 13,000 years of economic history.

As global markets form in food, health care, telecommunications, media, accounting, pulp and paper, chemicals, and most other industries, the profit opportunities will be in the hundreds of billions of dollars.

Consider personal financial services. The global market for personal financial services currently represents a $300 billion annual pretax profit opportunity. Over just the next decade, this profit pool will continue to grow at its historical pace to $600 billion. But the market will also integrate. Until recently, regulations and technology limits have kept this market segmented. Therefore, no one participant has been able to capture more than 2 percent of the total global profit pool. Soon this entire market will be accessible to all players. Anyone who can capture

EXHIBIT 1-1   The size of the globalized arena will increase nearly twelvefold by 2027 *($ Trillions)*

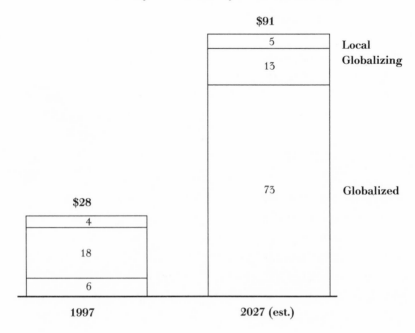

10 percent of this market will produce annual profits of about $60 billion—ten times the profits of the leading nationally based personal financial service providers in 1997.

In an economy without geographic boundaries, the rules change. The good news is that companies increasingly will have access to the best resources the world has to offer: the most talented labor, the most extensive customer markets, the most advanced technology, and the lowest-cost, highest-quality suppliers of goods and services. With such rich resources at their disposal, creative business people can go as far as their imagination, intelligence, and nerve will take them. But the risks are high because every business will be competing with the best in the world and because integrating markets are filled with volatility and uncertainty. Even those that now dominate their national and local markets will face white-hot competition. They will have to realize that what they have been calling global strategies are in reality little more than international expansion tactics.

During the transition, familiar geographically constrained economies will coexist with an emerging global economy, resulting in a confusing picture. But in confusion lies opportunity. To find opportunities in the transition economy, it is necessary to step back and reflect on the way in which geography has influenced the shape, size, business practices, roles, and economics of industries and markets.

THE POWER OF GEOGRAPHY

In the Pulitzer prize–winning book *Guns, Germs, and Steel,* Jared Diamond explores the influence of geography on human history.[4] He argues that a people's geography—comprising the food resources, climate, terrain, proximity to other peoples, raw materials, and technology accessible in their native land—is the key determinant of how societies and economies evolve: "History followed different courses for different people because of differences among people's [geographic] environments, not because of biological differences among peoples themselves" (25).[5]

Diamond tells the story of a Polynesian people, the Maori, who settled in the Pacific Islands between the years 1200 B.C. and 500 A.D. (Diamond, 53–56). We retell this ancient story here because it provides a clear example of both the potential and peril of economic integration and demonstrates the interaction of three key economic effects: access, specialization, and scale.

Some of the Maori colonized the Chatham Islands, with important economic effects on their economic development.

> *While those ancestral Maori who first colonized the Chathams may have been farmers, Maori tropical crops could not grow in the Chathams' cold climate, and the new arrivals had no alternative except to revert to being hunter-gatherers. Because, as hunter-gatherers, they did not produce crop surpluses for redistribution or storage, they could not support and feed non-hunting activities. Their prey were seals, shellfish, nesting seabirds and fish that could be captured by hand or with clubs, requiring no more elaborate technology. In addition, the Chathams are relatively small and remote islands, capable of supporting a total population of only about 2,000 hunter-gatherers. With no other accessible islands to colonize, the[y] . . . had to remain in the Chathams. (55–56)*

The Chatham Islanders had access only to each other and to the relatively sparse natural resources of their two isolated islands. Their economy could develop only to a primitive level. They lacked access to what they might have needed to develop a surplus: trading partners or agricultural techniques appropriate to their climate. They achieved economic equilibrium and remained hunters and gatherers for centuries.

Other Maori colonists, who settled in northern New Zealand, found a warmer climate that allowed them to employ their traditional agricultural methods and to accumulate surplus food.

Those Maori who remained in New Zealand increased in numbers until there were more than 200,000 of them. They developed locally dense populations chronically engaged in ferocious wars with neighboring populations. With the crop surpluses that they could grow and store, they fed craft specialists, chiefs and part-time soldiers. They needed and developed varied tools for growing their crops, fighting and making art. (65)

As their economy grew, it supported increasingly specialized, larger-scale economic activity. But every economy has natural limits to growth. If these cannot be overcome, the economy will stop growing and specialization and scale benefits will also be limited. The Chatham Islanders had reached their limit at a very primitive level of development. The northern New Zealanders faced limits as well—an agriculture-based island economy can support only so many people.

Growing beyond these limits required increased access. In 1835, "an Australian seal-hunting ship visiting the Chathams en route to New Zealand brought the news to New Zealand of islands where there is an abundance of sea and shellfish; the lakes swim with eels; and it is a land of the karaka berry . . . The inhabitants are very numerous but they do not understand how to fight and have no weapons" (57). In short order, an expedition of New Zealand warriors set forth for the Chathams promptly and slaughtered the Chatham Islanders.

Diamond's book provoked us to think about the influence of geography on the development of different industries and competitors within those industries. When we talk about geographic constraints, we mean not only physical obstacles such as mountains, oceans, and distance but also other geographic barriers to free economic exchange including interaction constraints (differences in language, standards, protocols, and cultural norms) and legal-regulatory constraints (tariffs, product-market restrictions, labor restrictions, and capital controls).

Business competition has evolved largely in response to the existence of strong geographic barriers to competition. What has differentiated economic winners from economic losers has been the ability to overcome these barriers. In a world bound by geography, privileged access to markets has been the overwhelming determinant of success. Just as geography has determined which human cultures wound up with particular economic advantages, it has also influenced which businesses wound up with competitive advantages. And as barriers erode, business competition changes. This is as true in the transition economy as it was in northern New Zealand. Indeed, the fate of the Chatham Islanders offers a cautionary tale: In the transition economy, sticking to your local markets and functioning in economic isolation makes you terribly vulnerable.

Different competitors, like different societies, have natural advantages derived from their geographic starting points. In particular, they enjoy differences in access, opportunities to specialize, and the ability to achieve scale effects. From an economist's point of view, *specialization effects* are the benefits gained from organizing work so that it is undertaken by the producers with the highest relative skill in performing each work activity. *Scale effects* are the benefits gained by being able to spread the fixed costs of production over a wider base, thus lowering average unit costs. Just as the northern New Zealand economy provided greater access, specialization, and scale benefits than the Chatham Island economy, companies growing up in large, integrated markets such as the United States or Japan have historically had much greater access to customer bases, technology, supply alternatives, and labor forces than companies operating in smaller or less economically developed or integrated economies.

However, a starting point is just a starting point. It is what you do with your native advantage that counts. Even more important than the opportunities provided by the economic home base has been skill in overcoming geographic boundaries. Companies such as Nestlé, Unilever, Shell, and ABB have proved enormously successful despite originating in small countries. A company that can systematically overcome geographic barriers gains new access, specialization, and scale advantages that lead to an even greater ability to overcome still wider geographic boundaries. This is not a new approach. Throughout history, economic advantage has been gained by leveraging these three effects. But *the means* of overcoming geographic constraints has changed greatly.

Once this was a matter of military skill. In the sixth century B.C., the Romans developed military and political techniques superior to those of its Etruscan rulers. Once free of the Etruscans, Rome used these same techniques to take advantage of political disarray among the Greek colonies of southern Italy, gaining control of the bulk of the peninsula by the third century B.C. As Rome's political and military influence grew, it overcame the geographic barriers that had historically limited social and economic integration. Roman roads facilitated the passage of armies and goods. The introduction of Roman coinage in 289 B.C. and the spread of Latin as a lingua franca facilitated economic interaction. Roman law, dating from the fifth century B.C., established a legal framework for social order and for commerce.[6]

Imperial expansion brought access to new sources of labor and raw materials, as well as an enlarged network of trade routes stretching from present-day England to India. Geographic expansion, prosperity, and growing consumer demand made possible increasing specialization of industries such as metal working in Gaul and luxury goods in the eastern Mediterranean. During its period of expansion, Rome was also able to gain scale effects, funding the costs of the empire by taxing subject territories and spreading its military officers over an army recruited from the provinces. Rome as an "active agent" became adept at overcoming geographic barriers, creating a reinforcing virtuous cycle of geographic expansion.[7] As it acquired greater geographic access, it developed increasing opportunities to gain specialization and scale effects. At its economic height in the early second century A.D., the Roman Empire created an integrated economic area embracing most of western Europe, North Africa, and the Near East.

In modern times, the active agent of economic integration shifted from conquerors to corporations. Consider the rise of Standard Oil. The modern oil industry was born in 1859 when

Edwin Drake successfully drilled for oil in western Pennsylvania. In its first decade, the industry was plagued with overcapacity and boom-or-bust cycles. Every new find depressed prices, as did each entrant that eagerly built a new refinery. John D. Rockefeller's genius lay in recognizing early on that preponderant scale would be necessary to bring order to the industry. In his words, "the larger the volume the better the opportunities for the economies, and consequently the better the opportunities for giving the public a cheaper product without . . . the dreadful competition of the late '60s ruining the business."[8] Rockefeller also recognized that access to suppliers and markets would be crucial to achieving scale.

In the formative years of the oil industry, access was rooted in geography. In the pivotal decades of the 1860s and 1870s, crude oil was produced only in the relatively inaccessible region of western Pennsylvania, and a majority of petroleum products were exported to Europe through Atlantic ports. By entering the industry through refining, Rockefeller placed himself at the center of the emerging network of petroleum flows. He then set about weakening the power of the railroads. His first refinery was built in 1863 at the conjunction of a waterway and a railroad line in Cleveland, giving him the leverage to negotiate favorable transportation rates from the oil fields and to the major terminals on the East Coast. He obtained concessions from railroads by promising constant, high-volume shipments and the necessary capacity by acquiring distressed competitors. In 1872, a scheme to establish a double cartel of refiners and railroads collapsed, but not before Rockefeller used the threat of denying others access to rail transport to buy up twenty-two of the twenty-six other Cleveland refineries. As the Standard Oil empire grew, it expanded its arsenal of competitive weapons: monopolizing the supply of tank cars to increase its stranglehold on rail transport, taking over East Coast oil terminals to control the flow of exports to Europe, and becoming the predominant builder and operator of the pipelines that served new wells in Pennsylvania. From drillhead to refinery to terminal, Rockefeller controlled access to the growing web of oil flows. Competitors had no choice but to sell out, and by 1877 he controlled 90 percent of U.S. refining capacity.

Rockefeller's strategy throughout was to use sheer size to dominate relationships with shippers and to use those relationships to increase his empire. By playing competing shippers against one another and controlling key components of the transportation system such as tank cars and pipelines, Rockefeller was able to create a virtuous cycle of geographic expansion based on ever-increasing access advantages and scale. Ultimately, by integrating backward into crude oil production and forward into retail distribution, he built Standard Oil into the world's biggest company.[9]

Not everyone who has attempted to be an active economic agent has enjoyed such success. The history of geographic expansion is littered with the failures of those who didn't quite get the formula right. At the beginning of the eighteenth century, the finest factory-made silk in the world was produced in Italy using techniques held secret for hundreds of years. In 1716, Thomas Lombe brought these techniques to Britain, where silk was made by hand. He set up a water-powered mill, hired people to run it, and began production. Lombe's strategy of specialization might have worked, but he lacked access to a sufficient volume of affluent consumers in Britain to generate scale effects, and his innovative factory failed.[10]

OVERCOMING MODERN GEOGRAPHIC BARRIERS

During this century, many of the most important geographic barriers have been man-made. After World War II, most national governments imposed controls on capital flows, foreign exchange, and interest rates, thus limiting capital mobility. Restrictions on national markets for goods, services, and labor, while promoting stability, dampened international economic activity by restricting access. Trade was frequently limited through tariffs and other barriers. Policies were put in place to subsidize or protect certain industries.

Such legal restrictions led individual nations to establish idiosyncratic industry and market structures. Bounded by regulation, consumer preferences, and culture, national and local economies evolved in distinct ways. There are local rules on how to compete for customers, labor, and capital. Often some parts of a business are overpriced relative to costs, and this overpricing helps subsidize the entire system. In telecommunications, for example, international calls might subsidize the system in some countries. In others, it might be interregional domestic calls or installation and user charges. In some countries, business customers might be favored at the expense of consumers; in others, the reverse.

The same is true within a country. In the United States, the practice of law differs so much by state that lawyers must qualify in each state in which they wish to practice. Fees earned for the same legal specialty vary enormously from state to state. Similarly in banking: until the 1990s, the states determined whether a bank could branch across state lines.[11]

It is easy to understand why a company that grew up in a geography with one set of rules and customer preferences generally has great difficulty entering another geography—even though the industry may appear very similar. Lacking access to local knowledge, customers, regulators, and politicians, foreign companies have struggled to penetrate local markets.

Some, however, have proved capable of overcoming geographic boundaries. Through hard work and patience, these active agents gained access to new customers, raw materials, labor, and technologies. As a result, they developed the capability to integrate over a wider geographic area, which enabled them to gain specialization and scale effects—leading to virtuous cycles of the sort enjoyed by the Romans and Rockefeller.

For many years, successful companies followed two basic geographic expansion strategies: *multilocal*[12] and *global*. The multilocal approach involves becoming an insider in multiple markets. This approach depends on gaining access to advantages not enjoyed by others—privileged access. Multilocal companies leveraged intangible assets[13] of course, but privileged access to capital was the power behind much of their success, allowing them to acquire local companies or build the local plants and distribution needed to become an insider.

Multilocals have historically operated in other geographic markets by building or acquiring a full business system in each geographic market—establishing production, acquiring access to local distribution channels as well as local talent, becoming adept at operating within local protocols and standards, sourcing local capital, and gaining regulatory approval. Nestlé, ABB, and Shell used this approach to cross national barriers. Bank One and the Hospital Corporation of America are examples of large companies that used this approach to overcome barriers within a single nation, the United States.

From the 1960s on, *global companies* began to emerge. The global approach leverages either specialization or scale effects (or both) to overcome geographic barriers in order to create a global market for a particular good or service. Companies seeking to globalize their products faced a set of challenges different from that facing the multilocal player: creating global demand and establishing global standards. Boeing's scale advantages in airframes and Canon's specialization advantages in 35 mm camera technology allowed them to deploy a classic global approach. In each case, their advantage "bought" them privileged access to local markets without making much local investment because local distributors and customers wanted their products so badly.

In a strange way, these global companies have much in common with the most local companies. As classic global companies grew up, they often relied on a single home-based research and development arm, located their production facilities largely in one country, and either developed a single "fly-in" or local representative sales force or relied almost exclusively on local distribution.

Global companies extrapolate what works in their own local market to the world. They are often run by managers from their home countries, and they use expatriates offshore. Their success is dependent on the quality and price of what they produce because they make little attempt to tailor to local tastes.

Global companies usually flourished in relatively large national economies where they could benefit from significant access, specialization, and scale effects. This enabled them to develop intangible assets such as patents and proprietary production techniques. Much of their success, however, was due to their access to as much capital as they needed. Historically, only a few companies succeeded by leveraging intangibles to expand globally with little reliance on physical capital. (Bechtel's leverage of its engineering talent is a rare example.)

In the last ten to fifteen years or so, leading multilocal and global companies have begun to converge around a *global-local* or *"transnational" model*, which combines the best features of the multilocal and global approaches.[14] This powerful model used by many successful companies relies on increasing the use of internal integration to capture global specialization and scale effects, while using local approaches to gain privileged access.

All these models—multilocal, global, and global-local—rely on integrating business activity across geography. They also rely on building and owning the entire business system, allowing for local distributors or captive suppliers where economical or appropriate.

ENTERING THE TRANSITION ECONOMY

The multilocal, global, and transnational models are built on privileged access to geography, capital, and technology. Now, however, we are moving toward an economic era in which privileged access will be rare if not impossible. Three forces are working together to lower most geographic barriers that have constrained economic integration since the end of World War II.[15]

First, national governments, under market pressure, are removing the legal and regulatory barriers to international economic interaction and welcoming those who have the ingenuity to turn possibilities into economic growth and profits. Second, a genuinely global capital market of enormous proportions has formed and is searching for returns. Participants who use capital wisely have incredible opportunities, as it has never been easier to tap into the capital markets. But this market is a harsh taskmaster. It rewards those who produce the results it demands but punishes those who don't. Third, rapid advances in digital technology are causing communication and computing costs to plunge. These combined forces are greatly reducing the importance of geographic barriers to commerce.

Access for all

Governments everywhere now understand they have no alternative to opening their national economies to world-class suppliers of intangible capital. Local companies that want to remain competitive seek to partner with world-class participants that have the intellectual property, talent, brands, and networks to compete in global markets. When governments open up their economies, they gain access to the skills and capabilities that companies based in other geographies have been developing for decades. In return, these companies have access to many more consumers hungry for their world-class products and services. Local companies can purchase internationally competitive inputs and know-how, dramatically raising their productivity. All players have the opportunity to generate vast new economic wealth.[16]

Until the late 1980s, there seemed little reason to expect the world's closed economies to give up the centralized management of state enterprises. Over the past decade, however, we have experienced a political and economic revolution. Around the world, governments and powerful insiders who sought to control national economies are in retreat. There has been wholesale privatization of state-owned assets in both developed and developing economies. Capital accounts are opening up as exchange and other monetary controls are lifted and foreign capital flows more freely. The shift to economic liberalism and to market-based economies is one of the defining political events of the late twentieth century, and it has happened nearly everywhere with remarkably few exceptions.[17]

This shift has not occurred because entrenched political and business leaders worldwide suddenly underwent a road-to-Damascus conversion about the benefits of doing business in an open, competitive economy. Rather, it became apparent that a certain historical approach was bankrupt. After forty years of growing state intervention in national economies, state-led development finally ran out of steam.

In many countries, the money quite simply ran out. Massive debts could no longer be serviced. Most spectacularly, we saw the collapse of the centrally planned economies of eastern Europe and the former Soviet Union. Across Latin America, we have witnessed a remarkable turnaround—from a world of import substitution and capital controls to policies that are both pro-market and pro–foreign investment. Even China has partially embraced capitalism, fueled by the influence of the extended diaspora of 57 million Chinese.[18]

These formerly closed societies have not been the only ones violently rocked. The financial market crisis that hit Indonesia, Thailand, Malaysia, and South Korea in 1997 and 1998 has reminded us how these relatively open countries nevertheless followed a central planning, state-subsidized economic model that used regulatory control over market forces and the banking system to achieve national objectives. All of these countries are now moving (however reluctantly) down the road of fundamental economic reform: removing restrictive regulation, eliminating protections and subsidies, and reforming the banking system.

Many politicians around the world do not like the loss of government control over economies. In the late summer of 1998, with emerging market countries from Southeast Asia to Russia experiencing severe economic downturns, there was talk of a globalization backlash and wishful thinking by some that the clock could be turned back. But turning the clock back is not only impossible, it is wrongheaded. The central problem with such thinking is the overwhelming evidence that open economies do better than closed economies.[19] Hong Kong and mainland China are right next door to each other. Fifty years ago, there was not much difference in the per capita GDP. Today in Hong Kong it is $20,493 (adjusted for purchasing power parity); in mainland China the figure is $3,561 even after a decade of spectacular growth.[20] Simply put, countries with open economic policies where the government has played a modest role by keeping taxes low and minimizing state ownership have done better than countries pursuing more interventionist paths (Exhibit 1-2).

As a result, an enormous array of hitherto closed markets is now offering real access to nonlocal players. Consider banking. In most of these formerly closed countries, foreign banks are being invited in for the first time. Many local banks have bankrupted themselves through a combination of government-directed loans to state-sponsored companies and ill-advised speculative lending to well-connected insiders. As the International Monetary Fund (IMF) and World Bank provide money to bridge the short-term crisis, foreign banks are being encouraged to step in with a more fundamental, long-term fix.

Perhaps less dramatic, but with equally important economic consequences, has been the deregulation of government, service, and utility sectors in many developed nations. A number of European countries, most notably the UK, realized that they can no longer afford the lethal mixture of increasing entitlements and slowing growth. They also realized the deep inefficiencies inherent in their utilities systems. As a result, global companies are emerging in the electricity supply industry, telecommunications, and water and waste management. In the future, we expect to see the emergence of global powerhouses even in education and health care provision.

It is true that in some countries the day of reckoning does not seem to have arrived just yet. Despite massive increases in the contingent liabilities of the public sector (such as underfunded social security systems) in France, Italy, Germany, and other European countries, there remains a fundamental reluctance to play by a more open set of rules. Many have met the new debt-to-GDP requirements of impending monetary union by raising taxes rather than by reducing the role of government.[21] Japan continues to drag its feet on economic liberalization, although the Asian financial crisis is accelerating reforms there as well. One way or another, the threat of financial crisis in nation after nation is forcing reform, and with reform, access.

Indeed, the real problem for companies going forward is no longer gaining access; rather, it is managing the risks of this

---

EXHIBIT 1-2   Economic freedom helps create real wealth

Freedom quintile*	Selected countries	Average per capita GDP $ Thousands, 1996	Growth of real per capita GDP Percent, 1985–1996
1	Hong Kong,** New Zealand, Singapore, Switzerland, UK, U.S.	$14.8	2.9%
2	Argentina, France, Germany, Mexico, Spain	12.4	1.8
3	Botswana, Estonia, Greece, Hungary, South Africa, Sri Lanka	6.4	1.1
4	China, Egypt, India, Nicaragua, Pakistan, Tanzania	3.1	0.1
5	Algeria, Brazil, Nepal, Nigeria, Rwanda, Zimbabwe	2.5	−1.9%

Sources: Data from I. Gwartney and R. Lawson, *Economic Freedom of the World: 1997 Annual Report*, Fraser Institute (Vancouver, B.C.), 1997.

*Freedom level determined by the following categories: money and inflation, government operations, takings and taxation, and restraints on international exchange.

**Prior to 1998 reunification with China.

more open economy. Laws and regulations are becoming far less important barriers to competition. By the same token, governments can no longer protect weak players from competition.

Capital for the strong

Accompanying the decline in the influence of governments around the world has been the extraordinary growth in the power of the global financial markets.[22] Increasingly, companies have no choice but to respond to the dictates of the capital markets.[23] If they do not, investors will look for other places to invest their risk capital or find an acquirer who will make better use of the assets. Companies will either quickly capture available opportunities through strategies the market respects, or they will be acquired or face obsolescence. Governments must also respect the power of capital markets or suffer significant premiums because their debt is judged to be of inferior quality.

In the early 1970s, the Bretton-Woods system that had essentially governed the world's financial markets since the end of World War II began to break down. The United States inflated its currency under the pressure of the Vietnam War, leading to its overvaluation relative to other currencies. As a result of persistent trade deficits by the United States, a significant stock of offshore Eurodollars built up. Everyone who could do so borrowed in dollars and invested in stronger currencies, until the pressure became too great. The system collapsed, and foreign exchange rates were allowed to float. Suddenly traders could capture "risk-free" pricing anomalies between the financial instruments in different markets. By using forward foreign exchange contracts, they could borrow at a low rate in one currency and lend at a higher rate in another without taking foreign exchange risk. Not surprisingly, as these practices quickly spread and volumes soared, the financial markets integrated speedily.[24]

By the end of the 1970s, the developed world's foreign exchange markets were substantially integrated into a single market.[25] With the subsequent integration in the 1980s of the developed world's bond market, over two-thirds of the world's liquid financial stock has now been integrated. The integration of the remaining third—the world's equity markets and the financial markets of the emerging economies—is well under way.[26]

As the global capital market integrates, the mobility of capital—driven by the need to find higher returns—increases. One illustration is the massive new flows of money into emerging markets. In 1996, foreign direct investment into these markets exceeded $138.8 billion, up from $24.2 billion in 1986.[27]

The amount of money available to finance attractive opportunities is overwhelming. In the 1990s the world became awash with liquid financial capital available for investment. We estimate that the world's stock of liquid financial assets will be nearly $80 trillion by the year 2000, more than seven times the $11 trillion total financial stock that existed in 1980 (Exhibit 1-3).[28] As a result, this glut of available capital caused risk premiums to fall worldwide. For example, the risk premium for high-yield (BB) debt above U.S. treasuries fell from the 5 to 6 percent range of the early 1990s to about 3 percent in early 1998. In early 1998, well after the Asian crisis was under way, the risk premium for emerging market paper was only 4 percent above U.S. treasuries.

This glut of capital available at low-risk premiums encouraged many players to develop the capacity and interest in making investments in physical assets throughout the world. As a result, the number of participants available to invest in physical assets to capture opportunities came to exceed the supply of attractive opportunities. In this process, the glut of liquid financial capital was transformed into a glut of physical capital exacerbating overcapacity in industries including automotive, petroleum, telecommunications, pulp and paper, chemicals, mining and metals, banking, and insurance. It is also one of the major reasons why there is already enough automotive assembly capacity built in Asia to satisfy expected Asian demand through 2010.[29] It is also one of the major reasons why deflationary pressures have developed worldwide.

By late 1998, though, fear came back, as the financial crisis that had begun in Asia spread to include most of the world outside the United States and Europe. Scared investors seeking safer havens dumped emerging market paper, small cap stocks, and the debt of highly leveraged companies in favor of U.S. and German government debt and the stocks and bonds of blue chip companies. Risk premiums soared. High-risk debt once again had high yields, as the risk premium for BB high-yield debt once again rose to 6 percent over treasuries. Emerging market debt premiums went from 4 percent over treasuries in May 1998 to 15 percent above treasuries in September 1998. Although the world remains awash in capital, there was suddenly little liquidity available for any asset viewed as risky.

EXHIBIT 1-3   By 2000, the world's stock of financial assets will be seven times larger than in 1980 *($ Trillions)*

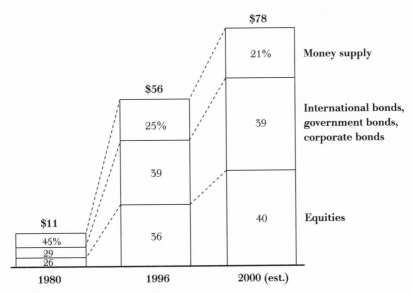

Sources: Data from International Monetary Fund; International Finance Corporation; IFC; McKinsey analysis.

These developments reaffirmed that easy access to capital is a double-edged sword. Tapping into this enormous supply of capital unwisely has proved dangerous because, while the market rewards participants who take actions that please it, it punishes those who do not. Even governments are not immune to the power of the global capital market. The crises in the Asian emerging markets in late 1997 and in Russia in 1998 offer the most powerful recent examples, but even developed world nations are not immune to its power. Canada and Italy in early 1995 had very high levels of domestic debt. As a result, their governments were paying real rates 2 percent to 4 percent over U.S. rates for debt of the same maturity. Within eighteen months, both Canada and Italy were obliged to bring their fiscal policies back into alignment, and they no longer pay such sizeable premium rates to borrow.

As long as capital has other places to flow, the capital market acts against institutions that fail to adhere to good management principles. As a consequence, the impact on companies and industries as the equity markets globalize will be immense. Companies that generate high returns while maintaining strong balance sheets will have ever-increasing opportunities to expand; underperforming companies and those with weak balance sheets face loss of control over their own destinies. The global capital markets are the servant of the strong, and the undertaker of the weak.

Technology for all

High interaction costs rather than physical geographic barriers or legal-regulatory barriers are the main reason services such as restaurants, health care delivery, and the distribution of personal financial services have remained largely local. *Interaction costs*[30] are the costs of all those tasks that result from coordinating the work of different parties. Until recently, for example, most financial service firms, even those operating nationally, delivered predominantly through physical distribution channels relying on the face-to-face interaction between customers and branch-based managers, service providers, or sales agents. The high costs of doing business this way kept financial services essentially local. At the national level, interaction costs represent as much as 51 percent of labor activity in the United States (the equivalent of over a third of GDP), and 36 percent in a less-developed economy such as India's.[31]

The cost of interactions is plummeting thanks to rapid advances in information technology. Take, for instance, the advances in raw microprocessor computing power. In 1980, microprocessors with a computing capacity of a million instructions per second (MIPS) cost almost $600. In 1995, one MIPS cost about $1.30 (Exhibit 1-4). Within a decade, a MIPS will probably

EXHIBIT 1-4   **Computing performance is increasing as cost is declining** *(Intel Microprocessors)*

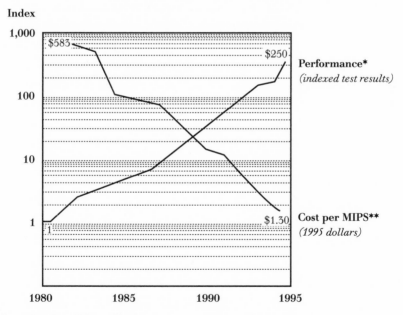

Sources: Data from McKinsey Global Forces Initiative; RISC vs. CISC: Microprocessor Report, January 23, 1995.

*1980 index.

**Million instructions per second.

cost about a tenth of a penny. The price-to-performance ratios of computer memory and different kinds of storage media have improved at 40 percent annually for the last decade. Within ten to fifteen years, most homes in the developed world will have access to bandwidth capacity of one megabyte per second or more—enough to permit electronic face-to-face customer relationships.[32]

These developments will fundamentally affect the way industries are structured, firms are organized, and customers behave to a degree likely to be at least as great as the changes in industry structure that occurred when transportation and infrastructure costs fell earlier this century.[33] Crucially, integration within a company will become less valuable, while cooperation *between* companies will increase as the balance between using outside specialists and internal integration will tilt toward specialists because it will cost less to work with them. Firms will move toward more networked forms of business configuration. The strategic value of aggregate size (as opposed to the benefits of economies of scale) will decline in many industries because doing everything for yourself will become a competitive *dis*advantage. Outsourcing will become the way to get the best at the lowest possible cost. The traditional role for intermediaries will change substantially because it will be far easier for customers to go direct as more and more efficient marketing mechanisms become prevalent, enabling more direct sales and distribution. Customers will increasingly need intermediaries who act as agents on their behalf rather than as agents working in the interests of suppliers.[34]

Digitization and the concomitant drop in interaction costs make specialization ever easier. Low interaction costs allow companies to dis-integrate and focus on a narrow specialty. More and more, they will be able to access reliably from others, at manageable costs, all the pieces of the value chain they have withdrawn from producing themselves. As the complication and cost of multiple suppliers declines, the logic of a world of world-class producers in every piece of the value chain becomes compelling.

Of course, digitization brings with it an additional bonus of its own in the form of electronic delivery of goods and services. In 1930, a three-minute call between New York and London cost $300 in 1996 dollars; today it costs only $1.26.[35] Electronics increasingly enables geographic distance to be overcome at lower costs. Widespread networks of communicating computers are spreading across the globe. Over the next decade, the number of people using computers and other networked electronic devices is likely to soar from about 100 million users today to over one billion people (from approximately 2 percent of the world's population to nearly 20 percent). Exponential growth is the norm here. As more people use the network, the value of the network increases. More people connected to the network also means more new ideas, which in turn create new sources of value.

As a measure of the power of electronic delivery, we need only note that it is actually allowing producers to customize their products and services to meet the needs of the individual customer—customer segments of one. Today, we see it in Internet products such as Firefly and My Yahoo! Soon enough it will be the ATM screen or any site where the means of product transfer is electronic.

This is not just a first-world story. The other 70 percent of the world's population currently makes do with less than 5 percent of the world's main telephone lines. But the number of lines in emerging markets is already approaching ten times its 1984 level. Penetration growth has been increasing at 9 percent annually for almost twenty years, and is expected to average 17 percent a year in low-income countries over the foreseeable future. China plans to install 75 million fixed new telephone lines by 2000.[36] Wireless communications are also expected to grow rapidly, especially in developing countries.

In fact, electronics are a way to overcome geographic market boundaries that is potentially even more powerful than the transplant model. Historically, business services have been delivered across geography only by trade or transplants. Electronics provide a new, third approach to delivering services. Its ability to replace traditional methods depends on whether an electronic producer can deliver a higher quality service at a lower cost. But the presence of a computer and communications infrastructure allows a service to be produced and consumed anywhere in the world at a marginal cost approaching zero. Given the low quality, poor availability, and excessive costs of traditional service delivery in many countries (in particular developing countries), the opportunity in global electronic delivery is very great, and we will soon see massive investment in overcoming the barriers.[37]

These are not blue-sky predictions. Our colleague Ted Hall led some research to see how much interaction cost could be saved by utilizing already existing technology. The results are impressive. The efficiency of data gathering could increase by a factor of at least 3, written and oral communication by around 2, and group problem-solving interaction by 1.5. The routine coordination of inventory reordering could be done in a tenth of the time it currently takes. Straightforward searches for a specific book title can be conducted many tens of times faster. Updating an investment portfolio, a basic act of monitoring, could take less than thirty seconds.

Historically, the most important fixed costs to most participants have been overhead costs, production costs, and physical distribution costs. *Overhead costs* are by definition all interaction costs.[38] Over time they will drop, decreasing the fixed cost advantage currently enjoyed by large companies.

A second set of fixed costs are *production costs*. In many manufacturing industries the optimum size of production facilities is actually *declining* because falling interaction costs lower the cut-off point where scale effects flatten out. As this takes place, it becomes easier and easier to trade off in favor of customizing to meet customer preferences as against standardizing to gain scale effects.

The third set of fixed costs are *physical distribution costs*, such as wires and networks in the telecommunications business and brokerage office branches, and stores in the retailing industry.

Now, many of the interactions between providers and their clients are beginning to take place electronically. The economics of these physical fixed costs diminish as electronic distribution takes marginal volume from these channels, thus obliging the channel to spread fixed costs over a smaller base—a painful process until the physical channels are reconfigured for the loss of volume.

Understanding these scale effects is important. In industries such as banking and telecommunications as much as 70 to 80 percent of costs is fixed. One of the major drivers behind the big telecommunications and bank mergers is the opportunity to eliminate redundant fixed costs. However, cost reduction is only one part of the interaction cost story. Digitization also brings with it an enormous increase in the aggregate capacity to conduct interactions cheaply, which will enable work to be performed better—a specialization effect. The trade-offs that shape economic activity (for example, firms trading off specialization against interaction costs or customers weighing current selections against further search costs) will each find a new point of balance as one side of the scale tips down. New ways to configure businesses, serve customers, and organize companies will emerge.[39]

Much of the expansion in interaction capacity will help overcome the physical barriers between markets by overcoming distance as well as reducing barriers between markets. The near impossibility of regulating electronic delivery of services will either make many of the remaining regulatory barriers moot or will be the final evidence of the need to reform regulation and laws. It will become impossible to maintain a closed market.

The impact of these developments is already visible in the U.S. financial services industry. Non-banks such as Schwab, Intuit, Microsoft Money, Fidelity, and Merrill Lynch, as well as traditional banks like Wells Fargo, Chase, and Citicorp,[40] are rapidly enlisting customers for electronic distribution of services. From a scant base that began to develop in the mid 1980s, Intuit, an electronic personal financial agent, now has over 12 million customers in the United States[41] and, in a telling development, has begun to receive unsolicited electronic inquiries for services from non-Americans. Now it has field sales and support in Canada, the UK, France, Germany, and Japan.

CHOICE CHANGES EVERYTHING

Digitization enables and enhances access, specialization, and scale. It is a technological discontinuity of enormous scope. As these three economic forces work together to overcome geographic barriers, one of the most remarkable effects will be the increasing power of customers. Throughout history the active economic agents have been suppliers. First through conquest, then through colonialism, then through the joint stock company, the drivers of economic integration were agents seeking to expand their access to new markets. For most customers, the interaction costs of finding better suppliers than those available in their local markets have been prohibitive, and so choice has been limited to local suppliers and companies able to overcome geographic boundaries. Now it has become far easier for customers to comparison shop outside their local markets. As a result, they now have a rapidly expanded range of choices and new price-value trade-offs.

In fact, there is an explosion in customer choice of providers, products, channels, and prices and terms. Comparison shopping is far easier for the customer to do than it is for local suppliers (with heavy fixed-cost investment in their business system) to restructure. This will, in turn, place greater customer pressure on producers to price off marginal costs in order to defend their market share.

Similarly, local producers that offer products of mediocre value will only be able to use price to defend their share from competitors offering superior value. As product availability increases, customers will be able to make this trade-off not only within categories of goods and services but also between categories. For example, customers will not only experience expanded choice among various consumer goods but also expanded choice between consumer goods and other new spending opportunities in telecommunications, health care, financial services, and so forth.

Historically, because of limited choice, customers have had relatively limited bargaining power. As choice expands, and as value becomes more transparent with falling interaction costs, their bargaining power will increase. Increasingly, they will demand more value at better prices. Often, this will translate into requirements to customize.

In such a world, marketing will be even more vital than it is today. Being able to match your capabilities with customer needs through crafting and delivering a superior value proposition will become an increasingly essential skill in the transition economy.[42]

INTANGIBLES: THE SCARCE RESOURCE

The companies that win in a world of increasing customer choice will be the companies that develop the most attractive value propositions. These will be the companies that make the most of their intangible assets. As every participant worldwide loses geographically privileged access to customers, labor, capital, technology, and techniques of production, many of the historical determinants of cost and value advantage disappear. In their place come intangibles such as talent, intellectual property, brands, and networks.[43]

Intangibles "buy" you the access that used to come with geographic privilege. Because intangibles have always been at the heart of specialization, they increase in value as an integrating global economy of six billion people allows more and more specialization.[44] And, as the world economy opens up, intangibles are now the differentiating capability required to generate enormous scale effects.

The costs of creating a world-class drug, software product, or movie do not vary much with volume. The marginal costs of producing more pills, more copies of the software, or more prints of a movie are truly insignificant relative to marginal revenue. Returns in the new world economy to Pfizer from Viagra, to Microsoft from Windows 98, or to Sony from *Titanic* are directly related to volume, which is why there is such a focus on market-ing and promotion in such intangible-rich businesses. More and more, it is intangibles that will be the scarce resource.

SAP, the German-based world leader in client-server environ-ments, demonstrates the payoff from intangibles. SAP began in 1972 as a five-person software manufacturer. In 1997, SAP made approximately DM 1.7 billion ($930 million) in pretax profits, an increase of 72 percent over 1996, on DM 6.0 ($3.4) billion in sales, three-quarters of which came from abroad. It operates in fifty countries. Currently, SAP owes its preeminence to its market leadership in enterprise management software.

The sheer amount SAP invests in R&D demonstrates the company's belief in the value of building intangible capital. In 1997, SAP invested an extraordinary DM 813 ($460) million in R&D—14 percent of its sales. By comparison, Intel's R&D investment was only 9 percent of total revenues in 1997; a typical pharmaceutical company invests about 10 percent in R&D.

SAP's chief advantage is its ability to dominate a specialty, in this case the provider of client-server applications to businesses. Because its name and brand have become synonymous with the best in this business, it is the supplier of choice and thereby benefits from enormous scale effects that it reinvests into enhancing its edge in its specialty. It has easy access not just to customers but also to partners who bring their own intangible assets to the party.

UNLIMITED POTENTIAL

Many people associate globalization with emerging market na-tions. However, the most important economic integration now under way is within the *developed* world—particularly *within* Europe, *within* North America, and *between* Europe and North America.

Europe, with some 450 million people (9.3 percent of the world) and 32 percent of dollar-denominated GDP, is on the verge of a dramatic increase in its internal economic integration. While the most visible manifestation of this process is the January 1, 1999 conversion by a majority of European nations to a common currency, other developments such as the movement toward harmonization of regulation across Europe, the opening of national borders to the free flow of traffic, and a host of other regulatory changes have dramatically lowered the importance of national boundaries.

Simultaneously, partially due to the movement to a common currency but also to the dramatic lowering of transaction and interaction costs brought by digitization and regulatory change, the formerly separate national equity markets are now integrating rapidly. This, in turn, is unleashing the power of capital to transform companies and industry structures across Europe. Given that Europe has a far denser population than the United States and a superior rail network, the physical barriers to geographic integration in Europe are less than in the United States. Over the next decade, the European economy has an incredible potential to integrate far more tightly, quite rapidly. While Europe does have some remaining significant interaction barriers, many due to language differences, as well as regulatory barriers such as labor laws, the next decade promises to produce a European economy that will look—in terms of economic integration—much more like today's U.S. economy.

The United States is the largest, most integrated economy in the world, with a population of 270 million (5.6 percent of the world total) and 26.1 percent of the world's GDP. The United States has long benefited from being an enormous single nation and having a common language, common currency, and common national regulation. As a result, it has achieved a remarkable degree of internal integration and been quick to benefit from any technological advances that help overcome physical barriers to economic integration. Advances first in automobiles, then airplanes, and now digitization have enabled rapid, sometimes transformational economic integration throughout the country. Combined with the low barriers to labor mobility in the United States, these advances have enabled the rapid development of new industries at a pace and scale not possible in Europe or Japan.

Much of the economic transformation of the U.S. economy over the last fifteen years has been driven by an incredibly vibrant internal capital market. This market has provided seed capital for start-ups and bridge money to commercialize promising intellectual property, initial public offerings (IPOs) to provide expansion capital, and principal investors and corporate acquirers to redeploy underutilized assets. Taken together with a dramatic reduction over the last fifteen years in state and federal regulatory barriers in industries such as trucking, public utilities, telecommunications, and financial services, these forces make it clear why the U.S. economy has been so robust.

Going forward, given that there remain relatively few regulatory barriers to economic integration and that capital within the United States is already incredibly mobile, the primary impetus to further internal integration within the United States will be through continuing rapid advances in communications. The United States is already the most "wired" society in the world, but the transformation of industry structures within the United States due to expanded customer choice and lowered interaction costs has barely begun.

Economic integration within North America does not end in the United States. The North American Free Trade Agreement (NAFTA), expanded capital mobility within North America, falling interaction costs, and expanded customer choice have all increased the integration of the Canadian and Mexican economies and the U.S. economy. When Canadian and Mexican populations are combined with the United States, North America represents a population of 390 million (8.1 percent of the world) and 29.3 percent of worldwide GDP.

It would be misleading, though, to overemphasize the internal integration within Europe and within North America relative to the importance of continued increased economic integration *between* Europe and North America. The same effects lowering barriers to regional integration are also lowering the barriers to cross-regional integration. Europe and North America are already more integrated with each other than are any other two regions of the world. Shared legal, cultural, political, and religious roots have kept interaction barriers lower than with other regions. Moreover, the relative size and sophistication of their economies create mutual attraction as companies and customers naturally seek access to the largest markets in the world outside their own region. Within ten years, barring the unforeseen creation of new regulatory barriers, it seems likely that the integration between Europe and North America will be far tighter than it is at present.

None of this, however, should minimize the long-term importance of integrating the emerging nations with the OECD economies. To date, the global economy's center of gravity has been in the developed world. In GDP terms, OECD countries still dominate. With 20 percent of the world's population, the developed countries still control over 80 percent of dollar-denominated world GDP—a figure that has remained almost constant over the past twenty years.[45] The emerging countries, in particular China, India, Brazil, Indonesia, Russia, and Turkey, have over 80 percent of the world's population, yet contribute only about 20 percent of dollar-denominated GDP. Despite the size of their populations, these economies were always relatively small, and companies going international generally found larger, less risky fish to fry closer to home.

Now, however, the emerging markets are within the global frontier. In 1996, constant dollar trade volume between the developed world and the emerging markets exceeded $2 trillion, compared to $802 billion in 1986.[46] In industries such as consumer goods, opportunities in the emerging markets are a lifeline to profitability today, given the intensity of competition elsewhere. In other industries, the prize will come in the longer term, but the race must be started today.

labor prod .33 — .56
labor rate 10 — 20

This is not just another set of opportunities to expand sales volume. These countries bring into the game a new resource: an almost inexhaustible supply of cheap, potentially high-skilled labor. Labor productivity levels are often only one-third to one-half the levels in the developed world. But labor rates can be ten or twenty times lower. If quality can be maintained, this translates into labor-cost advantages of 30 percent to 50 percent or more. Once focused skill-building leads to higher levels of productivity, companies will begin to capture this advantage. As more global competitors move their work to these nations, everyone else must follow or lose in the global arena.

The new supply of labor gives new access opportunities to companies in their role as intermediate consumers—as the arena expands, they have ever more places to buy the labor they need. Today these labor anomalies are being captured primarily by manufacturers. In the future, however, the pool of labor available at low cost will be enormous for players producing services that can use innovation and technology to overcome language, quality control, and skill-development barriers.

To take just one example, India has already become one of the leading players in writing computer software programs. In 1997 the industry generated U.S. $1.8 billion in sales—an eight-fold increase from five years ago[47]—the majority of which are exported. This trend shows little sign of abating. India possesses the world's second-largest pool of English-speaking scientific labor power in the world, and the cost of that labor is among the lowest.

It may take decades before the labor rates in these nations reach developed-world standards (it has taken forty years for Taiwanese labor rates, arguably now a developed-world nation, to catch up). But what we are seeing today are the very early stages of real globalization in the market for labor. For exactly the same job in Detroit and Guandong, workers are being paid fundamentally different rates of compensation relative to their productivity. Some of this is a function of purchasing power parity differences.[48] Nevertheless, there is clearly almost a 5:1

gap between standards of living for the same job. Even when labor costs are only a small portion of a company's total cost, the steady lowering of tariffs and transportation costs worldwide means that global and would-be global companies ignore these differentials at their peril.

Of course, this process will lead over time to labor-rate equalization. But this slowly lessening advantage will be more than offset by a massive improvement in the standard of living of billions of people in emerging markets. These effects are likely to be sufficiently great that by 2010 only 48 percent of the world's medium-income consumers will come from today's high-income countries, down from 78 percent in 1995.[49] This will represent a massive reserve of unmet demand, which will in turn generate an answering increase in sales volume in those companies poised to take advantage of it.

For those who can meet the challenge, the transition economy provides unprecedented opportunities. In geographically constrained markets, internal economic growth and innovation have been the primary means of expanding specialization and scale effects. Now, the impact of aggregating previously separate markets and the transfer of innovation between markets will increasingly swamp these local effects. The potential to specialize work, given the extraordinary diversity of skills and capabilities in a global economy, is incomparably greater than in even a large national economy. Ultimately, the ability to spread fixed costs over a $28 trillion global economy of 6 billion people dwarfs the potential in any local, national, or even regional economy.

TRANSITION AHEAD

The transition ahead of us will be bumpy, accompanied by the kinds of social unrest, market crises, and political stress we are seeing in Asia, Russia, and elsewhere. There is plenty of evidence that the path to a more integrated global economy is neither without its hazards nor its tragedies. With high growth must come, to some extent, high risk—but ultimately, we believe, high reward.[50]

All participants will face new challenges. Nearly every existing competitor has traditional advantages based on geography. As the barriers to global economic interaction disappear, these advantages will rapidly erode. *We are moving from a world where 90 percent of the competitive advantage was derived from geography to a world where 90 percent will be nongeographic.* This will undermine the competitive advantage of all producers whether they are currently local, multilocal, or global. Being better will become ever more important than having privileged geographic access.

Formerly durable competitive advantages such as physical distribution and breadth of offerings can quickly become competitive millstones. Local producers find they lack the profits to defend themselves. Insiders suddenly find their friends in government are either out of their jobs or no longer write the rules. As electronic distribution begins to parallel and even to bypass physical distribution, as installed capacity becomes obsolete before it has even been depreciated, and as focused competitors attack like piranhas—companies find they must restructure simply to survive.

In such an environment, the incentives of participants in local geographic markets change. Rather than colluding, incumbent local players find themselves in a competitive scramble to find partners from elsewhere who can deliver the most value to their customers so that they can maintain their customer base— albeit in a diminished role. New local players emerge from surprising places playing by different rules. Fully integrated producers begin to shed the parts of the business system in which they are not competitive. Broad-based distributors begin to focus on discrete segments. Large cracks appear in the local cartels.

Every market and every industry is being restructured at the micro level at an accelerated pace. Firms that fail to exploit the possibilities will see their value propositions deteriorate in comparison to those of their competitors. Over time, the only class that matters will be world class. All others will be forced to restructure or go out of business.

But what opportunities! To quote Schön and Ackoff: "Problems are interconnected, environments are turbulent, and the future is indeterminate" just insofar as managers can shape them by their actions. What is called for, under these conditions, is not only the analytic techniques traditional in operations research but also the active, synthetic skill of "designing a desirable future and inventing ways of bringing it about."[51] In other words, strategy is back and with a capital *S*. The sudden release of geographic boundary conditions creates a land rush to claim territory in the world economy—a race for the world.

2

RUNNING THE RACE

THE REMOVAL OF THE CONSTRAINTS imposed by geography makes life harder for most companies. Suddenly, a landscape of geographically bounded markets with protective regulations, loyal customers, known competition, and known technologies gives way to an increasingly unbounded world filled with unfamiliarity, complexity, and uncertainty.

Starting from various geographies, industries, and skill bases, different participants see the same opportunity and begin to pursue it. Electronic companies, software companies, telecommunications companies, cable television companies, publishing companies, and media companies all compete in a new global media industry. Banks, insurance companies, and mutual fund companies all compete for the global asset management business. In such a world, you are constantly in danger of being blindsided by unknown competitors.

In this environment, the first critical task corporate leaders face is understanding the nature of the race being run. This means avoiding the conventional wisdom that makes a conceptual leap from local to global without realizing that the transition from local markets and industries to an integrated global economy is a dynamic process that will take decades.

What matters is *how* you run. To succeed, companies must take advantage of the unique opportunities being made available by an economy in transition to global market structures. This requires understanding how global markets form as well as the dynamics of two distinct kinds of restructuring that are taking place simultaneously in industry after industry. With this understanding comes the opportunity to craft a strategy that takes full advantage of the opportunities afforded by a transition economy.

HOW GLOBAL MARKETS FORM

The test of whether a market has fully formed is whether or not all customers in the market can get the best product available at the best price. If the same item sells for the same price throughout a market, allowing for transaction and transportation costs, then it is one market. If not, multiple markets exist. This condition is called the *law of one price*, a fundamental law of economics advanced by Adam Smith to describe the equilibrium condition of aggregate, efficient markets. The law of one price provides a straightforward test to determine whether particular markets are global, national, or local.

A global market exists for commercial airplanes. An airplane produced by Boeing costs the same worldwide. (Because of competition with Airbus Industries and others, the industry structure among producers is global as well.) In contrast, beer is sold in markets that are largely national. For example, the supermarket price of a six-pack of Heineken in different countries (even after allowing for adjustments due to purchasing power parity differences between currencies) varies from $2.50 to $5.50.[1] This is because the price for the six-pack in each country is set by the competition in each market between Heineken and national beer producers, which in turn reflects differences in local costs, market production, regulation, competitive intensity, and so forth. While all of the world's markets are *becoming* global, most are far from global today. As we will describe later, only one-third of the world's output is in industries where meaningful global structures have begun to form. And we estimate that the global law of one price, as yet, applies to well less than 20 percent of the world's output.[2]

The end game

The race for the world is in large part a race to create global markets. Producers that can actively participate in the creation of global markets will benefit greatly. Once global markets are fully formed, the race gets harder. In a fully global market, all customers can get the best product at the best price. In that end state, all competitors will need to have world-class skills just to survive. It is more fun and profitable to compete in markets where customers still have limited choice and most of the competitors are local incumbents with mediocre skills.

In truth, competing in fully global markets is tough, especially in markets where output has been commoditized. Because customers have practically unlimited choice and the variation in perceived output is minimal, a global commodity market is close to a perfect market as an economist would define it. In the developed world, institutional (as opposed to retail) foreign exchange is essentially a commodity; the law of one price applies to literally thousandths of a percent of the volume traded. It is a scale-driven commodity game with relatively low returns for the suppliers, all of whom have to be world class simply to survive. It is a great market for large customers that are able to transact almost unlimited volumes of foreign exchange at virtually no cost. It is a struggle for competitors trying to make money out of the foreign exchange business.

Much of the world's globalized output is natural commodities such as crude oil, bauxite, iron ore, and manufactured commodities such as petroleum, aluminum, and steel. However, manufactured goods and even services can commoditize if there is insufficient variation in output as perceived by customers.

Take the market for personal computers (PCs), which is essentially global. A number of generic producers of PCs compete primarily on price. However, some innovative producers such as Dell and Compaq have managed to escape the commodity game. Dell, for example, has grown enormously by leveraging its proprietary intangible advantages. It entered the market as a low-end PC assembler but developed a business system that enabled it to provide customers around the world with customized computers at close to wholesale prices. It accomplished this by selling directly to customers, thereby saving the costs of retail distribution. Because Dell assembles the units only after orders are placed, it can customize to individual requests. This has proved to be a powerful draw. Customers exercise their expanded choice to find Dell, rather than Dell having to spend distribution dollars to find them. This manufacturing process means Dell has no need for finished goods inventory, saving both working capital and losses from the high rate of obsolescence in the industry.

Speed of formation

Global markets are forming faster than ever, but they do not form overnight. It took roughly twenty years for the global bond markets to form fully. It has taken Coca-Cola around fifty years to build a global market for Coke. It may take another twenty years to globalize the beer industry, which started down the path nearly twenty years ago. In contrast, it took less than a decade to globalize the PC business which was largely "born global."

Many factors affect the speed at which markets aggregate into global structures, including the specific geographic barriers in operation, the risks involved, the evolution of global standards and protocols, the opportunities to leverage specialization and scale effects, and the actions of individual participants. Moreover, in different industries, different parts of the market go global at different rates. For example, high-end segments such as luxury goods globalize faster than down-market segments. Some parts of the value chain go global before other parts do, creating new opportunities to specialize globally.

Take the automotive industry. While there is intense global competition in the sale of new cars, the businesses of repairing and maintaining cars and of selling used cars are still largely local, not even national. And these local businesses are, in combination, larger than the new car business.[3] Even in the manufacture of new cars, there are new opportunities to specialize in the manufacture of components parts. The automotive industry, in its entirety, is still a long way from perfect global competition.

As global markets form, local and national industry structures erode, but slowly. In the transition economy, local and national markets will coexist with growing global markets. Many companies will face the dual challenge of serving their local and national markets at the same time as they are building global capabilities.

KNOWING WHERE YOU START:
THE LOCAL-GLOBAL CONTINUUM

Before training for a race, you have to know how far you will be running and the best time of the highest-ranked competitor. Markets and industries are at different points in the transition from local to global. This means that each business leader must understand where their business is on the local-global continuum and how long it is likely to take each industry to reach its end state. Is it a 400-meter race, a 5,000-meter race, or is it a marathon? Generally speaking, the closer an industry is to being fully global, the faster the pace. Things speed up toward the finish line.

A continuum has an infinite number of points. But it is helpful to group industries into three broad categories: (1) locally defined industries; (2) nationally defined industries; and (3) globally defined industries (Exhibit 2-1). At this point in the transition economy (conveniently enough), roughly one-third of the world's economic activity now takes place in locally defined industries, one-third in nationally defined industries, and one-third in industries that are well on the way to global definition.

Locally defined

Food, print media, construction materials, health care delivery, retail distribution, and home construction—in short, every enterprise that is traditionally the province of small business—are all industries that have historically been locally defined. This category also includes services often performed by local governments such as waste management, education, and police protection. In each of these industries, local players now face competition from outsiders. Not surprisingly, global players are beginning to emerge. Some of these companies are well known, such as McDonald's or Wal-Mart. Others, such as Compass in catering services and Service Corporation International in funeral homes, are as yet little known.

In local industries, the degrees of freedom are almost unlimited. Industry structures are not yet defined, even at the national level. These industries offer incredible opportunity over the next twenty years because the forces at work in the new economy are opening up access, specialization, and scale opportunities not previously available. The trick is to discover new, winning approaches.

Consider cement and concrete production.[4] These segments of the construction materials industry are the most local imaginable.

EXHIBIT 2-1   Different industries are at varying stages of globalization

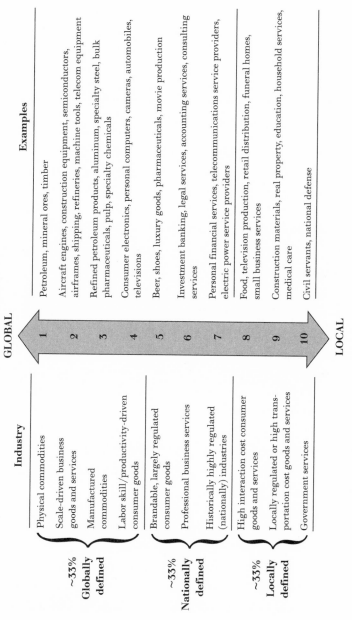

	Industry		Examples
		GLOBAL	
~33% Globally defined	Physical commodities	1	Petroleum, mineral ores, timber
	Scale-driven business goods and services	2	Aircraft engines, construction equipment, semiconductors, airframes, shipping, refineries, machine tools, telecom equipment
	Manufactured commodities	3	Refined petroleum products, aluminum, specialty steel, bulk pharmaceuticals, pulp, specialty chemicals
	Labor skill/productivity-driven consumer goods	4	Consumer electronics, personal computers, cameras, automobiles, televisions
~33% Nationally defined	Brandable, largely regulated consumer goods	5	Beer, shoes, luxury goods, pharmaceuticals, movie production
	Professional business services	6	Investment banking, legal services, accounting services, consulting services
	Historically highly regulated (nationally) industries	7	Personal financial services, telecommunications service providers, electric power service providers
~33% Locally defined	High interaction cost consumer goods and services	8	Food, television production, retail distribution, funeral homes, small business services
	Locally regulated or high trans-portation cost goods and services	9	Construction materials, real property, education, household services, medical care
	Government services	10	Civil servants, national defense
		LOCAL	

Sources: Data from World Development Report (World Bank); McKinsey analysis.

The distance between concrete mixing plants and construction sites is rarely more than twenty-five miles. In most cement and concrete markets around the world, producers are fragmented and inefficient. Now, French, Swiss, and Mexican firms, notably Lafarge, Holderbank, and Cemex, are acquiring local producers, transferring superior production methods and using advanced logistics techniques to increase productivity and lower transportation costs (the largest input cost).

Whether in construction materials, retail distribution, or health care delivery, most existing local players find the notion of pursuing global strategies absurd, if not terrifying. They have no idea what it will take to prosper in this new economic environment. There are few role models; many of the ways to globalize these industries have yet to be invented. This means opportunity. Because there are tens of thousands of players in each of these industries, it is safe to say some global players will emerge.

For participants in local industries, the race has barely begun. It is impossible to see the end game. It will take decades before these industries and markets are fully global. But the opportunities that lie ahead are truly enormous.

Nationally defined

Approximately one-third of the world's output is produced in industries where structures exist at the national, or in some cases, regional level. Industries in this category include personal financial services, telecommunications, public utilities, rail transportation, and trucking. Most have been highly regulated by governments and have significant fixed costs, which means enormous scale effects when access is expanded. Absent the regulatory constraints historically imposed in these industries, they would be significantly more global than they currently are due to these scale effects.

Because global industry structures are not yet fully formed, participants still have a great many degrees of freedom. But the same forces that are opening up the cross-border opportunities are also opening up the various national industry structures. In many nations, even the national structures are not yet fully formed in many of these industries. For example, in the United States, public utilities, telecommunications, and personal financial services are just now moving from regional to national structures at the same time as global opportunities are opening up. Participants in these industries are thus torn between pursuing the still-available national opportunities and the newly available global opportunities.

For participants in national industries, the race is well under way. They can see that global industry structures will develop, but it is not clear what form they will take. The stakes are high: the opportunities are huge, but so are the risks that others will win the race.

Globally defined

Another third of world GDP already has well-defined global markets and industries, including such early-to-globalize industries as raw materials (e.g., crude oil and timber), manufactured commodities (e.g., paper and aluminum), and scale-driven capital goods (e.g., aircraft engines and construction equipment). The raw materials industries began to globalize more than fifty years ago because producers had huge incentives to spread their fixed investment costs over as large a market as possible. Every developing and developed country needed raw materials, so most national governments kept regulatory barriers to importing raw materials low. Companies with technology and capital advantages worked together with countries in possession of the relevant raw materials, more or less to the benefit of both. For similar reasons, global markets quickly developed through exports and imports for manufactured commodities and for scale-driven capital goods.

In the 1970s and 1980s, integrated markets formed for several manufacturing industries throughout the developed world, including consumer electronics, pharmaceuticals, and automotive manufacturing. During the same period, capital markets businesses, particularly foreign exchange and fixed income, globalized. Most of today's PC–based electronics industry was "born global" in the late 1980s and 1990s, replacing the older, mainframe-based global computer industry created in the 1960s and 1970s by IBM.

In addition to these mature global industry structures, industries such as consumer packaged goods, electronically delivered media, apparel, and professional business services (e.g., legal services, accounting, consulting, and investment banking) began to reach global markets in the 1990s. In these industries, global structures are only now beginning to emerge.

All of these global markets, with the exception of the PC–based electronics industry, were created by companies using either classic multilocal or classic global approaches. Most of these companies grew, country by country, through patient expansion over decades.

Unlike the participants in nationally defined industries, participants in global industries have no choice but to focus on the world. Unfortunately, in more mature global industries, the degrees of freedom are becoming more limited as more and more firms enter the competitive arena pursuing similar strategies. Often, the core business is a virtual commodity or is becoming one, and the end game is becoming visible. Participants in mature global industries do not necessarily have to face a future of head-to-head worldwide wars of attrition, but such a future is a possibility unless they act to change it.

TWO KEYS: DURATION AND PACE

Geography will be an obstacle to economic integration for a long time, particularly as it restricts access. The speed at which barriers fall, and the relative skill and ability of participants in overcoming the barriers that remain, will be highly industry specific. The pace and duration of the race will differ tremendously by industry. To illustrate, let us look at four examples—power, telecoms, beer, and accounting—and explore how their starting points and drivers of pace are affecting the nature of their global race.

The *electric and gas power businesses* start off at a very early stage of globalization; most economic activity in this industry is still organized at the local and national level. Furthermore, it will probably take decades for fully global industry structures to evolve. This race will be a marathon. Why? Most geographic barriers in the delivery of power to businesses and consumers remain intact. The major geographic barriers have been, and remain, regulatory and legal ones; these are eroding, but the process is very slow.

Digitization has even less impact because power still needs to be delivered through wires into homes and businesses. Thus, digitization cannot enhance the end users' (i.e., households and businesses) ability to choose among suppliers because the wires can only be owned by a single provider. Customer choice is therefore constrained. However, the combination of capital mobility and active agents is having some impact. They enable geographic expansion to take place in two ways: through changes in the ownership of the wires and by creating global markets for the components of the value chain other than the wire-based local delivery of power.

The AES Corporation has become the world's largest global producer of power by pursuing a global integrator strategy based on acquisitions and a transplant of their world-class management techniques. At the time of its IPO in June 1991, AES Corporation (founded in 1981) owned and operated three coal-fired plants and one natural gas–fired plant in the United States with 700 megawatts (MW) total capacity, had two plants under construction, and managed the operations of one other plant. Revenues totaled $330 million and market capitalization was $1.4 billion.

In 1991, AES began aggressively searching the world for high-return projects. The results have been impressive. By 1997, AES had an interest in 100 power plants in 17 countries with a total capacity of 31,000 MW. Revenues totaled $1.4 billion, and market capitalization had reached $7.5 billion.[5]

AES achieved such phenomenal growth through an aggressive strategy of acquisition and greenfield growth. Analysts' reports suggest that before allocation of corporate costs, 42 percent of AES's value creation for the 1991 to 1996 period came from legacy assets (via operating efficiencies), 43 percent through acquisitions, and 15 percent through greenfield growth options.[6] In 1997 alone, AES raised $5.9 billion in additional financing for acquisitions and new plant projects.

At the same time, specialists have chipped away at other elements of the value chain. CellNet Data Systems (CNDS) has pioneered a wireless data communications network that allows utilities to monitor their residential, commercial, and industrial usage meters remotely. This product will allow CNDS to collect minute-by-minute usage data from utility customers, which will enable utilities to improve load management and outage detection while providing additional services to customers, such as demand-side management service or time-of-use pricing. CNDS's wireless fixed data network is the largest in the world, with more than one and a half million endpoints connected in August 1998 and growing at a rate of 100,000 additional endpoints per month.

While a large number of businesses can potentially use wireless remote monitoring technology (e.g., security alarms, copy machines, vending machines, "smart" home devices), CNDS has chosen to focus on utilities (electric, gas, and water) for the near term. The market is huge. In the United States alone there are roughly 225 million electric, gas, and water meters; internationally there are several hundred million additional meters. Currently, CNDS operates only in metropolitan areas in the United States, but its future opportunities embrace the world.

CNDS's strategy for growth is to develop close partnerships with regional utilities. As the utilities industry deregulates state by state, CNDS will be well positioned to install a statewide wireless data communications network. The potential for growth in demand is immense, given the pace of development in many of the world's emerging markets. CNDS is taking advantage of rising global energy demand, which includes growing demand for meters. It has partnered with Bechtel Enterprises to gain access to distribution infrastructure opportunities worldwide and with Siemens Measurements (UK) to integrate its radio technology with Siemens' leading-edge metering hardware. In the United States, CNDS has partnered with Schlumberger to integrate its radio technology with new state-of-the-art, solid-state metering products. CNDS has captured a desirable position as a specialist player in a global micro industry. While metering is less than 1 percent of the total utility business, annual revenues in this micro industry are expected to reach $25 billion within the next ten years. CNDS has positioned itself to grow at a faster pace by using existing national structures versus a greenfield approach.

The *telecom industry* is also at an early stage of globalization, but the pace at which it is globalizing is far faster. Like power, telecom has been largely locally or nationally defined— dominated until recently by large national monopolies operating in industry structures defined by national regulation. However, this industry is now undergoing wrenching, fast-paced change.

Digitization is transforming this industry. Unlike the power industry, wireless and digital technologies mean that providers can deliver services without maintaining physical connections to homes and businesses. Coupled with deregulation and cheap capital, new entrants and heightened competitive intensity have become a reality. Active agents—the newly formed British Telecom–AT&T joint venture, Telefónica de España's extensive presence throughout Latin America, and others—are beginning to create links across borders. Not surprisingly, consumer choice is also on the rise, accelerating the pace of change even faster.

The *beer industry* starts the race as a largely national industry. Currently, geographic incumbents enjoy privileged access in national markets and control nearly 70 percent of the industry's profits. In addition to legal and regulatory barriers, these access advantages are based on strong local preferences for national brands and beer recipes, as well as entrenched distribution relationships that are difficult to overcome.

In recent years, however, the forces at work in the transition economy have begun to erode the geographic barriers, much as they have in soft drinks under Coca-Cola's leadership. Beer has been a slow business to globalize. For example, in the nineteenth century, Guinness decided to take its draught beer global. In 1821, stout made up over 80 percent of Guinness's output. By 1886, it had the largest brewery in the world. In 1936, it constructed its first brewery outside Ireland (in West London). As it expanded abroad, new products were launched, for example, nitrogenated, kegged Guinness draught in 1961 and Guinness in cans with a nitrogen-filled widget in 1989. By 1995, only 14 percent of their total volume of 26 million hectoliters was sold in Ireland. Now Guinness is brewed in over 50 countries and sold in more than 150.[7] However, despite how long Guinness has been attempting to globalize the beer industry, it has only been able to capture a small percentage of the worldwide market. The pace is picking up, but for different reasons than in the telecom industry. The race is on in the beer industry among fully integrated competitors such as Guinness, South African Breweries, Interbrew, and Anheuser-Busch, while others, such as the Boston Beer Company, are playing a specialist's game. Boston Beer Company is a virtual beer company. It outsources brewing, packaging, and distribution while specializing in the intangible elements of the business—product development and marketing.

Because reduced interaction costs make it easier now than ever before to create global brands, it may take only ten to fifteen years for the beer industry to evolve to global industry structures it took Coke fifty years to achieve. Here some pioneering companies are beginning to realize the opportunities afforded by capital mobility and digitization. Greater consumer choice is beginning to affect the mix, and the pace of change is accelerating.

The *accounting industry,* by contrast, is already quite global, driven so by clients who are themselves global and want consistent audit services and information technology in all their operations. They also face increasing pressure from the global capital markets to adopt accounting conventions that are standard around the world. The consolidation in little more than a decade of the industry, in which the Big Eight has become the Big Five—Ernst & Young, Deloitte & Touche, PriceWaterhouseCoopers, KPMG, and Arthur Andersen—is just one manifestation of this trend. Interestingly enough, the need for global standards and the power of reputation have provided little room for global specialists in the audit business. Here the pace of change is remarkably fast as these various forces converge to turbocharge a final sprint to the global finish line.

So while the duration and pace of the race varies from industry to industry, it is possible—and greatly advantageous—for individual companies to move into global markets at a faster pace than their industry as a whole. Those that do so successfully will be well rewarded.

THE PRIZES

The prizes available to participants who can run the race for the world well are breathtaking because the transition economy allows unique opportunities not available in a mature, geographically bounded economy. Specifically, there are unique opportunities to establish self-perpetuating virtuous cycles of geographic expansion, to increase returns on financial capital without making commensurate increases in investments, and to expand the capture of cross-geographic arbitrage of productivity and factor cost differentials.

Virtuous cycles of geographic expansion

The transition economy provides producers with superior value propositions to continuously gain new access, specialization, and scale advantages, enabling them to benefit from a virtuous cycle of geographic expansion. Gaining such advantages does not necessarily require gaining access to the entire world. In largely local industries, these advantages can be gained by expanding nationally faster than competitors. In national industries, these advantages can be gained by expanding regionally.

As producers successfully expand geographically, profits increase, further enhancing their abilities to invest more into gaining greater geographic access, penetrating their existing markets more deeply, increasing scale and specialization advantages, and investing even more in intangibles such as intellectual property and talent, which further enhances their value propositions. A virtuous cycle of geographic expansion gets under way as initial advantages are used to gain even greater advantage.

When it comes to creating such virtuous cycles of geographic expansion, Coke is it! Coca-Cola now claims 49 percent of the global soft drink market. Its closest competitor, PepsiCo, has only 17 percent. In 1997 Coca-Cola generated close to $4 billion in operating profit outside the United States. PepsiCo has never generated more than $200 million outside the United States in soft drinks.[8] The heart of Coca-Cola's virtuous cycle of geographic expansion is a superior value proposition.

Coca-Cola creates a superior value proposition thanks to the approach it has adopted toward physical and intangible assets. Pepsi owns most of its operations. Coke, on the other hand, owns very few physical assets. While the company directly employs about 31,000 people, its bottlers and associates employ over 600,000 people. Its market-to-book ratio at the time we wrote these words was about 27, an indicator not only of the market's dizzying expectations for its future earnings but also of its high-return strategy. Coke has typically generated an ROE of 50 to 60 percent over the past few years, while its bottlers are lucky to reach the mid-teens.

Coca-Cola owns only those pieces of the value chain with high returns and low asset intensity (i.e., Coke is a specialist in certain value chain elements). Coke owns the globally leverageable intangibles—the brands, the technology, the management and marketing expertise, the relationships—and leaves the intangibles such as the trucks and the bottling plants and the locally leverageable intangibles, such as local relationships and customer knowledge, in their local partners' hands. The combination of Coca-Cola's world-class marketing and its local partners' manufacturing and delivery expertise means that Coca-Cola can offer the customer superior benefits.

Coca-Cola's bottlers purchase over 95 percent of the raw materials required, such as glass, plastic caps, sugar, water, and machinery. They manufacture the soft drinks—with the exception of the "secret formula" for the syrup concentrate—and the bottles. Coke prefers that the bottlers own their own operations. Only 16 percent of Coca-Cola's bottlers are consolidated. It is unlikely they would be able to attract such high-quality local talent if the bottlers were Coca-Cola employees.

This asset-light approach enables Coke to focus ever greater investment into its proprietary intangible assets—brands, marketing skills, global talent—to gain intangible scale economies and to generate specialization effects, particularly in marketing. These intangible assets allow it to grow its volume faster and to further refine and develop its intangibles, while simultaneously growing its profitability and its capacity to invest in geographic expansion. In particular, Coke has been able to invest in its brand—it has spent over $30 billion on advertising in the last twenty years around the world as it has pushed into country after country. As it achieves ever greater differentiation from its competitors by building superior brands and distribution, Coke feeds a virtuous cycle of geographic expansion.[9]

While companies such as Coke generate a virtuous cycle of expansion, it is easy for the old national or regional competitors with mediocre value propositions to get caught in a cycle of decreasing profitability. Companies offering inferior value lose volume because their formerly captive customers exercise their increasing power to choose at the same time that new suppliers enter their once-protected market. The loss of volume starts out slowly but soon the company has a growth problem. Unless the company's ability to add distinctive value is renewed, it loses access and scale effects and experiences a declining ability to invest.

Increasing returns

The transition economy also offers the intelligent competitor access to huge profit pools and the means to capture these profit pools without making correspondingly huge capital investments. The key to this is increasing economic returns.

The idea of increasing returns is the opposite of the traditional economic notion of diminishing returns. Diminishing returns exist when incremental investment yields diminished marginal returns. For example, as you mine ore you lift the easiest-to-extract ore first; as you exhaust the bed, it becomes progressively more expensive to get the same yield. Therefore, your returns on investment diminish. In contrast, you experience increasing returns when incremental investment yields increased marginal returns. This is possible in the transition economy because the removal of geographic barriers, to extend our example, makes all the ore easier to extract.

There is an old Wall Street adage attributed to the former Soviet premier Nikita Khrushchev that "trees don't grow to the sky." Any growth process, at some point, runs into limits. Throughout history, most of the relevant limits to growth have been geographically based. As geographic barriers fall, the historical limits that have constrained producers from capturing market share outside their home base are continually being relaxed. Companies with superior value propositions to offer have increasing returns on capital invested partly because they can enjoy a free ride on past investments. They will not have to seek out new customers. Customers will come to them. A movie intended for a U.S. audience turns out to be popular throughout the world. A new drug for the developed world is also demanded throughout the emerging markets.

Increasing returns occur partially because intangible assets, unlike physical assets, often have marginal production costs of close to zero (i.e., the marginal cost of printing an extra movie or copy of software is practically nothing) and therefore have huge scale effects. But what makes for increasing returns (rather than simply increased returns) is that superior intangibles also have virtuous cycle effects. As Brian Arthur and others have pointed out, intangibles also appreciate with use.[10] For example, the more customers in a telephone network, the more value the network has to everyone who uses it. Moreover, superior talent attracts other talent seeking opportunities to interact. Superior intellectual property attracts potential partners who want to work with you. And so forth.

The key to increasing returns is that superior intangibles continually benefit from the expansion of choice in the transition economy. If you possess superior intangibles, customers will seek you out without your having to invest to find them. Other participants seeking opportunity will seek you out as a partner and will be willing to share in the capital investments needed on terms that you find attractive. For all these reasons, returns on invested capital can continue to increase or, alternatively, can provide the resources to continually step up investment levels to gain ever greater intangible asset superiority.

Cross-geographic arbitrage

Arbitrage in the financial economy focuses on tradable instruments denominated in different currencies. Arbitrage in the real economy focuses on differences in the costs of production. These arbitrage opportunities in the real economy exist because in each area of the world local methods of production developed independently over time. As a result, factor costs and productivity levels in delivering various goods and services vary enormously from geography to geography.

Companies can arbitrage both these differences in factor costs and in productivity. Of the major factor costs of production—raw materials, capital, labor, and land—only raw materials and capital are priced in global markets. Raw materials such as crude oil, bauxite, and iron ore have long been traded global commodities subject to the law of one price. Over the last twenty years, the capital markets have also globalized. Roughly two-thirds of the world's financial assets, including money and bonds, are priced in truly global markets and now even equity markets are globalizing rapidly.[11]

Most other factor costs are very different in different geographies. The cost of land varies enormously by geography, as do the taxes to produce and distribute goods and services. Perhaps most important, the price of equivalent labor varies extensively by geography. Well over 90 percent of the world's labor markets is still predominantly local. Labor is relatively immobile, and geographic differences in economic opportunity, language, and education are obstacles to the formation of global markets. The principal exceptions are the markets for world-class talent (e.g., movie stars, soccer players, investment bankers), which have become relatively global.

Differences in labor and capital productivity between countries can also be quite large (as much as 50 percent, according to a McKinsey Global Institute study; see Exhibit 2-2). Productivity differences between the developed world and emerging markets are even larger, while factor cost differences (i.e., labor, rent, taxes, etc.) can be downright enormous (Exhibit 2-3). Combining world-class productivity with the lowest local factor costs can create potential savings of close to 80 percent compared to the production costs of an equivalent product in the developed world.

A producer specializing in supplying goods and services where it enjoys both world-class productivity and factor cost advantages has the potential to earn extraordinary returns. Strategies built on cross-geographic arbitrage can provide lucrative and enduring advantages in specialization and scale over slower-moving geographic incumbents living within the constraints of local or national value chains. The good news is that roughly 90 percent of the world's market share and capacity is in the hands of competitors with a limited capacity to capture such arbitrage opportunities.

This way of doing business has long existed. But the opportunities have mushroomed as a result of the communication revolution and developments of standards and protocols that make arbitrage far more accessible. Astra, Motorola, and IBM are building R&D capabilities in India to take advantage of factor cost differentials. In India, they have a ready source of cheap, high-quality research talent who can work with the rest of the

EXHIBIT 2-2   **Capital productivity levels can vary significantly even among developed countries** *(Index: U.S. = 100)*

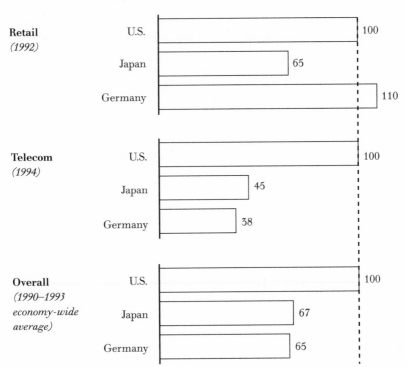

Retail (1992)
U.S. 100
Japan 65
Germany 110

Telecom (1994)
U.S. 100
Japan 45
Germany 38

Overall (1990–1993 economy-wide average)
U.S. 100
Japan 67
Germany 65

Source: McKinsey Global Institute.

organization through high-speed data links. Cross-geographic arbitrage also underpins the globalization models of Citigroup, Enron, and SAP. All of these companies are leveraging superior business-system productivity costs in different geographies.

When firms combine their ability to arbitrage productivity and factor cost differentials with scale effects, they can create overwhelming advantages over locally constrained participants. A global firm has the potential to produce goods and services using factor costs from whichever nations have the lowest cost of labor with the highest labor productivity, employing world-class techniques of production not used by local producers. Because they can also benefit from the scale effects of being able to spread investment and overhead expenses over a larger geographic base, they are able to achieve an enormous potential advantage over local producers. Whether they use this cost differential to overcome the insider access of local producers by compet-

EXHIBIT 2-3   **Labor productivity and cost differences make emerging markets an attractive arbitrage opportunity—1992** *(Index: U.S. = 100)*

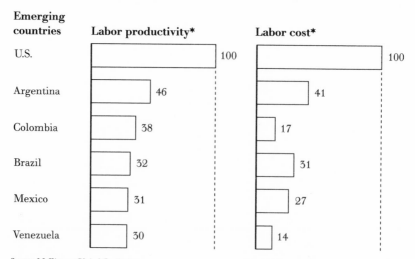

Source: McKinsey Global Institute.

*Weighted average of four industries: steel, processed food, retail banking, telecom.

ing on price, or simply pocket most of the differences as profits, they will be hugely advantaged. Some idea of the magnitude of the opportunity may be grasped from the fact that automotive experts place the theoretical limit on the ability of a company using Indian labor, world-class plant design, and scale effects to produce the Asian "world car" at less than $2,000. The developed world equivalent costs some $10,000 per car.[12]

The existence of such large cross-geographic arbitrage potential is direct evidence of just how separate have been the world's markets and industry structures. As we said, the test of a globalized market is that any given item being sold has the same price throughout the market, allowing for transaction and transportation costs. If large differences in price exist, then great differences in markets, that is, in demand curves and supply curves, must also exist. Pricing evidence indicates that most of the world's markets, particularly for factor costs, are still geographically distinct, despite the increased pace of the integration of the world economy over the last decade.

Arbitrage opportunities have access effects. The more access a firm has to different geographic markets, the greater the variety of arbitrage opportunities it can see. Many of the most attractive arbitrage opportunities also have specialization effects (e.g., the arbitrage opportunities for a participant with world-class productivity in a given function are greater than for other participants). Toyota has shown over time that it obtains a 30 to 40 percent greater labor productivity advantage over other participants in developed world markets.[13] It has also shown it can transplant this advantage in emerging markets as well.

Cross-geographic arbitrage also has significant scale effects because much of the investment required to capture arbitrage opportunities are fixed costs (e.g., technology platform costs and development of proprietary techniques to capture arbitrage). Much of the costs Toyota has built up to capture cross-geographic arbitrage are semi-fixed (e.g., training manuals, quality control methods, model designs permitting the use of standardized component parts in multiple models assembled in multiple countries).

This yields scale effects because as more countries to be arbitraged are added, the costs of capturing the arbitrage do not increase pro rata.

People often wonder about whether such arbitrage differentials are sustainable, given the relentless push of the forces at work in the transition economy. The answer depends on how close an industry is to its end-state condition. When comparison shopping is relatively easy, due to the availability and accessibility of information, demand curve aggregation—and global integration—can be relatively complete. This is why the price of a barrel of crude oil or an integrated circuit is always the same worldwide net of transaction and transportation costs. The customers for a barrel of oil or an integrated circuit are corporations that can easily comparison shop. Over the next decade or so, as interaction costs plummet through electronics, retail and small business customers will gain increased power to choose. This will speed up the formation of global markets in many industries. Internet shoppers already have more information more easily accessible than most large corporations could afford just a few years ago. As products such as Yahoo!, Firefly, and the like continue to evolve, single market conditions will be created for goods and services that have historically represented distinct markets.

However, the aggregation of global demand curves over the next decade or so does not imply that cross-geographic arbitrage opportunities will be fleeting. Not all demand aggregates globally at the same time; as described earlier, it will take a long time in any market for the bulk of local demand to migrate to global markets. At some stage, inevitably, local and national markets will lose such a mass of customers that the existing market and industry structures will lose their viability and will collapse into more aggregated, and far more specialized, global markets. Until then, however, cross-geographic arbitrage opportunities will remain.

For example, the beer-brewing industry in Ireland may eventually lose its existence as a separate industry structure; however,

Irish beer can simultaneously become a global micromarket. Guinness, in fact, is trying to promote the development of "Irish pubs" outside of Ireland. While this transformation to global structures is occurring, however, price differences are likely to vary by 50 percent or more from country to country for the same brand of beer (net of transaction costs and after currency adjustment).

It will take time, certainly several decades, for local factor costs such as labor and rent to converge worldwide and for productivity differences between different suppliers to disappear. In other words, producers with world-class productivity who are able to access low-cost factors of production will be able to live under the price umbrellas of high-cost, marginal local producers, who will hold much, if not most, of the market share in the world for a long time in many industries.

Why will it take a long time for both factor cost and productivity differences to converge globally? If a company is arbitraging a cheap source of skilled labor or a well-located plant site in a particular country, the costs of that labor or the rent for the plant site do not quickly adjust to a world market rate even if the market for the output globalizes (i.e., even if there is a worldwide price for the product). Local factor costs are the result of a myriad of local market effects, none of which are directly influenced by the action of the global market for the final product. For example, if a company decides to produce software written by low-cost programmers from India, the decision has little effect on the labor rate paid to Indian computer programmers. But even if the labor rates of computer programmers are bid up by the collective action of all global participants, other individuals in India with appropriate educational backgrounds can be recruited away from other, less rewarding jobs and trained in programming skills. Moreover, even if a particular local factor cost does begin to converge to world price levels in one locale, the arbitrageur can often simply shift production to another locale with lower factor costs, for example, as other emerging countries become skilled in writing software.

Similarly, if a company has a proprietary productivity advantage based on superior intellectual capital, it can arbitrage that advantage by either self-producing or by licensing or franchising that skill to local participants. In most industries, productivity advantages appear to be surprisingly durable, probably because they are derived from intangibles owned uniquely by the firm itself and are therefore not easily copied. Despite twenty years of trying to imitate Toyota, no automotive company has been able to equal Toyota's productivity advantages.

While we can imagine a fully globalized world economy in which the demand and supply curves for all goods and services are fully integrated into single market and industry structures, we are a long way from that world. The differentials in prices worldwide are the legacy of a world economy that has been organized around highly differentiated, geographically segmented markets. It will take decades for fully integrated markets to exist throughout the world, where the law of one price applies fully to all markets for capital, goods, services, labor, and other factor costs.

Even in relatively open, integrated national economies such as the United States, large variations in prices exist for equivalent goods and services, as well as for factor costs, from one region to another because of local supply curve differences. The price of carpenters and electricians in Mississippi is about half the rate of equivalent labor in New York City. The variations in supply curves between countries are far larger and far more durable than are those between the regions of a nation.

RUNNING THE RACE

The transition economy is extraordinarily attractive to strong competitors with superior value propositions. It provides the opportunity to gain the virtuous cycle effects of geographic expansion, enabling the capture of profits from weaker competitors who had previously been protected by geographic boundaries.

It also provides opportunities to earn increasing returns and to profit on cross-geographic arbitrage.

Winning players will tend to take full benefit of all three of these unique opportunities simultaneously. They will be continually investing in the intangible capital needed to create superior (i.e., world-class) value and will then use that superior value to put in place a self-perpetuating virtuous cycle of geographic expansion that gains access to more markets. Moreover, this same investment will benefit from increasing return effects because customers with increasing choice will seek out superior value on their own. If the company can also capture cross-geographic arbitrage, it can simultaneously reduce costs and increase margins. This also increases the ability of the company to invest. The combination provides the potential to make huge investments to expand while increasing returns on the capital and broadening profit margins through capture of cross-geographic arbitrage. If a company can take full advantage of these opportunities, it can easily out-distance all of its competitors.

All of this is easier said than done. Most competitors do not currently possess superior intangibles and, as a result, do not offer a superior value proposition. Therefore, they can neither put in place a virtuous cycle of geographic expansion nor benefit from increasing returns. Moreover, they have little capacity to capture cross-geographic arbitrage. Finally, they live in a world that seems to be filled with confusion, complexity, and uncertainty. Any action they take seems to be exposed to overwhelming risk.

This is why developing a winning strategy is so essential. Most companies have limited resources and must make careful choices about how to deploy those resources if they are to find a way to win the race. In most cases this will involve thinking through how to begin creating a virtuous cycle of geographic expansion, how to begin to earn increasing returns, and how to capture cross-geographic arbitrage. Just as the economy is making a transition from a geographically bounded world to a globally integrated world, so must a company. It needs a transition strategy.

These transition strategies are "midgame" strategies because they are strategies not about winning but rather about putting the company in a position to win. Just as it is a mistake to underestimate the pace of the transition to global market and industry structures, it is a mistake to overestimate it. Underestimating pace causes you to wait too long to act, allowing yourself to fall hopelessly behind your competitors. Overestimating pace causes you to make your moves too early, exposing you to unnecessary risks. For example, if you build strategies based on earning increasing returns but find that geographic barriers are still strong, you may lose to players gaining virtuous-cycle effects from geographic expansion. Companies will need to bear in mind that most end games in most industries lie far in the future. They must act now, but must act wisely, crafting strategies that account for pace, flexibility, and timing.

3

MIDGAME
STRATEGIES

GAINING THE HIGH GROUND

WHILE THE HEADLINES HAVE GONE to the mega-mergers, such as Citicorp–Travelers, Daimler-Benz–Chrysler, British Petroleum–Amoco, BankAmerica–NationsBank, and AT&T–TCI, "globalization," as we have now defined it, is also taking place in less visible industries among less well-known companies.

Consider Service Corporation International (SCI), the world's leader in funeral home services, or "death care services," as it is commonly called in the industry. SCI is well on its way to defining a new global industry. Founded and headquartered in the United States, SCI has made significant acquisitions recently in Europe, Australia, and Asia. It expands by purchasing either individual mom-and-pop firms or groups of firms assembled by funeral home consolidators and then transferring superior marketing and production processes. While keeping the local brands intact and building on family-based customer relationships, SCI transforms internal operations using a strategy in which local groups of apparently independent (to the public) funeral homes share vehicles, personnel, accounting staff, and embalming facilities. On the marketing side, SCI is skilled at offering extra services (e.g., flowers, better caskets) to the bereaved. In other words, it acquires access to privileged local intangible assets and then leverages specialized skills (i.e., proprietary processes) to gain significant local scale effects. At the global level, it builds world-class skills in such areas as negotiating and structuring acquisitions and in understanding demographics—vital in an industry that must anticipate and accommodate local death-rate changes.

SCI started small, with one funeral home, the Heights Undertaking Company, in Houston, Texas. The founder, Robert Waltrip, began experimenting with the idea of "clustering" several funeral homes in the early 1960s. After successfully implementing this strategy with three funeral homes in Houston, Waltrip established the Southern Capital Company in 1962 to facilitate an aggressive acquisition strategy. Southern Capital expanded first in Texas. In 1968, it purchased a funeral home in Chicago. In 1969, Southern Capital crossed geographic boundaries again, this time into Canada. That same year, Southern Capital changed its name to Service Corporation International. In early 1970 it began trading on the American Stock Exchange.

SCI has superior economics. In 1993, in a typical transaction, SCI acquired the Pine Grove Funeral Group, the largest Australian funeral house and crematorium operator. In the first year alone, SCI increased Pine Grove's sales by 13 percent and operating income by 40 percent, without raising prices. In other words, SCI is able to achieve higher returns as it acquires and expands. It has established a virtuous cycle of geographic expansion. Since 1992, SCI has had earnings growth of 32 percent annually, accompanied by annual market capitalization growth of 48 percent.

SCI achieves superior returns because it is competing with locals who cannot match its specialization or (local) scale advantages. The local funeral homes with which it competes have high costs and therefore create a price umbrella for SCI. By transplanting its methods of production (forgive us), SCI is able to arbitrage its productivity advantages. Essentially, SCI has begun to shape a new global industry where it is emerging as the dominant force. While it is several times larger than its next-biggest competitor, it has only a 1.1 percent share of the global funeral market. Its opportunities are virtually unbounded. There is no reason it could not contemplate eventually capturing a global market share of 10 percent or greater.

SCI is thus in a position to win in its industry even though it will be decades before the funeral home business fully forms global market and industry structures. Most firms do not enjoy such a position. For most firms, the challenge today is not so much to win as to position themselves to win—in other words, to accomplish what SCI has spent the last decade achieving.

MIDGAME STRATEGIES

Midgame strategies are about gaining position relative to other competitors. Midgame strategies take into account pace, flexibility, and timing as well as anticipating the competition's moves. The focus is on making "no regrets," high-return moves while avoiding "big bet," high-risk moves until they can be made with a reasonable degree of confidence in the outcome.[1]

Midgame strategies focus on such strategies as creating a virtuous cycle of geographic expansion or searching for opportunities to earn increasing returns or to capture cross-geographic arbitrage opportunities. As these midgame strategies succeed, competitive advantages that at first seem small will eventually push you out in front of the competition. This makes time your ally, not your enemy. Once you get a competitive edge that benefits from the transition economy, it is easy to stay ahead because you can go faster and faster as virtuous-cycle effects provide you with ever increasing advantages. Moreover, when the end-state dynamics of your industry become clearer, you will be in a better position than your competitors.

TWO TYPES OF INDUSTRY RESTRUCTURING

In 1996, approximately $1 trillion of merger and acquisition activity took place worldwide. In 1997, the volume reached $1.6 trillion.[2] Through mid-1998, the pace had accelerated. Spectacular mergers and acquisitions were being announced on an almost weekly basis; if the rate of the first half of 1998 had continued for the entire year, nearly $3 trillion of merger and acquisition activity would have taken place.

These mergers are the most visible manifestation of the strategies pursued by companies as they jockey for position in the transition economy. In fact, during the course of our research, we observed companies engaged in two fundamentally different midgame strategies: the "integrator" strategy and the "specialist" strategy. Each responds to one of the two kinds of industry restructuring that characterize the transition economy.

Integrators

In the *integrator* midgame, you take advantage of falling geographic barriers by acquiring or merging with similar companies in adjacent geographies. The intent is to gain the virtuous cycle effects of geographic expansion while capturing cross-geographic arbitrage through internal integration of operations. As you roll up others, you gain access and scale advantages while your competitors lose both relative position and the opportunity to do the roll-ups themselves. As you get larger, you can acquire bigger and bigger competitors. This increases your absolute earnings and expands your geographic base, relative to others, while eliminating potential rivals.

In the integrator midgame, a company expands across geography and across the business system by either owning or controlling all parts of the value chain. Depending on the industry, integrators' strategies can be based on going from local to national, from national to regional, or from regional to global. Integrators usually connect to customers by owning or controlling direct distribution channels. They either produce the goods or services themselves or use captive suppliers for this purpose. Either way, integrators try to control how work is undertaken throughout the business's value chain, enabling them to capture cross-geographic arbitrage.

Exxon is the classic global integrator in the petroleum industry, although John Rockefeller, in retrospect, played the integrator midgame in this industry by rolling up competitors over a hundred years ago. What is unique about the transition economy is that this can be done in every industry, and it is happening fast. The Daimler-Benz–Chrysler merger, the BankAmerica–NationsBank merger, the UBS–Swiss Bancorp merger, the Bell Atlantic–NYNEX–GTE mergers, and the British Petroleum–Amoco merger are all examples of companies pursuing integrator strategies over an expanded geographic arena.

Specialists

The second type of restructuring happens when companies pursue specialization in a focused area of the economy—that is, a "micromarket."[3] In the *specialist* midgame you focus on doing more business where you have relative skill advantages and less business where you lack world-class skills. The intent is to gain increasing return effects and to capture cross-geographic arbitrage opportunities through partnering with others. As you do more business in your specialty, you learn more, attract more talent, and find other specialists to acquire. As you gain specialization advantages, others want to work with you and help you expand your market access. As your reputation grows, more customers search you out, enabling you to capture greater intangible scale effects while increasing returns.

In the specialist model, a company competes across geography by leveraging specialization advantages and intangible scale effects (i.e., leveraging the fixed costs of building intangible assets). These players work as part of an industry value chain. They do not own or control the entire value chain. They accomplish much of the work of producing and delivering their output through contractual arrangements with integrators or other specialists. Component-parts manufacturers in the automotive industry (e.g., TRW, Bosch, Delphi) and payments-processing specialists in the financial services industry (e.g., ADP, FDC) all pursue the specialist strategy. Many of these specialists were originally owned by or were captives of integrators but are now independent active agents. For example, the credit card processor FDS used to be owned by American Express. Lucent, the telephone equipment maker, was formerly owned by AT&T. It is now an independent company, selling its products to AT&T and its competitors. Delphi, the component-parts maker, is being spun off by General Motors.

Specialists have learned how to compete in a world of entrenched integrators and geographic incumbents in spite of the fact that, in comparison to integrators, they often bear both access and fixed-cost scale disadvantages. They often find ways to take their specialty global, often through acquisitions that both deepen their ability to specialize and strengthen their ability to pursue cross-geographic arbitrage through contracting. For example, the number of automotive component manufacturers with over $2 billion in sales grew from 16 to 47 between 1992 and 1997.[4] They are now able to become big players themselves as the forces at work in the transition economy are making specialization ever more valuable in the global markets, which in turn enables them to create businesses of significant size in their specialties by meeting worldwide demand.

GLOBAL INDUSTRY STRUCTURES

Because most people are familiar with the roll-up model of industry restructuring, they assume that global industries come into existence when national industries merge, that existing industries somehow simply conglomerate into single global industry structures, different in size but not in shape. In reality, what happens is much more complicated. As traditional boundaries to economic activity disappear, the most aggressive, innovative, and intelligent players search the world for opportunities to create global markets. At the same time, equally well-motivated customers are looking in nontraditional places for opportunities to purchase products and services that precisely fit their needs. From the point of view of players in existing industries, competition appears as if from nowhere, and customers disappear as if into a void. Kimberly Clark, a pulp and paper company for most of this century, is now vying with consumer goods giant Procter & Gamble (P&G) for dominance in disposable diapers. Both are taking on the world. This puts a great deal of pressure on the vertically and horizontally integrated local and national industry participants. But more is going on than a simple collision of industries. All of a sudden, or so it seems, customers are demanding different, highly specialized products and are purchasing them from a new generation of competitors who focus with laserlike precision on particular customer segments, products, or elements of the business system. For example, local commercial banks find themselves in competition with specialists in credit cards, mutual funds, and mortgages based in different geographies.

The competitive attack takes place wherever the local or national supplier offers the customer the worst deal. If there is a local cartel that overprices a particular good or service or part of the value chain, that is where the attack takes place. If one customer class is cross-subsidizing another, the attackers will go after the class being discriminated against.

As this process goes on, the range of choice available to customers expands and competition intensifies. Traditional local players lose the ability to cross-subsidize unproductive elements of their business system. They are forced to outsource to the suppliers that have the best production techniques. This creates room for yet more specialists, and the entire business system begins to separate into component parts. Then, the new generation of specialists begins to rearrange the pieces—not just through acquisition and organic growth but also through alliances and counterparty agreements—to create new global markets and more specialized businesses. In the process, they begin to create new microindustry structures.

At the same time, well-run, integrated companies are looking for opportunities to acquire or merge with other integrators, particularly in high-fixed-cost businesses. As integrated producers lose volume and therefore scale effects, enormous pressure develops to merge with other integrators to recapture them. This is a robust strategy for defending against the attack of the specialists.

These two kinds of industry restructuring are being played out simultaneously in industry after industry. We see them in action today in telecommunications. Over the past several years, many of the regulatory prohibitions that once limited activities in this industry have been removed. Simultaneously, large business customers operating in multiple geographies have become dissatisfied with the high rates charged by their local telecommunications suppliers. They have actively sought out alternatives from newly emerging global specialists[5] in business telecommunication service, which will offer these large corporate customers exactly what they need: superior service at better prices designed particularly for companies operating in multiple countries. Traditional suppliers will continually become less competitive. Eventually, these customers will form a new global market. The universe of telecommunications specialists who serve them, such as the joint venture between AT&T and British Telecom, will make up a new global microindustry. Meanwhile, the local phone companies, having lost some of their most profitable customers, must either increase the prices they charge their remaining customers or lower their costs. Often, large integrated companies resolve this dilemma by divesting the parts of the business in which they can no longer compete. In the telecommunications industry this breakup of integrated production creates room for specialists to develop in each customer segment, from high-end retail to small business, and in every value-chain element, from data communications to equipment manufacturing. What was once an integrated telecommunications business system operated by a handful of companies is breaking apart into a number of global microindustries operated by many specialists with global scale.

A reasonable strategy for the traditional integrated suppliers in this situation is to merge with other integrated providers, which are also losing share to specialists. The Bell Atlantic–NYNEX–GTE merger that we mentioned above and the SBC–Ameritech merger provide scale effects in the U.S. telephone service provider industry through consolidating operations to spread the fixed-cost base over a far larger volume; the mergers also provide the combined companies with the mass needed to specialize internally and with larger networks of customers who can be served without incurring access charges.

What we see, therefore, as we survey the global landscape are two trends: the creation of cross-geographic specialists and the consolidation of traditional, integrated companies. Both trends are driving the unending wave of mergers, acquisitions, alliances, and divestitures.

These midgame strategies are viable only as long as the industry retains its geographically bounded structure. As global microindustries form, geographically determined industry structures will gradually erode. Eventually, superior players will emerge—*shapers* who will dominate the global microindustry structures now being created. Before explaining how the battle between integrators and specialists will play out, however, we must first describe the role of geographic incumbents in this process.

Geographic incumbents

Geographic incumbents are the broad class of players who, as yet, have not developed the world-class skills needed to play an integrator or specialist role beyond their current geography. In most industries, geographic incumbents hold from 60 to 90 percent of market share. In the financial services industry, the geographic incumbent category includes most regional and national banks and insurance companies. In the telecommunications industry, it includes most regional and national telecommunications service providers. In the automotive industry, it includes most regional and national components manufacturers.

Worldwide, these geographic incumbents are struggling as they lose their historical geographically derived advantages. As these advantages erode, geographic incumbents find themselves at access, specialization, and scale disadvantages relative to integrators or specialists. Unless they overcome those disadvantages, geographic incumbents will increasingly find themselves in a vicious cycle of decreasing profitability and facing the prospect of extinction. This is particularly true in industries like banking, telecommunications, automobiles, capital markets trading, and semiconductors, where a high proportion of total costs do not vary with volume and where loss of volume has large declining scale effects. For geographic incumbents in such a position, the only option may be to form alliances with specialists or be acquired by an integrator.

The relative size of the market share held by geographic incumbents versus integrators and specialists tells much about an industry's future. It is the geographic incumbents' share that is up for grabs by integrators or specialists. What happens to the geographic incumbents' share of the market will significantly determine the ultimate structure of the industry. The midgame is largely a battle to capture the geographic incumbents' piece of the pie.

CAPTURING EXTRAORDINARY
TRANSITION PROFITS

As they take market share and profits from geographic incumbents, integrators and specialists are, in effect, competing to capture the extraordinary virtuous cycle, increasing returns and cross-geographic arbitrage opportunities available in the transition from local and national structures to global structures.

Virtuous cycles for integrators

Integrators can create virtuous cycles of geographic expansion by taking share away from geographic incumbents. In SCI's case, the difference between its access and scale advantages and those of the geographic incumbents is so great that the local geographic incumbents are simply overmatched. Compared to SCI, local funeral home operators are also at a severe specialization disadvantage. Given enough time, integrators with such huge specialization advantages over local incumbents can gain share through organic growth (i.e., growing internally without relying on acquisitions) as well as through acquisition. Organic growth is the most important indicator of the quality of an integrator's value proposition; those who do not offer superior value propositions with world-class benefits to customers will not grow organically. However, given the increasing mobility of capital (as described in Chapter 1), many integrators, such as SCI, have also chosen to expand by acquiring disadvantaged geographic incumbents, which nonetheless have valuable intangible assets including customer bases, labor forces, and local brands. Acquisitions enable integrators to grow more quickly. While it is easier than ever before to gain geographic access, doing so by organic growth alone is frequently difficult and always slower than growing by acquisition because the remaining geographic barriers are still strong enough to ensure that only a fraction of potential customers switch to a new supplier at any one time.

If you grow through acquisition you get instant access to customers and an operating entity complete with a labor force, physical facilities, and so forth. In the midgame, speed is often critical because if *you* don't "roll 'em up," your competition will.[6] Once a strong base is established in a new geography, it becomes far easier to grow organically in that geography.

One of the masters of this approach is NationsBank, which just took on the name of its newest partner, BankAmerica. Based in North Carolina, the then-NCNB first expanded beyond its state in the early 1980s to acquire a small bank in Florida. At the time, NCNB had earnings of $95 million and a market capitalization of $325 million.[7] Over the next two decades, under the leadership of Hugh McColl, NationsBank acquired and integrated bank after bank in state after state. NationsBank developed world-class skills in acquiring and integrating banks, moving to common operating systems platforms and cross-geographic customer group and product organizations. As a result of the merger with BankAmerica, it became the biggest, most profitable bank in the United States, with pro forma earnings approaching $10 billion[8] and a pro forma market capitalization of $130 billion—400 times its market capitalization in the early eighties. NCNB accomplished this without moving much outside the United States. The new BankAmerica is now one of a small group of players, along with the new Citibank–Travelers group, Lloyds, GE Capital, AIG, and Hong Kong and Shanghai Banking Corporation (HSBC), to occupy the critical high ground as the financial services industry begins to create global industry structures: these players have market capitalizations sufficient to acquire geographic incumbents around the world.

Not all acquisitions by integrators deliver higher returns on invested capital. The key is whether the access and scale advantages following the merger are sufficient to create a virtuous cycle of organic growth. Which is to say that if an integrator cannot grow the business after acquisition, it will have gained only a temporary advantage. The key to SCI's success is not simply acquiring local companies, but growing the business after the acquisition. If all the growth is acquired, and if the sellers are paid the full value of the synergies, then little progress is made.

This gets to the one big—and obvious—disadvantage of acquisitions. They are capital intensive. When an acquirer pays a high price for a company, most of the value of the synergies is captured by the seller. In industries where there are a large number of small geographic incumbents and few integrators, the bargaining power is in the hands of the acquirer. However, in industries where there is a large number of acquirers with deep pockets, the premiums paid can approach the full value of the potential synergies as well as the potential to increase returns through the acquisition. For example, in the 1997 NationsBank–Barnett Bank merger, NationsBank paid $14.8 billion, which was approximately a 43 percent one-week premium over Barnett's trading price before it put itself up for sale. This premium enabled the former owners to capture much of the fixed-cost scale advantages created by the combination. In this case, NationsBank's objective was to eliminate roughly 50 percent of Barnett's costs. Despite the premium paid, NationsBank stock rose to a premium in the thirty days following the announcement of the transaction.

In industries where the sellers are capturing much of the benefits of acquisition, the best approach may be to merge two strong players and pay more modest premiums to the seller. Daimler–Chrysler, BankAmerica–NationsBank, and SBC–Ameritech are all examples of mergers in 1998 between relatively strong players in which only modest premiums were paid. This approach enabled both companies' stockholders to share, largely pro rata, in the access and scale effects of the merger. Moreover, because almost all large, successful companies have some real specialization advantages, these mergers also provide both parties with instant access to each other's specialization skills.

Consider the Daimler–Chrysler merger. In this merger, Chrysler shareholders received about a 15 percent premium. However, the equity markets liked the deal so well that both Chrysler and Daimler shares appreciated by about 15 percent in the month following the merger's announcement. Perhaps investors liked this transaction because it provides many benefits to both companies. Both companies have unique skills and intangible assets and merged from a position of strength, enjoying record revenues and earnings. Through the merger, Daimler gains access to world-class purchasing and supplier management skills, an area of increasing importance in the automotive industry. Chrysler has proven expertise in efficient product development and in the areas of fast time-to-market and sound design-to-cost, both of which are critical to success in all but the luxury-car segment. Daimler's attempts to get into the small-car segment, which have not been very successful, could get a boost from specialized skills and resources of Chrysler. While the automotive industry is global, there are still substantial national industry structures in place, particularly distribution networks (including in some cases thousands of local dealerships). While it is arguable how much synergy exists from access to each other's home markets, partly due to concerns about brand dilution, it is widely agreed that over a period of time, geographically complementary distribution networks will be advantageous. This is particularly true for Chrysler, largely a North American player. For Daimler, an immediate advantage is sharing parts distribution and other logistics in North America.

This merger has also provided each party with access to each other's factor costs and techniques of production. This creates the potential to capture cross-geographic arbitrage. North America is already the low-cost luxury-car manufacturing location, and Daimler's plant in Alabama produces its successful high-end sports utility vehicles. Other opportunities abound, and complementary geographic presence will eventually allow the new company to capture these. Along with Toyota and Ford, the Daimler–Chrysler combination now occupies some of the most important high ground as the automobile industry begins to move toward an end game.

Cross-geographic arbitrage for integrators

Integrators capture cross-geographic arbitrage largely through internal operations. The ability of large companies operating across geographies to do so has long provided much of the impetus needed to overcome the geographic barriers between markets. Citibank is a good example.

Up through the late 1980s, Citibank used a multilocal approach to conduct operations in its credit card business. It essentially replicated its full business system in each country—card manufacturing, printing and mailing, processing, marketing, customer service, and collections. In the early 1990s, after a few rough years in the U.S. market, Citibank transformed its model from multilocal to global-local. It centralized many of its business system functions to be run either from a single global location or on a continent-by-continent basis. It set up a global utility in the United States to manufacture all its cards. It established a global brand. It moved all its European processing to the United States and all its European printing and mailing to the Netherlands. It centralized its Asian data center in Singapore and established a global data network, outsourced to AT&T and run out of three hubs in North Carolina, London, and Singapore. It centralized its branch design and created an integrated product set for its various operations. As any Citi customer traveling abroad and using the Citi ATM will know, the ATMs have the same look, feel, and functionality regardless of location. Some of Citibank's credit card operations, however, are still almost entirely locally determined—local marketing, customer service, and collections. This global-local approach enabled Citibank to capture the benefits of its global reach by realizing internal arbitrage opportunities—scale economies in low-cost, high-productivity locations.

Much of the historical success of integrators—oil companies such as Exxon and Shell, personal financial services companies such as Citicorp and American Express, and other leaders such as Toyota, IBM, and Caterpillar—is due to this ability to capture internal arbitrage. *The key to internal arbitrage is to achieve integration across different geographic markets through internal organizational processes and internal standards and protocols.* For example, Toyota, through standardization, can produce parts in many different countries, depending on which is cheaper, for use in assembling cars in a variety of countries. The profits from the arbitrage have been used to support overhead and other interaction costs required to maintain the integration of the company's operations and to coordinate activity across the entire value chain.

Although internal cross-geographic arbitrage is not a new technique, it is becoming much more attractive to integrators. As markets liberalize, as capital becomes more mobile, and as electronics lower the interaction costs of work performed in separate geographies, it becomes easier and easier to capture such internal arbitrage in more areas including, in particular, arbitraging higher-skilled, nonmanufacturing labor. For example, a recent study suggested that pharmaceutical companies could locate global product development functions in India to capture labor anomalies in the form of cheap Ph.D.s.[9] They estimated that the average cost of a multinational's R&D could fall by up to a theoretical potential of 95 percent. If an entire drug were developed and manufactured in India, the cost could fall by approximately 75 percent (Exhibit 3-1). As the Indian government simplifies or abolishes regulations that have in the past blocked capturing such opportunities, the total value of using India as a base for sourcing pharmaceutical formulations for export and for R&D could rise to $800 million for a sophisticated global player.

We are beginning to see this trend spread well beyond manufacturing and product development. Using electronics to locate global utilities—administration, data processing, finance functions—in the lowest-cost labor markets in the world also has the potential to reap major cost savings. IBM and Dell now have some call centers in Ireland, as does Citigroup with its data processing. Motorola, Cadence, Hughes Network, and Temic have all opened software-design centers in India. All these companies are realizing global scale economies by capturing skilled labor anomalies through advanced computing and communications technologies.

Increasing returns for specialists

Specialists have extraordinary potential for increasing returns benefits because of their ability to leverage intangible capital

---

EXHIBIT 3-1   Combining world-class productivity with lowest factor costs can yield savings of close to 80 percent

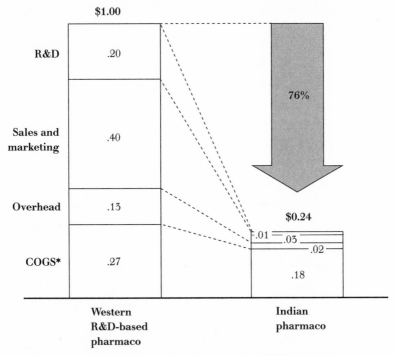

Source: Adapted from "Four Opportunities in India's Pharmaceutical Market," by Rajesh Garg, Gautam Kunra, Asutosh Padhi, and Anupam Puri, *McKinsey Quarterly* 1996, No. 4, 139.

*Cost of goods sold (COGS) assumes 50% raw materials and 50% other manufacturing costs; Indian pharmaco COGS assumes raw materials costs equal to Western R&D-based multinational pharmaco; other manufacturing costs (labor and infrastructure combined) are estimated to be about 65% less than R&D MNC pharmaco costs.

scale effects and to out-invest everyone else. Consider MBNA. MBNA has undertaken customer-based specialization primarily in the U.S. credit card industry. Spun off from a nearly bankrupt bank holding corporation in 1990, MBNA is now the second largest credit card company in the United States after Citibank, with a market capitalization of about $40 billion. The company generated $623 million in net income in 1997.

MBNA is in the business of lending money; its success is built on several specialized skills including affinity marketing and data mining. Essentially, MBNA differentiates itself by how it attracts new customers and how it serves those customers. It seeks out formal organizations that endorse MBNA products—sports associations, professional associations, universities—and codevelops branded credit cards. It also markets to attractive customer segments that share common interests or affinities. Thus, its specialized marketing and segmentation skills enable it to cherry-pick the most attractive customer segments—those that carry higher balances (45 percent above the industry average)[10] while simultaneously generating lower loan losses.

Integral to its success are its data-mining skills. By leveraging sophisticated technology and highly predictive models, MBNA is able to make better credit decisions. It gathers data on members and conducts refined analyses of its databases, while putting in place processes to learn more about customers and creating cards that give the customer segment special breaks on rates for services that are of particular interest to them. In this way MBNA induces the best risk-reward relationships by encouraging loyalty and above-average card usage, but below-average defaults.

MBNA's specialization generates intangible assets—customer knowledge and relationships—that it converts into valuable intangible capital—databases and networks. These intangibles are then applied to create ever more targeted marketing strategies. These strategies don't use much capital because credit card receivables can be securitized. MBNA has thus created a business system that leverages intangibles without requiring a large capital base. As a result it has generated huge returns—consistently over 30 percent ROE. However, MBNA has begun to hit the limits of its exceptional growth in the United States and is now beginning to go abroad. After only a few years, it has attained a 7 percent market share in the UK.

World-class specialists gain access to expanded geography without having to use too much financial capital. Furthermore, they are better able to manage the risks because they stick to expansion where they have deep skills. Customers seek them out because they offer better value. Geographic incumbents seek them out to help overcome their own specialization disadvantages and to gain access to specialty skills to offset scale or access disadvantages. Even large integrators often contract out to specialists for parts of the value chain because the specialist can often do the function at higher quality and lower cost. Further, when world-class specialists in different parts of the value chain cooperate, they can establish common standards and protocols, which are key to controlling work across the value chain. If they can succeed in this, they neutralize much of the value integrators' gain by controlling or owning all pieces of the value chain. For example, Microsoft and Intel, working together, established common standards that negated much of IBM's historical control over the computer business.

The principal tools of specialists are alliances or webs.[11] Rather than acquiring to gain access or fixed-cost scale effects, they contract or work with others to gain those benefits. If they do make acquisitions, it is usually to deepen their specialization skills or to increase their intangible scale effects. Specialists have huge advantages in capturing increasing returns. But specialists in many industries are often less able to capture cross-geographic arbitrage.

Cross-geographic arbitrage for specialists

In most industries, it has been relatively difficult for specialists to capture cross-geographic arbitrage because of the existence of multiple, distinct markets with huge interaction costs between them. Unlike integrators, who can, as we described earlier, internally integrate across geographic markets, the interaction barriers that prevent specialists from working together across geography are difficult to surmount until standards and protocols are developed. Over time, this will change as global value chains emerge, as global protocols and standards are developed, and as specialists expand their geographic reach.

The development of protocols and standards often starts with a company's attempt to capture arbitrage opportunities by outsourcing. In relatively simple industries, such as toy or shoe manufacturing, this process is well under way. Some players are capturing huge arbitrage opportunities by outsourcing to captives—dependent companies—or partnering. Manufacturers including Nike and Mattel have been able to move most of their production to emerging markets. Nike sources components for their footwear from more than thirty plants across Asia, including China, Thailand, Indonesia, and Vietnam. One of their signature shoes, the Air Max Penny, is made up of fifty-two different components from five nations. In the past decade, Nike has reduced production costs as a percentage of revenues from 67 percent in 1988 to 60 percent in 1997. In the early 1990s, Nike was able to use its increased operating income to invest in their core intangible: the Nike brand. Selling and administrative expenses grew from 20 percent to 25 percent of revenues during the same period, largely due to increased advertisement and promotional spending outside the United States.

In some industries, companies have begun to contract externally with other specialists through arm's-length counterparty arrangements in an effort to capture cross-geographic arbitrage. Most notably in the capital markets and computer industries, it has become possible for specialists to do this by contracting with one another, with integrators, and with geographic incumbents. In these industries, producers can capture internal arbitrage for themselves in their area of specialty, while sharing in the arbitrage the others are capturing through counterparty transactions.[12]

In fact, the potential arbitrage opportunities in an industry organized for external contracting is far greater than can be achieved by a single company through internal arbitrage. An industry fully structured for arbitrage capture through external contracting has access to the lowest factor costs, everywhere, and has specialists with productivity and risk-taking advantages in every business function. The resulting products are frequently superior and cost less. This increases aggregate demand worldwide because high quality at low cost attracts customers who might otherwise find their way to other sectors.

It is not surprising that it has been the relatively simple manufacturing businesses, like shoes and toys, in which it has proved easiest to capture the arbitrage potential through external contracting. In such industries, there is little need for global industry restructuring to permit the capture of arbitrage. Use of partners or captives is sufficient to gain the benefits. But it is arguable whether the Nike or Mattel approach can work everywhere.

In more complex industries—such as automotive, health care, or personal financial services—much of the entire industry must reorganize globally to create the conditions for external-contracting–based arbitrage to take off. While integrated local players still dominate local markets in these industries, the ability to find attractive counterparties is limited. The incumbent has few incentives to act as a counterparty, and bargaining power over it will be limited. One lesson here for participants is that efficient contract-based, cross-geographic arbitrage among specialists will not take place until counterparty structures evolve. Trying to capture arbitrage too early can be costly and risky. There is another lesson here for participants in large complex industries: *The capture of cross-geographic arbitrage is heavily dependent on reducing the complexity of the arbitrage transaction.* Just as complex financial arbitrage transactions need to be decomposed into a series of simpler trades, complex arbitrage in the real economy will best take place by disaggregating the complexity into a series of simpler transactions.

When conditions are right, however, arbitrage can yield powerful benefits. Consider the success the electronics industry has had in capturing cross-geographic arbitrage in the personal computer business. Participants as diverse as Microsoft, Intel, and Dell work together in a global value chain. The key has been to use a wide variety of very specialized suppliers, each focusing on a single part of the value chain, working together through standards and quality control collectively enforced by the industry. In the future, external cross-geographic arbitrage through contracting is going to become an even more important element of strategy because the global economy is becoming sufficiently specialized and enough global standards are emerging to make successful counterparty transactions easier to undertake.

THE BATTLE TO DEFINE INDUSTRIES

Competition between geographic incumbents, integrators, and specialists drives the industry restructuring described in Chapter 2. Even industries that have already formed global structures are being redefined. Large geographic integrators merge with one another; specialists create new subindustry structures by dominating elements of the business system; and integrators and specialists learn to work together in new ways through contracts, standards, and collective quality control. In the electronics business, integrated players such as IBM, Compaq-DEC and Hewlett-Packard compete with specialized players such as Microsoft, Intel, Oracle, and SAP for share of value added. In the oil business competitors from all parts of the industry are competing for position: the major integrated petroleum companies (Exxon, Shell), the independent oil producers (Hess), the national oil companies (Pemex), oil service companies (Schlumberger), oil and gas traders (Enron), and independent refiners (Tosco).

Each industry restructures in its own idiosyncratic way. Access, scale, and specialization advantages are highly specific. However, there are some elements that will heavily influence the particular profit opportunities and roles available. It makes a big difference whether the geographic structure of the industry prior to entering a transition period was local, national, or global.

In nationally structured businesses, nationally integrated producers as a group are, in general, losing share and earning less on capital invested than specialists. In the telecommunications industry, large national players including Deutsche Telekom, NTT, and Bell Atlantic clash with emerging global specialists such as MCI–WorldCom and the AT&T–British Telecom joint venture in international telecommunications. In the personal financial services business, large integrated national banks including the new BankAmerica, DeutscheBank, and Lloyds grapple with emerging global specialists such as GE Capital, MBNA, Schwab, and Fidelity.

In general, most of the national integrators in these industries lack the skills necessary to compete outside their home countries and are rightfully concerned about the risks of doing so. In contrast, the specialists in these industries usually are better able to manage the risks because they stick to expansion, where they have deep skills. Their difficulty in crossing borders comes from the well-entrenched national business standards to be found in each country. Moreover, the access and scale advantages of nationally based incumbents are formidable. So creating global industry structures in nationally structured industries is a struggle for both integrators and specialists alike.

In local industries, the battle looks different because the existing incumbents are small and markets are fragmented. In these industries, players such as McDonald's, Wal-Mart, Compass, and SCI are defining new global industries where none have existed by deploying an integrator model. In industries with global industry structures, there are already several global integrators that have powerful incumbency advantages and are adept at leveraging access and scale advantages and internally capturing cross-geographic arbitrage. However, they have less room left for geographic expansion, particularly in the developed world. In most of these industries, numerous specialists are emerging rapidly. At some stage, few geographic incumbents will remain in these industries, leaving the large global integrators with no more roll-up acquisition opportunities. Consequently, mergers in the relatively mature global industries such as automobiles (e.g., Daimler–Chrysler) or aerospace (e.g., Boeing–McDonnell Douglas) are now often between peers.

In general, then, the pattern across industries is that integrators as a group are losing share to the specialists. However, roll-up acquisitions are making individual integrators bigger even while, as a class, they lose market share.

FROM MIDGAME TO ENDGAME

Midgame strategies are viable until the transition opportunities from those strategies are exhausted. At some stage, integrators run out of acquisitions and specialists achieve global scale. As we described in Chapter 2, once an industry fully globalizes, growth opportunities slow down to overall market rates and participants face the prospect of decreasing returns as the markets become increasingly perfect. The only real defense against becoming trapped in a mature, commoditized global market is to become an industry shaper (Exhibit 3-2).

The shaper strategy

Industry shapers combine elements of the approaches pursued by geographic integrators and winning specialists. They create virtuous cycles of geographic expansion, earn increasing returns, and capture cross-geographic arbitrage both internally and from external contracting. Shapers create unique, enduring roles that others cannot easily imitate. Rather than matching the capabilities of the company to the opportunities afforded by the historical geographic structure of the industry, shapers create compelling value propositions so that the industry rearranges itself around the company's unique capabilities. Multiple shapers can coexist in the same industry; for example, Microsoft, Intel, and SAP all have shaped unique roles for themselves in the global personal computer industry and work together as part of a global value chain.

Shapers understand the economic interests of all players in the industry and are often skilled in crafting alliance propositions that are appealing. They do not try to do everything themselves, but rather are willing to involve others. But they keep the best parts of the business for themselves. The result is both rapidly growing earnings and high returns on financial capital. As the shaper continually captures an increasing share of profits, the

---

EXHIBIT 3-2   The four types of industry participants can be identified by unique strategies

Specialists

- Become world-class in areas of specialization
- Leverage intangible capital scale
- Gain intangibles-based access
- Generate high returns, but capture small piece of profit pool
- High ROE with little book equity growth

Shapers

- Dominate "slivers"
- Become intangible-heavy and capital-light
- Capture increasing returns and arbitrage opportunities
- High ROE and book equity growth

Geographic Incumbents

- Lack world-class skills
- Access and scale advantages limited to geographic region
- Geographic advantages erode
- Low ROE and low book equity growth

Geographic Integrators

- Gain access to customers and scale effects
- Gain advantage through cross-geographic arbitrage
- Earn lower returns, but larger share of total profit pool
- Constant ROE with high book equity growth

geographic incumbents, integrators, and specialists find they have no choice but to work with it.

Geographic integrators can become industry shapers. Specialists can become industry shapers. Even a geographic incumbent facing a vicious cycle of decreasing profitability can become an industry shaper if it can craft winning value propositions. The trick is to discover the unique intangibles that can be used to create new industry structures, which the shaper then dominates. This intangible-based approach follows the path of the leading global specialists and creates powerful increasing-returns effects.

When do you want to become a shaper? At the same point you move to an endgame in chess: whenever you have the opportunity. If you are successful at playing a midgame, at some point you must move to the endgame in order to win.

Shaping telecom equipment

Let's look at what "shaping" means in the telecom equipment industry. Despite a great deal of consolidation in the early 1980s, this industry's structure is still in flux, driven by the technology changes described in Chapter 1. The top eight players have 55 percent of the market, with another twenty companies sharing the remaining 45 percent. Increasingly, open standards and compatible interfaces mean easy interoperability of equipment from various suppliers. Global standards and protocols have made it possible for specialists to enter the industry on a global scale.

Today, the battle in this industry is between specialists that have come to dominate a particular technology, like Cisco in routers or Ericsson in wireless, and large entrenched full-line telecom producers such as Lucent and Nortel. Because of the speed with which technology is advancing, all of these producers have found that business is robust. These companies still have potential to capture global scale in specialties and to acquire and consolidate other companies. By this measure, midgame strategies are still viable.

Continuing to pursue such midgame strategies, however, is becoming dangerous. Why? Because global shapers are beginning to emerge, and long-term global industry structures are beginning to form.

One clear shaper has begun to emerge in the industry: Cisco. Cisco has come to dominate the markets for routers—the critical equipment needed to facilitate the movement, at switching "hubs" of data and voice communications, between one network point in, for example, one service provider's network to another network point in another service provider's network. In particular, Cisco has specialized in the routers that facilitate global Internet-based communication.

As Internet traffic has taken off, Cisco has turned its investments in intangibles in this arena into a virtuous cycle of geographic expansion while also capturing increasing returns. Started by Stanford researchers in the eighties, Cisco invested heavily in the intellectual property and talent needed to dominate the routing of data. In the nineties, it bolstered this strategy by making a flurry of acquisitions to supplement its technology and product development capabilities and to ensure dominance of router technology not just in data but increasingly in voice as well. (Cisco is one of the most acquisitive players in the industry.)

Through astute investment in technology, by leveraging early market share, and by developing an excellent sales force, it has achieved remarkable organic growth in revenue and earnings, riding the exponential growth of Internet-based traffic. Cisco is an industry shaper because, more than any other company in its industry, it is redefining telecommunications on its own terms through its dominance of the markets for routers. From a market capitalization of $3 billion in 1992, Cisco grew to $100 billion by mid-1998. Despite its size, Cisco has a much smaller product line than traditional telecom players like Lucent. However, its dominance in its specialty is unrivaled.

There are other players in the telecommunications equipment industry that have the potential to become shapers due to their heavy investment in intangible assets. For example, Ciena is a specialist start-up that has invested heavily in technology to expand the bandwidth capacity of fiber. The large, broad-line players such as Nortel and Lucent have also invested in intangibles, but the core of their business is still supplying traditional voice communication products to service providers—mature businesses that are hard to shape. European players such as Ericsson and Nokia have focused on high-growth technologies. For example, Ericsson made an early push into wireless, where it now earns 70 percent of its profits.

In the next few decades, as the technology continues to evolve, it is likely that the telecom equipment industry will enter an endgame that resembles the personal computer industry. The telecom equipment industry will likely become, increasingly, a series of global scale specialists working together in a value chain, each of which will have shaped, and come to dominate, specific global microindustries.

SHAPERS WILL WIN THE RACE FOR THE WORLD

The second half of this book is devoted to the subject of shaping industries. Pursuing either a specialist or an integrator approach can be rewarding in the midgame, but there are fundamental business and strategic reasons for believing that shapers will be the players who win the race for the world. From a business point of view, shapers create new industry structures built on their own intangibles and thereby create stable industry platforms on which to stand. In contrast, integrators eventually run out of candidates to acquire. Unless they can become shapers themselves, by specializing in parts of the business system that give them abilities to capture disproportionate returns, they become more and more vulnerable. After all, integrators who just become bigger, but not better, eventually become geographic incumbents to be attacked as the forces at work cause them to lose their privileged geographic access. Moreover, just as integrators run into limits by running out of acquisition opportunities, specialists eventually saturate their global markets in that specialty. Specialists are also vulnerable to shapers that may redefine the industry in a way that eliminates the need for their expertise.

Shapers will also win because they will enjoy, like Cisco, superior market capitalizations, enabling them to acquire whatever they want. Geographic incumbents who fail to act, specialists who become ever-smaller players, and integrators who run out of consolidation opportunities and thereby begin to disappoint the market, are all, over time, vulnerable to shapers with superior market capitalizations. We now turn to that challenge.

4

KEEPING CONTROL OF YOUR DESTINY

THE MARKET-CAPITALIZATION IMPERATIVE

RETURNS ARE NOT THE ONLY THING increasing in the transition economy. So are market capitalizations. There is pressure on all to increase market capitalization. It comes from two directions. As the world's equity markets continue to integrate, capital will be attracted to the high performers and run from those that are standing still or losing ground. And as performance pressure spreads throughout the world, market capitalization will be a firm's only form of protection. Participants that are not able to get high performance from their assets are likely to lose control of those assets to others that can make better use of them. You must resolve to maintain a superior market capitalization or risk losing control over your own destiny. On the other side, superior market capitalization is the ultimate offensive weapon. It gives you the strength to acquire the assets, structure the alliances, and attract the talent you will need to capture the opportunities ahead in this transition economy. This, then, is the market-capitalization imperative.

While the Anglo-Saxon world has had a relatively open market for what we might call strategic control for the last twenty years, this has not been true in the rest of the world. Now, more and more business people worldwide are recognizing the importance and value of market capitalization. Over the past two years we have witnessed in continental Europe, Latin America, and Asia a meaningful shift in the attitude of the world's corporate leaders. Driven by global institutional investors—forcing spin-offs, divestitures, and a focus, albeit often grudging, on shareholder value—the leadership of many of the larger European corporations, who used to dismiss market capitalization as largely irrelevant outside the Anglo markets, are beginning to change their minds. At the same time, many state-owned enterprises are being privatized and now face the same pressure. Previously insulated equity markets have been pried open, and foreign share ownership is on the rise as mutual funds, pension funds, and other institutional investors seek attractive returns abroad. More and more privately controlled and family owned companies are tapping into the global capital markets, and in so doing are being forced to accept its terms in order to gain access to cheap capital.

The restructuring of the Asian markets in the face of various financial crises has brought with it the need to open up ownership to foreigners. In Latin America, financial crises have also catalyzed the opening up of large portions of the local economies. While Latin America is much farther behind Europe and North America in terms of the wide-scale conversion of family controlled conglomerates and companies to publicly controlled ones, the trend is clearly accelerating. A large for-sale sign is going up in many sectors.

MARKET CAPITALIZATION IN THE TRANSITION ECONOMY

Until the summer of 1998, the world's stock markets, except for Japan, had been on an unprecedented run-up for five years.[1]

From 1945 to 1990, total returns to shareholders (that is, stock appreciation plus dividends) averaged about 9 percent compounded; from 1992 to 1997 they were at 15.3 percent compounded.[2] In historical terms, equity prices are at extraordinary market-to-book value ratios and price-to-earnings ratios despite the market correction in 1998.

Some believe that this increase in stock values is evidence of a temporarily irrational market, one similar to the Japanese market in the late 1980s when speculation drove a classic bubble in equities and other assets, particularly real estate.[3] As of early 1999 when this book was going to press, this bull market has overwhelmed every corrective move—including the scary period in late summer 1998 when there was talk of worldwide depression in the wake of Russian default and the rescue of hedge fund Long-Term Capital. There is little evidence, however, that the sustained bull market is due either to speculation or to the fundamental overliquidity and incautious lending that drove the Japanese market. There are few signs of excessive speculation in real estate or other assets, or indications that investors are unaware of the risks in equities.[4]

As a result, the market has produced remarkable valuations of stocks. Even start-up companies can raise almost unlimited funds. Yahoo!, an Internet directory, was started by two Stanford students in 1994. Two years later, with only $1.4 million in revenues, Yahoo! was able to raise $34 million in equity through a public offering of 10 percent of its stock. The market value of the shares immediately shot up to more than twice the offering price, placing a market-capitalization value on the company of a whopping $850 million on the day it went public. Yahoo! had a market capitalization of $8.5 billion on annual revenues of around $140 million and book equity of $147 million as this book was going to press. Such valuations seem incredible. However, given that Yahoo! benefits from nearly every trend described in this book, perhaps the market is not being completely irrational. Given the trends described in this book, you would expect the stocks most favored by the world's capital markets to be those that represent the best claims on those trends; thus, as global integration proceeds, we expect to see a continuing revaluation of corporate equities relative to historical experience.

Even if a good portion of this is due to a degree of "irrational exuberance" in the capital markets,[5] particularly in the "Internet" stocks, there is a greater force at work here. We looked at U.S. stocks, where the best historical data are available and where effects have been most pronounced in the 1990s. Over the forty-five–year period between 1945 and 1990, book values and market values for all U.S. companies were roughly equal; that is, the market-to-book ratio fluctuated in a range around 1.0. This means that for all U.S. companies over this time period, the market capitalization was roughly the same as the tangible value of the company. During the 1990s, however, the market-to-book ratio increased sharply and is now greater than 3 (Exhibit 4-1).[6]

We believe that this increase is partly due to a fall in the cost of equity. In an attempt to validate this hypothesis, we took a list of the 200 largest companies worldwide as measured by total market capitalization as of year-end 1996. We then identified the 25 companies within the group with the lowest earnings growth and with the least change in return on equity. Between 1991 and 1996, the earnings of these companies grew at a compounded rate of 1.0 percent, while their return on book equity fell from 11.2 percent to 10.0 percent in 1996. In other words, their performance hardly changed. Their market capitalizations, however, grew at a compound rate of 11.4 percent. Some believe this increase in value without an increase in performance is proof that the market is filled with wild speculation. We believe the explanation behind the rise in the value of these no-performance-change stocks is more straightforward: Just as the price of a bond issued at par will rise to a premium if interest rates fall, the value of stock in companies whose earnings and return on equity capital remain constant will rise if the cost of equity falls. As we will explain a few pages later in the chapter, such a fall in the cost of equity capital is understandable given the changes in the supply and demand for all capital and, in particular, equity capital that have occurred in the 1990s.

EXTRAORDINARY VALUATIONS EXPLAINED

But the falling cost of equity does not adequately explain the extraordinary market valuations of some of the world's global firms. We looked at another group of companies: the 100 global companies with the greatest increase in market capitalization since 1993. The list includes players from a diverse set of countries and industries but excluded large national companies (e.g., in telecommunications and banking). Fifty-eight on the list had their headquarters in the United States, 30 were European, 11 were from Asia (mostly Japanese), and 1 was Canadian. Thirty-two of these companies were in largely global industries (such

EXHIBIT 4-1   **The ratio of market capitalization to book value of U.S. stocks is sharply on the rise in the 1990s**

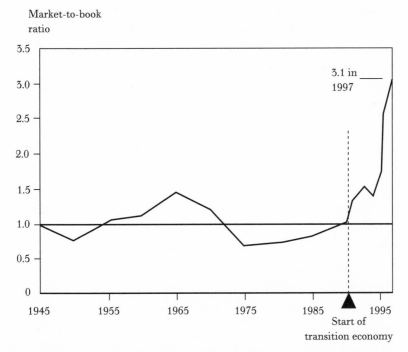

Sources: Data from U.S. Federal Reserve; *IFC-Stock Market Fact Book;* Compustat; IRS: Sourcebook; *DAI Factbook.*

as petroleum and automotive), 16 were in the "born global" electronics industries (computer and software companies), 31 were in rapidly globalizing industries (consumer packaged goods, pharmaceuticals), and 21 were global companies operating in largely local or national industries (food, insurance, banking).

These companies all had spectacular increases in their market capitalization in the 1993 to 1998 period—collectively growing from almost $1.7 trillion to $5.9 trillion—a compound growth rate of 28 percent versus the market average for all stocks world-wide of about 13 percent. The outstanding stock market perfor-mance of these companies is not surprising given that, as a group, their earnings increased at a compound rate of 25 percent during this period, and their return on equity increased from about 9 percent to 18 percent.[7]

We broke the growth in market capitalization for each of these companies into two components: (1) increases in book value and (2) increases in market value over book. Not surprisingly, the rapid market-capitalization growth is primarily due to growth in the market value over book value—$3.8 trillion of the $4.2 trillion growth—rather than growth in book capital. The collec-tive market-to-book ratio of the 100 global companies improved from 2.4 to 5.2 during this time period (the U.S. average was about 3 in 1998).

To understand this increase in market-to-book value, we divided the 100 companies into four quartiles of 25 each in order of their market-to-book ratios: (1) a very high market-to-book group (i.e., a collective market-to-book ratio in 1998 of 14.2); (2) a high market-to-book group of 6.3; (3) a somewhat high market-to-book group of 3.7; and (4) a below-average market-to-book group of 2.2 (Exhibit 4-2). The compounded growth rate in market capitalization varied across these four groups, with the highest market-to-book quartile growing at 37 percent and the lowest quartile growing at 16 percent.

Interestingly, the earnings growth of the highest market-to-book quartile was good at 17 percent but was only slightly more than half the lowest market-to-book quartile, which grew earnings

at 33 percent. (Many of the lowest market-to-book quartile companies were turnarounds.) In other words, the highest earnings
growth did not lead to the highest market-to-book ratios. What,
then, explains the differences in market-to-book ratios? Very simply, the differences are due to the return on book equity. The highest market-to-book quartile had a return on book equity in 1998
of about 31 percent, nearly three times that of the lowest market-
to-book quartile, which had a return of 13 percent.

The implications of this analysis are straightforward. Market-
to-book ratios are related more directly to returns on book equity
than to earnings growth. Earnings growth can be achieved by
simply raising and deploying financial capital, particularly
through acquisitions. But, as long as return on book equity does
not increase, the market-to-book ratio is not likely to rise more

---

**EXHIBIT 4-2   100 global companies with greatest increase in
market capitalization** *(Sources of high market-to-
book ratios—May 1998)*

	Market-to-book ratio	Market cap growth compounded over 5 years	Compounded annual earnings growth May 1993 to May 1998	1997 year-end return on book equity
Highest quartile	14.2	37%	17%	31%
2nd highest quartile	6.3	29	30	22
3rd highest quartile	3.7	25	23	17
4th highest quartile	2.2	16	33	13

than the increase caused by the decline in the cost of equity. Companies that have achieved strong income growth by issuing new stock, while maintaining a reasonable return on book equity, can be successful at growing their market capitalization. However, those that have produced more modest earnings growth but at very high returns on book equity have established enormous market capitalizations for themselves without diluting the stake of existing shareholders.

The indication is that if you can both grow earnings rapidly and achieve a high return on book equity, you can propel your market capitalization to extraordinary levels and make your existing shareholders very rich. As some companies get this right and their valuations soar, it becomes necessary for all to manage both their size and their performance to increase their own market capitalization.

How do you accomplish this? The long answer is the subject of the rest of this book. The short answer is that you build and leverage intangibles to tap into the newly accessible profit pools opening up around the world.

VALUING COMPANIES IN THE TRANSITION ECONOMY

We are witnessing a fundamental redefinition of how a company is valued in the transition economy, a redefinition driven by two factors: (1) the commoditization and fall in the cost of equity capital, in combination with (2) a great increase in the value of intangibles.

Equity capital: Available—and cheap

For most of recent history, access to equity capital has been a hard-earned privilege. As the world's liquid financial markets are integrated into a true global capital market, however, access to equity capital has become more of a commodity. Part of this is simply due to the increasing mobility of equity capital in search of high returns. But if equity capital were simply being reallocated among private companies, one company's gain would be another company's loss. That is not the case. Companies are increasingly able to raise vast amounts of equity on very attractive terms. In other words, the cost of equity capital is falling.

There are several reasons for this. In terms of the overall supply of all financial capital, research has shown that the aging of the developed world's population will bring about an enormous shift in the proportion of savers in the developed world to borrowers. This research also indicated that household financial assets would grow by $12 trillion between 1992 and 2002 and that this demographically driven demand for financial assets would continue to increase through at least 2010 and remain at a peak level for most of the following decade.[8]

It has also become apparent that many of these savers have developed a clear bias toward equities rather than bank deposits or bonds as the vehicle for asset accumulation—particularly in the United States, which, due to the size of its baby-boom population and the financial wealth of the nation, accounts for half of these demographic demand changes worldwide. Recently, the shifts in this flow of funds have been particularly visible. For example, from 1994 to 1997, annual inflows to equity mutual funds in the United States grew by 94 percent, from $119 billion to $231 billion.[9] At the same time, bank deposits have grown relatively little in dollar terms. Bank deposits have fallen from about 45 percent of the world financial stock in 1980 to a level of about 29 percent today.

This trend is likely to become more compelling over time, as non–U.S. investors follow the U.S. pattern of risk-migration from bank deposits to money-market mutual funds, then to bond investment vehicles, and eventually to equity investment vehicles. Efforts in Europe to move from government-sponsored entitlement-driven retirement programs to personal and corporate-sponsored pension programs will accelerate this shift. In other words, not only is real savings from households increasing, but households increasingly want to hold those savings in equity investments.[10]

In August and September of 1998, it became clear that, while the capital markets have come to view equities as more attractive investments, they seem to be viewing bonds issued by players other than developed world governments or by single A or higher corporations as being riskier. For example, the debt of emerging market countries went from being priced at roughly 5 percent over U.S. treasuries to over 16 percent over U.S. treasuries. High-yield (BB) corporate debt went from 3 percent over to 6 percent over U.S. treasuries. If investors feel they are taking equity-like risks for these kinds of investments, then they seem to be saying they expect equity-like returns.

As important as increases in demand for corporate equities, many developed world countries (particularly the United States) have slowed new debt issuance, thus making more of the world's financial stock available for investment in corporate equities. In just the last five years, the projected volume of government debt outstanding in the year 2000 has dropped from $28.9 trillion to $18.6 trillion, or some $10 trillion less![11] In other words, governments are soaking up the world's savings at a far lower rate than they were in the 1980s and early 1990s.

At the same time that more financial capital is available for investment in corporate equities, the need for a company to invest in tangible assets is declining. In the United States, driven largely by technology advances, the ratio of revenue to the sum of property, plant, equipment, and inventory has increased from an average of about 2.8 in 1975 to 3.1 in 1985 and to 3.5 in 1995.[12] With the rate of technological development continuing to rise due to the availability of massive, cheap computing power, this trend is likely to become even more pronounced as we move into the next century.

The productivity of financial capital has been increased through innovation. For example, developments such as the securitization of mortgages and other assets and the addition of new, less capital-intensive services have driven the ratio of revenue to capital of the finance, insurance, and real estate sectors in the United States from 2.4 in the 1970s to over 4.5 today.[13] There is great potential to increase capital productivity further. For example, the world's banks hold approximately $6 trillion in corporate loans and have to maintain over $300 billion in equity capital to meet the requirements of the world's bank regulators.[14] Securitization of these assets alone, through innovative structures developed by banks such as J. P. Morgan and Goldman Sachs, could eventually free up much of this equity capital.

Significant sums of capital invested by corporations worldwide can be freed up simply by transferring best practices across borders. Significant capital productivity differences still exist even between major developed countries in many industries, creating capital productivity arbitrage opportunities, which, as they are captured, will further decrease corporations' demand for capital.

The emerging markets are sometimes cited as a source of demand for liquid financial capital that will offset these trends, but this will not be the case in the near term. First, it will take a decade or so before emerging market needs make a significant difference to the balance of supply and demand for capital. In 1992 they represented about 2 percent of the world's total stock of financial assets. Despite rapid growth, they will represent little more than 7 percent in the year 2000.[15] Second, savings rates in emerging markets are quite high. Today, this is largely offset by the inefficiency of their financial systems: the costs of bank intermediation is often 8 to 12 percent of assets or more, as against 3 to 4 percent in developed countries.[16] Closing this gap through labor and capital productivity transfers from the developed world should independently offset much, if not all, of the increased demand for capital from the emerging markets in the next decade.

The combination of these supply-and-demand factors means that for the next decade, if not longer, companies are likely to be able to raise equity capital on very attractive terms relative to history. For all of these reasons, it is not surprising that the cost of equity has fallen. In fact, the pricing evidence indicates that the risk premium for equities has fallen by roughly 3 percent in the 1990s.

Intangible capital: Valuable—and scarce

We asserted in Chapter 1 that we are moving to a world in which intangibles are the dominant source of value creation. Talent, patents, brands, software, customer bases, intellectual capital, networks, protocols, and so forth are the heart of the ability to grow earnings while increasing returns on book capital. These intangibles should be considered true capital in the sense that they can produce real cash returns even though they use little tangible, physical capital.

The scarce capital resource that companies will be driving for in the transition economy is not financial capital, but intangible capital. Global companies owning scarce intangible capital can generate extraordinary returns on the financial assets they do deploy because they can get other players needing those intangibles to put up most of the financial capital needed and to take most of the associated financial risks. Because of differences in comparative advantages, this approach can be attractive to both parties; that is, participants with excess financial capital can increase returns by gaining access to intangible capital. Even when it is necessary for them to raise financial capital themselves, intangible rich companies can do so on attractive terms.

We believe that global companies that pursue strategies of growing and deploying intangible capital, while minimizing their ownership of tangible assets, will be rewarded with extraordinary market capitalizations.

THE ACCOUNTING TRAP

The spending that companies undertake to create this intangible capital is, however, accounted for as an expense on the income statement rather than as capital on the balance sheet. For example, a rough estimate of the invested costs of the installed base of software in the United States is some $1 trillion,[17] but most of this investment has been expensed, even though the software will be used for years. Advertising and promotion expenses, R&D expenses, systems development expenses, people development and training costs, and so forth are not routinely capitalized. The intangibles being created as a by-product of this spending, however, have value that can endure for years.

We have no standardized accounting methodology for recognizing the ongoing value of these assets.[18] For example, the sum total of just the advertising, software development, and R&D expenses in the United States in 1997 was $354 billion[19]—a large number relative to total corporate profits in 1997 of $735 billion.[20] Because these expenses are growing rapidly to stake durable claims across geography rather than to undertake business-as-usual operations, current profits are being understated. In such a circumstance, the market is not being irrational in placing high valuations on companies making such investments because the steady-state earnings of these companies are much higher than current-year accounting earnings. So is the companies' real capital.

The straightforward reason that high returns on book capital are the primary source of high market-to-book ratios is that our accounting conventions understate both "real" earnings and "real" capital in the transition economy. Therefore, earnings growth is understated, and returns on book equity are overstated.[21]

Take company X, which had an initial book value of $1 billion and reported rapidly growing earnings in the past four years of $150 million, $200 million, $300 million, and $350 million. Assume it paid out all of its reported earnings using today's accounting conventions in dividends or used the earnings to buy back stock. As a result, its reported return on book equity would have climbed steadily from 15 percent to 35 percent. Assume, as a result, that its market-to-book ratios increased from

3 to 4.5 (i.e., its market capitalization grew from $3 billion to $4.5 billion). Assume further that it had spent $400 million each year on intangibles such as software development, advertising, and R&D.

Now assume it was able to use a different accounting convention that capitalized, rather than expensed, half of this spending (under the rationale that the intangibles created had value measured in decades). Ignoring tax and depreciation effects, this would mean that in the first year the return on equity had been 29 percent rather than 15 percent. By year four, book equity would have been $1.8 billion, since some $200 million extra a year would now be included as equity. And earnings in the fourth year would have been $550 million, or a return on book equity of 31 percent. Therefore, the company, rather than reporting an increase in return on equity from 15 percent to 35 percent using today's accounting conventions, would have instead reported a modest increase of 2 percent in return on equity (from 29 percent to 31 percent). And its market-to-book ratio, instead of increasing from 3 to 4.5, would have remained constant at 2.5. In other words, the valuation ratios of the company would seem more reasonable even though all that had changed was the accounting.

While this example is grossly simplified, the same point can be made by applying a more rigorous analysis to a real company with heavy expenditures on intangible assets. Take P&G, for example, whose annual expenditures on advertising and R&D combined have averaged 13 percent of sales in the 1990s. Using conventional accounting standards, the ROE and market-to-book ratio for P&G in 1997 were 33 percent and 9.4, respectively, up from 25 percent and 4.6 in 1990![22] If 50 percent of the advertising and R&D expenses made by P&G in the 1990s were capitalized instead of expensed,[23] the current ROE and market to book ratio would be 25 percent and 6.5, which seem much more reasonable. The increased value of intangibles in the years ahead necessitates a change in the way intangible expenditures are treated. The market is already taking this into account in its stock valuations.

Companies, in addition to their R&D and advertising expenditures, are spending significant money to acquire options on potential future global businesses. Again, the premium being spent to acquire these options is being expensed, despite the real value being placed on them by the market. The valuation of a company like Yahoo!, mentioned earlier for the huge difference between its market capitalization ($8.5 billion) and its book equity ($147 million), is based not on its reported profits but on its acquisition of business options derived from its intangibles.

One problem that many companies (particularly geographic incumbents) face is that they are being misled by the inadequacies of current accounting conventions and, in an effort to improve their reported financial numbers, are underinvesting in developing the intangible capital and in acquiring the options they need to capture global opportunities. Although equity capital is increasingly cheap and a company has more bargaining power than before if it wants to raise new equity, executives tend to feel they have less bargaining power than ever before if they fail to meet investor expectations. As stock prices get bid up to higher multiples of expected future earnings, the potential consequences of a change in market expectations become greater. Most CEOs care a lot about meeting the market's earnings expectations. The market clearly does not like earnings surprises. Such a response is consistent with the equity risk premium having fallen—the market does not want to find out it was wrong in believing equities are less risky!

At least in the United States, the market is increasingly willing to replace managers who fail to deliver. From the late 1980s to the mid-1990s, the rate of annual CEO turnover has increased by 54 percent, with the average tenure of a CEO falling from ten years to just under six.[24] As a result, many companies are intensely focused on short-term earnings performance. Unfortunately, this causes them to cut back on expense-based investments in order to meet a budget. Advertising budgets, R&D expenses, recruiting, training and development expenses, software projects, and so on are almost always done on a "what we can afford" basis as opposed to "what is needed." In many companies, getting capital is easy, but getting expense dollars is hard. In the transition economy, however, the potential return on investment of expense dollars in the right intangibles is higher than ever before.

Part of the challenge is that many companies do not differentiate between investors spending that is a true investment in intangibles and spending that is simply a cost of doing business. Given a lack of better information, the market will assume that the spending is for current consumption. Companies that make large expenditures on intangible development or global options without making the nature of the expenditures clear may actually lead investors to undervalue their stock.

Living with today's accounting conventions

Even though we complain about accounting conventions, you and we both are, for the time being, stuck with them. So the near-term challenge is to use them in a better way.

In business schools and among financial analysts, it has become conventional wisdom to believe that book equity means little and that what really counts is market capitalization. As we have said, we also believe that market capitalization is critical. But we also believe that the importance of book equity has been dismissed too readily. Book equity is a convenient proxy, using current accounting conventions, for the value of the firm derived from its ownership (net of debt) of tangibles. In contrast, the difference between market capitalization and book equity is a proxy for the value of the firm derived from its ownership stake in intangibles (and options). We therefore use the market-to-book ratio as a proxy for how much of the value of the future cash flows of the company is stored in intangibles.[25]

Swedish management consultant Karl Erik Sveiby has recently highlighted this approach.[26] Sveiby, who also believes intangibles, particularly knowledge-based assets, are the key to success today, attributes all the market value of a company's stock above book value to intangibles.

The premium of market value over book value is by no means a perfect measure of intangible value. On the one hand, as we saw earlier in the chapter, a premium on book value can also be derived from a fall in the cost of equity capital, which makes all of a firm's existing earnings and assets (tangible as well as intangible) more valuable. On the other hand, an acquisition that results in goodwill in effect capitalizes the acquired firm's intangibles. These flaws notwithstanding, the premium that the market places on a company's book value can be a reasonable proxy for the value of its intangibles.

As we showed earlier, high accounting earnings on book equity are a relatively good proxy for explaining high market-to-book ratios. Therefore, until we have better accounting conventions, using performance metrics that measure reported earnings on book equity over time is a reasonable approach to testing the attractiveness of a strategy in terms of its ability to add to market capitalization through intangible spending.

The problem with net present value

It is out of fashion even to look at the estimated return on book value to make capital budgeting decisions. Instead, most companies tend to use NPV-based approaches for capital budgeting. Unfortunately, NPV has some real problems.

Net present value (NPV) takes the estimated future cash flows from an investment and discounts them back to the present to estimate their current value. If the net present value is positive, the investment is thought to be attractive. The valuation is quite sensitive to the discount rate used, with higher discount rates reducing the value of future cash flows. For example, the net present value of $10 million paid in 10 years' time at a 5 percent annually compounded discount rate is $6.1 million; at 20 percent it is $1.6 million.

The discount rate used most typically is the estimated weighted average cost of capital, which is calculated using the company's cost of debt and an estimated cost of equity (based on the Capital Asset Pricing Model methodology). Using an NPV approach, the economic value of an investment is the absolute value of the cash flows above the cost of capital. The economic value of an investment with an NPV of $1 billion that has estimated net present value capital costs of $900 million is the same using this methodology as the economic value of an investment with net present values of $200 million that has net present value capital costs of $100 million.

Using this methodology to make capital budgeting decisions has some severe limitations if you want to increase your market capitalization. First, a classic NPV approach works best when the firm faces a large current investment where the range of outcomes is largely predictable and the primary uncertainties can be clearly defined, where it is possible to make reasonable assessments of the probabilities of how the uncertainties can be resolved, and where, under reasonable sensitivity testing of the assumptions, the terminal value does not swing the decision of whether to invest.[27] It is much less useful when the unfamiliarities and uncertainties are large—where there is a huge range of possible future investment decisions and significant flexibility in the timing of appropriate investments, and where the assumptions used to estimate the terminal value swing the decision of whether to invest. Unfortunately, these latter conditions quite accurately describe today's transition economy.

Second, NPV does not take into account the intangible assets or the new strategic options being created as a by-product of the investment. Spending on intangibles is simply treated as a negative cash flow and the capitalized value of the intangibles created is not often included in the assumed terminal value of the investment. Moreover, much of the global opportunity derives from the almost unlimited degrees of freedom available today and the ability to avoid committing to massive financial investment until some of the uncertainty and unfamiliarity have been removed. The ability to use flexibility to overcome unfamiliarity and uncertainty cannot be estimated reasonably up front and therefore is not taken into account by the NPV approach. Winning global companies will need to create high upside options for themselves by making many small and medium-size investments in intangibles to pursue opportunities such as acquiring knowledge on unfamiliar subjects or assembling teams of talented people, none of which are very susceptible to NPV analysis. Many of these relatively small investments are needed to uncover unfamiliar opportunities to capture profits in new geographies or to find increasing returns or cross-geographic arbitrage opportunities. These companies will also see embedded options in potential acquisitions that make an otherwise "too expensive" acquisition seem cheap.

Third, NPV and economic value assume that capital is the scarce resource. To the contrary, capital has become abundant and (relatively) cheap to raise. What is now scarce is the talent and the ability to mobilize (that is, focus) a company's intangibles to capture the best available opportunities in the transition economy. Committing the company's capacity to investments that earn returns only slightly above the cost of financial capital has huge opportunity costs because the company will be allocating scarce talent that could be used to find and capture better opportunities with less investment of financial capital.

Fourth, as the cost of financial capital falls, it becomes ever easier to justify low-return investments in familiar, relatively low-return businesses. This, in turn, through parallel analysis and parallel planning among many participants in an industry, tends to exacerbate overcapacity in capital-intensive heavy industries such as automotives, telecommunications, pulp and paper, chemicals, metals, banking, and insurance. This is the trap for many integrators. Their historical success has been due to using tangible capital investments to gain access to markets and to gain scale effects. As long as capital was scarce, their privileged access to capital gave them an advantage.

We are not saying that companies should abandon NPV. Rather, we are saying that they should supplement NPV with other analyses that include, for example, the estimated return on invested tangible capital, the estimated capitalized value of intangibles, the estimated value of the options created, and the opportunity costs of the talent deployed in capturing the opportunity. The world needs new metrics for evaluating strategy and capital budgeting decisions. The NPV approach is no longer sufficient for today's dynamic global economy.

Just as companies underinvest in the expenses needed to build intangibles, they overinvest in tangible assets, which create predictable earnings but earn low returns on the tangible assets deployed. Both underinvestment in intangibles and overinvestment in low-return tangible assets make it difficult for a company to grow its market capitalization faster than its competitors.

STRATEGIC CONTROL

We have argued that market capitalization gives you an edge in acquiring other companies and new opportunities while at the same time protecting your company from takeovers. A slow-growing market capitalization makes you vulnerable. As the equity capital markets of the world integrate, any company with a relatively low market capitalization is vulnerable to being acquired by any company that has a much larger market capitalization and the ability to make better use of the firm's intangible and tangible assets.

Additionally, as more and more companies capture the profit pools that are opening up as global markets form, market capitalization will be increasingly measured on a global rather than a domestic basis. Indeed, we believe that capturing transition economy opportunities will represent the single most important source of growth in many industries. And it is capturing these opportunities that will drive market capitalizations upward.

What this means is that large domestic companies that fail to capture these pools will find that their market capitalizations shrink compared to their competitors'. At the same time, small companies that capture these pools, leveraging opportunities to gain increasing returns and capture cross-geographic arbitrage, can create large market capitalizations relatively quickly. In short, market capitalization will become the scorecard for the players in the transition economy. But geographic incumbents, integrators, specialists, and shapers will all have to take different approaches to the game.

Geographic incumbents, most of whom have yet to develop winning value propositions, are under the most pressure from the market-capitalization imperative. Large integrators can continue growing their market capitalizations and controlling their own destinies as long as they can roll up geographic incumbents and maintain a virtuous cycle of geographic expansion. However, in industry after industry, integrators who once thought they were predators are finding out that they are being hunted instead.

Specialists earning high returns on capital, but lacking relative size, are also vulnerable to acquisition by either other specialists or by an integrator who decides to become more specialized (i.e., become more of a shaper). Only shapers who are able to both grow earnings rapidly and earn high returns on capital simultaneously will be in full strategic control.

The dynamics of market capitalization

It is important to understand the two dimensions of market capitalization: size and performance. We use book equity as a proxy for size and the market-to-book ratio as a proxy for performance. That is, we define *performance* as the ability to get the most market value from the company's tangible assets (book equity) with the market value above book value attributed to intangibles. Given the analyses shown earlier in the chapter, this, in turn, means we define high performance as high reported earnings relative to the book capital invested (i.e., return on book equity). Or said differently, spending money on the right intangibles provides high returns on the deployment of financial capital into tangible assets.

All companies—geographic incumbents, shapers, specialists, and integrators alike—must actively manage both dimensions to have large market capitalizations. As we showed earlier, however, increasing returns on book equity is the most important driver for increasing market-to-book ratios. Increasing book value from retained earnings has a relatively small impact unless the capital retained earns high returns. Obviously, though, increasing size by making large acquisitions can have a big effect, even if it does not increase returns on book equity. Generally, for companies of relatively equal size, the acquiring company will be the company with the highest market-to-book ratios (that is, the highest returns on book equity). Of course, companies with a very large market capitalization can usually acquire smaller companies with very high market-to-book ratios if they do not mind the dilution.

Getting superior performance requires active redeployment of both intangible and tangible capital to the highest risk-return opportunities. Yet, historically, sufficient size has often allowed companies to retain control of tangible and intangible assets that were inappropriately owned. In many cases today, inappropriate ownership may result from continuing to hold tangible and intangible assets that provide options to capture global opportunities without undertaking the spending needed to exercise those options. Over time, as global equity markets continue to integrate and as shapers of global industries develop staggering market capitalizations, the ability of companies to continue to retain inappropriately owned assets will erode. Increasingly, the incentives created by the market should stimulate divestitures and acquisitions until assets find appropriate ownership.

Many companies are too focused on absolute earnings growth rather than on performance as we have defined it: earning high returns on book equity through deploying intangibles. In fact, a weighted average cost-of-capital approach to capital budgeting results in aspirations for returns on financial capital that are too low. Approving all projects showing forecasts above the cost of financial capital fails to take into account the high global opportunity costs of committing not just the firm's financial capital but its intangibles, particularly its talent, to marginal projects.

Rather, given the degrees of freedom made available by the transition economy, companies should not be satisfied until they find opportunities to create intangibles that benefit from intangible scale and increasing returns effects. All companies have a finite capacity to focus and therefore should be making hard choices.[28] If most of the energy of a company is consumed by pursuing familiar but low-return projects, then the capacity to focus on finding intangible-based opportunities in the transition economy is diminished. Instead, the energy of the company needs to be focused on finding high-return opportunities founded on intangible capital.

Companies should therefore be aspiring to invest their financial capital in projects that will generate high returns on equity (e.g., 25 percent or more). This is another way of saying that companies should be relying far more on intangible capital, rather than financial capital, for returns given the value of owning the right intangibles in the transition economy. As we saw earlier, such companies can get market-to-book multiples of five or more for such returns. Companies that can earn return on equity of only 13 percent or so, given the cost of not capturing abundant, high-return global opportunities, will increasingly be viewed as inappropriate owners of valuable tangible and intangible assets. Companies earning returns on equity of less than 13 percent usually have market-to-book ratios of 2.0 or below.

Returns on equity of 25 percent or more may seem an impossible objective in industries filled with overcapacity. Yet such an approach is reasonable in most industries. A large number of companies that grew up in capital-intensive overcapacity industries earned very high returns on equity in 1997 despite low average return on equity in their respective, traditional industries. Examples include General Electric (24 percent return on equity), Du Pont (22 percent return on equity), Allied Signal (27 percent return on equity), Chrysler (25 percent return on equity), and Lloyds (41 percent return on equity).

And the winners are . . .

The natural winners in this environment are the global firms that have the capacity to deploy significant amounts of capital while also obtaining high returns on that capital. As shown earlier, the ability of companies to move their market capitalization by increasing returns on book capital and therefore their market-to-book ratio has been spectacular. But companies that have been able to deploy massive amounts of capital through acquisitions have also been able to improve their market capitalizations spectacularly, even if they have not been able to increase returns.

A strategic control map[29] can help companies think about the dynamics of market capitalization. The map provides a useful picture of the relationship between the size and performance dimensions of market capitalization (Exhibit 4-3). It plots book equity as a proxy for size on the horizontal axis and market-to-book ratio as a proxy for performance on the vertical axis.[30]

When we place all the players in a given industry on the strategic control map, we have a snapshot of that industry's racecourse and the relative positions of each competitor. The map shows how you measure up to the competition and what you have to do to win. Geographic incumbents, integrators, specialists, and shapers each start in a different quadrant of the map and each take different paths across the field as they play out their strategies.

Taking control in financial services

When we look at a strategic control map of the financial services industry (Exhibit 4-4), we see an industry dominated by geographic incumbents. Geographic incumbents tend, by definition, to be relatively small and to be earning relatively low returns on capital. They are clustered in the lower left-hand corner of the map (there are too many such players to show individually on a simplified map).

A few competitors have separated themselves from the pack and are leading the race in financial services. The integrators, located at the lower right-hand of the map, include players such as BankAmerica–NationsBank, Chase, First Union, and Bank One, which have been highly successful in acquiring to integrate across the various local markets comprising the U.S. banking

EXHIBIT 4-3   A strategic control map can help a company set its goals

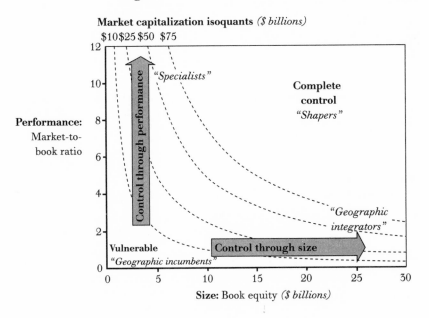

EXHIBIT 4-4   Strategic control map of the financial services industry (*Simplified to display a few of the hundreds of large institutions*)

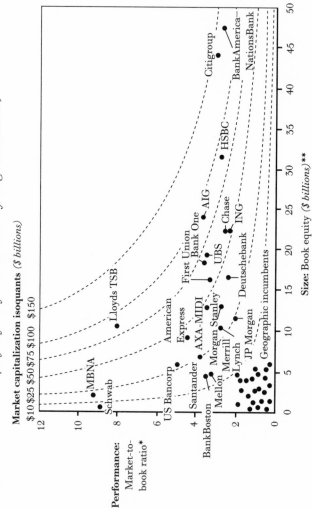

Sources: Data from Compustat; *Global Vantage;* Bloomberg.

*Market value calculated as price of common stock on March 31, 1998, times most recent available shares outstanding.

**Shareholders' equity as of March 31, 1998, or most recent previous reporting date.

market, and players such as HSBC, ING, Deutschebank, and UBS, which have been pursuing multilocal expansion to expand their global presence. These players have grown through both acquisition and organic growth to increase their customer access. The best of the pack have simultaneously increased their market-to-book ratios by realizing cost savings—closing branches, eliminating duplicative overhead, creating large utilities—and scale advantages that improve their returns on book equity.

Specialists, located at the upper left-hand of the map, include such companies as MBNA and Charles Schwab. These players have achieved very high market-to-book ratios due to the high returns generated by an asset-light focus on the higher-return pieces of the business. However, their market capitalizations are small relative to the geographic integrators because they do not deploy much capital. As a result, they may still be vulnerable to acquisition. In the U.S. market, several specialists have been acquired by larger local or global players—First USA and Scudder being two such examples.

Finally, there are a few shapers in the financial services industry. GECC[31] in leasing and AIG in insurance have pursued shaper strategies. They deploy massive amounts of capital while earning high returns on that capital. As a result, they are moving toward the upper right-hand quadrant of the map.

Even though they perform poorly, geographic incumbents today capture approximately 75 percent of the earnings in this industry worldwide. Geographic incumbents in this industry include most of the regional and national commercial banks, savings banks, insurance companies, finance companies, mortgage companies, and the like throughout the world. Specialists capture approximately 10 percent of the industry earnings, integrators a further 12 percent, and shapers a further 3 percent. As the financial services industry integrates globally, more and more of the earnings will be captured by geographic integrators and specialists. Eventually, more shapers will emerge and will capture an ever greater share of value added. Market capitalizations will be driven ever higher as the leading players take a greater share of industry value added or acquire and restructure geographic incumbents around the world.

The map is also interesting when one looks back over time. Exhibit 4-5 plots the course of a few of the main active agents in the industry between 1992 and 1997. Their movements are truly remarkable. Integrators grow market capitalization by deploying massive amounts of capital while earning relatively constant returns on that capital. Integrators move horizontally on the strategic control map primarily through maintaining a virtuous cycle of increasing returns and capturing cross-geographic arbitrage internally.

As Exhibit 4-5 shows, NationsBank has achieved extraordinary market capitalization by pursuing an integrator strategy through acquiring C&S, Boatman's, Montgomery Securities, and Barnett and by merging with BankAmerica (among others) in the last five years.[32] First Union, Bank One, and US Bancorp are other examples of acquisition-minded integrators in the United States. All of these players have been using capital to acquire access to new geographic markets and to gain scale effects from eliminating redundant overhead, distribution, and operations costs. European players such as UBS–Swiss Bancorp, ING–Barings, and AXA have played an integrator game to gain access but have not derived the same scale benefits partly due to restrictions on their ability to shed employees. Citicorp is unique among this group of integrators since prior to its merger with Travelers, it pursued an integrator strategy based on organic growth.

Specialists grow their market capitalization by deploying small amounts of capital while earning high, increasing returns on that capital and capturing cross-geographic arbitrage through alliances and partnerships. Specialists move vertically on the strategic control map, as MBNA and Schwab have done in this industry (we described MBNA's approach earlier). Schwab is a specialist that focuses on serving investors through its own direct brokerage operations, indirectly through financial planners, and

EXHIBIT 4-5   Strategic trajectory of the financial services industry

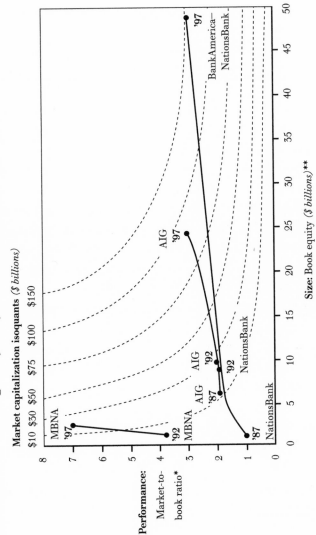

Sources: Data from Compustat; *Global Vantage;* Bloomberg.

*Market value calculated as price of common stock on March 31, 1998, times most recent available shares outstanding.

**Shareholders' equity as of March 31, 1998, or most recent previous reporting date.

through electronic delivery. It also uses little capital while earning high returns on that capital.

Shapers deploy large amounts of capital and earn high, increasing returns on that capital. They achieve such performance by being able not only to enter a virtuous cycle of geographic expansion but to earn increasing returns while they do so. They also capture cross-geographic arbitrage internally and externally. Their movement on the strategic control map is diagonal. By evidence of their results, GECC and AIG would qualify as (emerging) shapers in an industry that is largely just beginning to develop global industry structures.[33] GECC and AIG are both classic shapers in that they are using both capital and superior intangibles to acquire access to markets and are utilizing specialization and scale effects to dominate portions of the global marketplace. We will describe these approaches in greater detail later in the book.

Lloyds TSB forms an interesting but different case. It has followed a more focused domestic strategy over the past few years, growing through acquisition of other local players—TSB, Cheltenham, and Gloucester—and pursuing an aggressive cost-rationalization path to achieve above-average returns on book capital (i.e., 41 percent). In other words, Lloyds has been deploying capital to gain access (primarily access to an existing customer base and to underpenetrated geography) and has then specialized largely by rationalizing and shedding low-return activities. Its market capitalization has grown to a remarkable $76 billion as a result. Presumably Lloyds is in a position to repeat such an approach in continental Europe.

There are other leading lights in the financial services industry we could have described, such as American Express, Axa, Merrill Lynch, Credit Suisse, Morgan Stanley Dean Witter, and Swiss Re to name a few. As all of these companies go on the attack, the thousands of geographic incumbents that have the bulk of the existing customers and profits begin to look small and vulnerable. As the map clearly shows, the race has evidently begun in the financial services industry, and great market capital-izations are already being achieved.

Taking control in telecoms

Consider another industry, U.S. telecommunications services, which is only now developing regional structures to supplement more local ones.[34] In providing local telecom service in the United States, the primary response to the 1996 deregulation has been consolidation. Or, in our terminology, geographic incumbents began playing an integrator's game, as seen in Exhibit 4-6, which shows the movement of some major telecom players from 1992 to 1997.[35] Leading the race into the lower right-hand quadrant is WorldCom, a classic integrator.

An anomaly among geographic incumbents has been Cincin-nati Bell, created, like all the Bells, by the AT&T divestiture in 1984. Rather than playing the consolidation game, it has chosen to specialize in, among other areas, billing and information systems for telecommunications companies and teleservices through its CBIS and MATRIXX subsidiaries. This is a classic specialist approach and, as you can see on the strategic control map, Cincinnati Bell is moving vertically. Another specialist on the map, QWEST, is a new company that has installed a state-of-the-art long distance fiber-optic network across the United States, with a capacity greater than the entire U.S. long-distance market—at a cost of only $2 billion.

In the long-distance market, MCI has focused increasingly on leveraging its expertise in pricing and service—intangible assets it believes will propel it forward. WorldCom, on the other hand, started out as a reseller and focused on owning network assets. When it acquired MCI, it leaped to the fore as a full-service provider. It looks more and more like a classic integrator; the question remains whether it can leverage the unique intangi-bles it now owns (e.g., MCI's expertise in service and pricing)

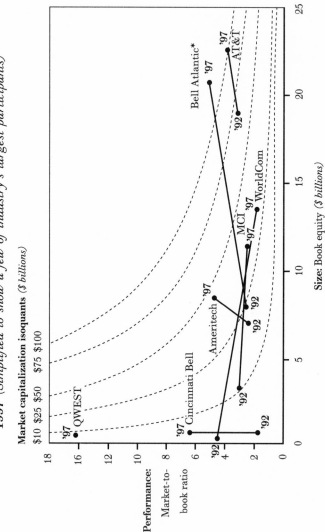

EXHIBIT 4-6   Strategic control map of the U.S. telecom service provider industry 1997 *(Simplified to show a few of industry's largest participants)*

Source: Data from Compustat.

*Bell Atlantic year-end 1997 results include the effects of its recent merger with GTE.

to generate substantial performance improvement (and vertical movement on the strategic control map).

Geographic incumbents, then, can choose to become integrators, like WorldCom or NationsBank, provided they are in an industry where they are not yet at fundamental access and scale disadvantages, or to specialize, if they have distinctive capabilities such as those developed by Cincinnati Bell and MBNA. However, if they do not act, they will likely lose their independence. For many geographic incumbents, accepting their fate is, unfortunately, the path of least resistance.

II

WINNING
THE RACE

5

THE NATURE OF THE CHALLENGE

T O SAY THE CHANGES created by the transition economy as we have described it are far reaching is an understatement. So it is disturbing that when we talk to executives, we find few focused on the transformations rocking their industries. Fewer still have thought hard about how wide-scale industry restructuring will change their roles in the future. All are aware that much is changing, but most do not really seem aware that these changes will affect them too. Most are not highly motivated to take action or even to understand their own position. Many seem almost bemused.

This isn't entirely surprising. Most of us have learned to function in an economy built within markets defined by geographic boundaries. In the transition economy, however, where in industry after industry we see the development of value chains that cross previously separate geographic markets, the existing strategies and organizations of almost all companies are increasingly inappropriate. As are our perceptions of what we do and how we do it. Up until now, in Part I, we have been describing what to do in today's world—pursue midgame strategies. In the remainder of the book, we will focus on how to win in the future world through shaping global business arenas. Challenged, many managers confess that pursuing genuinely global strategies based on shaping business arenas strikes them as undoable, sometimes terrifying. They have little idea of what it will take to succeed in this new, continually integrating world economy. There are few role models, and many of the strategies for industry restructuring in the transition economy have yet to be invented. What should they do?

In Part I we described the microeconomics of the transition economy. In this part, we turn our attention to what we, as managers and executives, must do to thrive in this confusing, complex, and uncertain environment.

INTERNAL CHALLENGES

The first step is to recognize that there are obstacles to success inside, as well as outside, the firm. The existence of internal obstacles was brought home to us by the 200 managers we interviewed in twenty companies in late 1996 and early 1997. Bear in mind that most of these organizations are large and globally oriented. Although we did not think in these terms at the time, we would now label most of them *integrators*. Most were in industries with global, or emerging global, structures. Thus our sample of interviewees was significantly biased to global rather than national and local companies. Nevertheless, we found the following:

1. Many individuals and companies lack sufficiently demanding aspirations given the market capitalization imperative and the speed of global industry restructuring. This manifests

itself as a lack of urgency. Even when companies believe that there are plentiful opportunities, they are in no great rush to capture them.

2. Many executives assume away the complexity of the world. As a result they are unable or unwilling to see clearly the opportunities or the risks in the transition economy.

3. Almost everyone found it hard to balance the pressures for current performance against highly unfamiliar and uncertain—but potentially very attractive—global opportunities.

4. Almost everyone found organizational issues—in particular, a shortage of talent—to be the most pressing constraint.

Challenge 1: Insufficiently demanding aspirations

Nearly 80 percent of those interviewed in our research believed that their companies had far more opportunities than they could effectively pursue (Exhibit 5-1). Most of them also acknowledged

---

EXHIBIT 5-1   **"We have more global opportunities than we can deal with"** *(Percentage of total respondents)*

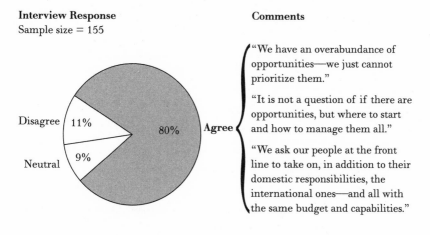

Interview Response
Sample size = 155

Comments

Disagree 11%   80% Agree

Neutral 9%

"We have an overabundance of opportunities—we just cannot prioritize them."

"It is not a question of if there are opportunities, but where to start and how to manage them all."

"We ask our people at the front line to take on, in addition to their domestic responsibilities, the international ones—and all with the same budget and capabilities."

that they were experiencing a step-function increase in competitive pressure. And yet this prompted few worries. There seemed to be little concern that leaving global opportunities on the table for competitors to capture was a real problem. Only 20 percent mentioned urgency as an issue. *Almost no one at the time (1997) mentioned issues of strategic control.* When prompted, few were at all concerned, even though in the year after we completed the interviews some of the companies we interviewed were acquired or were talked about in the press as merger targets. And few non-American companies acknowledged any real market pressure at all.[1]

This complacent attitude surprised us until we realized these managers did not yet see the world as we have described it in Part I of this book. Not one of the people we interviewed articulated the effects of the removal of geographic barriers, such as opportunities to launch virtuous cycles of geographic expansion, to earn increasing returns, or to capture cross-geographic arbitrage opportunities. To be fair, at that time we were also blind to these distinctions. At that point, both the interviewees and our team tended to be thinking primarily about international expansion rather than the opportunities available in the transition economy. There are good reasons for this.

Most managers still operate as if opportunities are bounded by geographic constraints. They do not fully comprehend what the lowering of those boundaries means in terms of the sheer size, lack of constraints, expansiveness, and accessibility of the new playing field.

Even those managers with international experience have difficulty grasping the scope and magnitude of the possibilities. This is because much of their experience still comes from country environments in which headroom and degrees of freedom have been limited. As a result, these managers have run businesses where they have enjoyed durable competitive advantage from owning the right local or national assets, and excel at playing "games of inches" and transferring operational improvements across geographic boundaries (i.e., capturing the benefits of internal geographic arbitrage).

Most of these managers grew up in a world in which financial capital, rather than intangible capital, was the scarce resource. Therefore they continue to see low incentives for spending money on unproved ventures or exploring unfamiliar arenas. Not accustomed to competing in global industry structures or to having too many options, they are more worried about defending existing territory than claiming new territory. Geared for competing in geographically protected markets, many find it easier to close down their options, narrow their choices, and "stick to their knitting."

A company rarely performs above its own aspirations. If it is happy with earnings growth of 10 percent, a return on capital of 15 percent, and a market capitalization growth of 12 percent annually from slow, steady, "two countries a year" expansion, it is unlikely to do better. If it thinks it has all the time in the world, it will be cautious and move slowly. And it will do just fine—until a hungrier, more successful company decides it wants to own it.

So, while some firms are acting as if there is a race to capture opportunities in a rapidly integrating world economy, a far larger number seem unaware that a race is being run.

Challenge 2: Assuming away complexity

Given the complexity of an economy in transition, the natural response of human beings and companies is to assume it away rather than embrace an exploding set of possibilities. One of our most interesting findings was the response to our assertion, "You are being unreasonably stretched. Your job is undoable." Almost 85 percent of those interviewed disagreed with this statement. Yet—as we discuss in Challenge 4—69 percent believed that their companies did not have enough leaders to manage and develop global businesses. No one's job was undoable, but every company had a shortage of managers! It became clear that individuals were cutting back their own jobs to what they could personally do.

In this process, much opportunity and perspective on risks is lost. In particular, companies and managers tend to restrict their thinking to either a multilocal or one-world perspective. The *multilocal viewpoint* assumes that the world is a series of local markets. The strategic goal is to tailor your approach to—and become an insider in—each and every local market. The *one-world perspective* sees the world as a single market. The goal is to convert the world to your way of doing business. Sometimes we found these perspectives within the same company. Managing tension between "local" and "one world" was often cited as one of the company's biggest challenges.

The distinctions between the perspectives are observable in the different ways multilocal companies and global companies operate. The classic multilocal approach is for a company to leverage its natural skill set as a local player. Multilocals are often highly skilled in tailoring their business to market conditions. Many of these companies grew up in the smaller European countries. When their need to grow outstripped the potential of their markets, they went cross-border looking for growth. Historically, successful multilocals have had superior access to capital and been able to attract high-level talent in different countries. This has given the multilocal significant intangible-asset advantages over local players.

But they are now competing with the world. While they have considerable skill in mobilizing information *within* local market boundaries, their ability to mobilize knowledge and talent *across* these boundaries is usually quite limited. Therefore, they cannot easily capture cross-geographic arbitrage opportunities (e.g., factor cost differentials).

As the industries they compete in integrate, multilocals become vulnerable to players gaining the benefits of virtuous cycles of geographic expansion as these players gain progressively greater scale advantages, better cross-geographic focus, and, most important, better cross-geographic integration of knowledge and mobilization of talent. One of the challenges facing multi-locals is capturing the enormous power that resides in the field. It is often difficult for even top management to be able to mobilize the company to capture cross-geographic opportunities.

At the opposite end of the spectrum is the global, one-world-market approach. Most of the companies with the most pronounced one-world mindset are U.S. or Japanese. Many of these companies leverage globally the scale or specialization advantages, or both, that they have gained from competing in their large, highly competitive domestic markets. They typically want to own, and control, all aspects of their business system (i.e., they are often geographic integrators capturing virtuous cycles of geographic expansion and internally capturing cross-geographic arbitrage).

Many of the most successful firms in the world follow this strategy. Usually, they are in industries that rely heavily on intangibles, have scale effects derived from their home market, and basically believe that the world ought to play by their rules. After all, their products are the best in the world! Consequently, they are often reluctant to tailor their products to local markets, and they rarely draw top managers from nationalities outside their domestic base.

Companies that are able to play this game are at a significant advantage. They reap huge scale-driven benefits and minimize the complexity of their business system and product range. They are the benchmark for all the players in their industry. But as the superiority of their products is challenged by new global industry-shapers, capturing increasing return and external cross-geographic arbitrage effects, it will be harder for them to insist that the whole world play by their rules.

Challenge 3: Balancing current performance against capturing global opportunities

Almost all executives we spoke to felt it was very difficult to balance the need to manage current markets with the need to expand into new markets (Exhibit 5-2). Part of this challenge relates to the challenges discussed above: It is difficult to emphasize expansion if aspirations are low and people are put off by the overwhelming complexity and sheer quantity of global opportunities.

But we found a deeper issue. Many people felt that the pressures for performance from the stock market required them to deliver current earnings growth no matter what—even if that meant sacrificing the future. Global opportunities were often described as both unfamiliar and uncertain. People noted that pursuing these opportunities was filled with risk and required using scarce expense dollars, which would depress current earnings and not become profitable for years. Moreover, the benefits would be realized by their successors! Nor, as we have seen, could the investments required to pursue global opportunities be justified using NPV–based capital budgeting methodologies.

So, although only 13 percent of the managers interviewed a capital constraint, very few had been willing to invest expense

---

EXHIBIT 5-2   **"We find it hard to balance managing today's core markets with the need to expand aggressively into new markets"** *(Percentage of total respondents)*

Interview Response
Sample size = 159

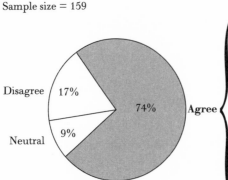

Disagree 17%

Neutral 9%

74% Agree

Comments

"Our mentality is that international stuff is interesting but we don't have time or energy for it."

"How do the people running the U.S. get some perspective about what is happening outside the U.S. without burdening themselves unduly?"

"It takes two to three years to develop products. In the meantime, we still have to do business and get people to stay the course."

dollars in acquiring global options. Many did recognize the need to develop a portfolio of low-cost options, but most simply placed a few large bets or deferred exploring the issues.

Our conclusion is that most companies simply do not have the performance metrics for pursuing opportunities in the transition economy. People behave based on how they are measured. They have few incentives to pursue the uncertain and unfamiliar.

Challenge 4: Organization issues and the talent shortage

Organizational barriers—particularly a shortage of talent—were cited almost universally as the fundamental impediment to capturing global opportunities.[2] Many managers thought the problem was related to the organizational structure, but many did not. Perhaps not surprisingly, CEOs and top managers tended to be much happier with the organizational structure than other managers. But without fail, CEOs and top managers in every industry identified talent as an important—if not the most important—constraint (Exhibit 5-3). Overwhelmingly, managers agreed that they do not have enough leaders to drive their global businesses. They affirmed repeatedly that the difference between failure and success in a given market is almost entirely due to managerial talent. Furthermore, nearly two-thirds of the managers we interviewed volunteered that they had real difficulties developing and retaining local talent.

STANDING ON THE SIDELINES

The overall sentiment of many business leaders seems to be that the opportunities presented by a transition economy are nice to have, but not vital to the continuing success of the firm. Many leaders deny the need to do anything special. Those from large global and multilocal companies are confident because they already operate internationally. Local and national companies lack the perspective to understand what these diminishing geographic barriers mean.

Most companies are overwhelmed with "business as usual." Taking on the challenges of the transition economy never seems to make the top-three list of things to do. It strikes people as too hard. Many apparently feel that they have a choice *not* to run the race. The truth is that the reason they feel overwhelmed with business as usual is that they are coping with the pervasive effects of the transition economy whether they realize it or not!

Economic integration is taking place everywhere—within countries as well as between countries. What most companies perceive as a "growth" problem is often, in reality, other players' capturing virtuous cycles of geographic expansion or earning increasing returns. What they perceive as irrational price compe-

---

EXHIBIT 5-3   "I do not have enough leaders to manage and develop my global business" *(Percentage of total respondents)*

Interview Response
Sample size = 175

Comments

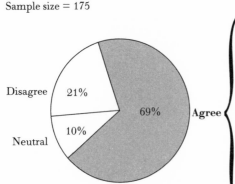

Disagree 21%

69% Agree

10%

Neutral

"Our number one problem is talent—identifying, enabling, and energizing good people."

"Our biggest problem is that we have more opportunities than people to go after them."

"We have weak bench strength— there are far fewer individuals around to fill in slots when someone goes, and poaching is prevalent."

"The secret is the people."

tition is often competitors that have developed cost or productivity advantages from cross-geographic arbitrage.

Although these companies think they are "sticking to their knitting," in reality they are standing on the sidelines. They are failing to focus on where they have real opportunities in this new world economy—even as their core business is attacked by competitors with better access to the world, better skills, and superior scale. They hire local people, to see the best leave. They introduce products to see them rejected by the local market. They seal alliances or joint ventures with local players to see them fail.

Most of the companies that are standing on the sidelines are doing so because they fear the consequences of acting. They view taking action as risky—and they are right. Unfortunately, standing still is also risky.

RISK MANAGEMENT:
THE OVERARCHING CHALLENGE

When we began our research, we thought that the internal constraints companies faced were an organizational challenge, particularly a talent challenge, because all of our interviewees told us so. As a result, we invested considerable time in how to use traditional organizational levers to surmount these internal obstacles. We thought hard about such issues as which axis of management should dominate (geographic, product, customer, functional, etc.), which organizational model to use, and which core processes to use (strategic planning, talent development, etc.). But everywhere we looked we found ourselves unable to generalize, in view of the wide variety of organizing approaches being used by successful and unsuccessful companies alike.

Given that all companies we interviewed, even the relatively successful global ones, were struggling with organizational issues, it eventually became apparent that we were observing symptoms—inadequate aspirations, assuming away complexity, difficulties in balancing the short term with the long term, and talent shortages—of a more fundamental problem.

When we saw global companies succeeding, it was because they had learned to manage the risk-reward trade-offs of the transition economy. This enabled them to capture high-return opportunities whose riskiness scared off everyone else and to do so without taking much risk. They were skilled in risk-reward management—and it is this we finally identified as the essential skill needed to overcome the internal constraints on action and thereby unleash a firm's potential.

People and corporations alike naturally avoid taking new risks in an uncertain and unfamiliar environment. Instead people quite sensibly choose risks with which they are familiar. Unfortunately, the result is that they narrow down their options and avoid using the many degrees of freedom afforded by the transition economy.

In *Against the Gods: The Remarkable Story of Risk,*[3] Peter Bernstein argues that the notion of bringing risk under control is one of the central ideas that distinguishes modern times.

> *In particular, modern economic man has come to believe that when we take a risk, we are betting on an outcome that will result from a decision we have made, though we do not know for certain what the outcome will be. The essence of risk management lies in maximizing the areas where we have some control over the outcome while minimizing the areas where we have absolutely no control over the outcome and the linkage between effect and cause is hidden from us* [italics added]."

One of Bernstein's contributions in this book is bringing out the implications of research by a number of people—among others, Amos Tversky, Daniel Kahneman, Craig Fox, Meir Statman, Hersh Shefrin, Daniel Ellsberg, Richard Thaler—on how real people make real decisions, a field now called behavioral finance. These researchers have demonstrated such phenomena as *ambiguity aversion,* which means that people prefer to take risks on the basis of known rather than unknown probabilities. Research has also shown that people will bet on vague beliefs primarily in situations where they feel especially competent or knowledgeable. Their research elucidated for us why so many companies are having such difficulty taking advantage of the opportunities in the transition economy.

We came to believe that risk management is the essential skill companies must develop if they want to win the race for the world. We believe it is lack of confidence in their own abilities to manage risk-reward relationships that places the real internal constraints on companies. Managers fear that with high aspirations comes a high likelihood of failure. They fear that if they spend money on unproven ventures, they will look foolish. They fear trusting people who do not think and act like themselves to make decisions—so they are always short of talent. They fear investing money in intangibles because these kinds of investments may lead to underperforming the market's short-term earnings expectations.

In an attempt to protect themselves from personal risks, managers avoid the unfamiliar and the uncertain. Instead, managers must learn how to manage unfamiliarity and uncertainty.

Geographic constraints that limited industry structures bounded not only opportunity *but also risk*. Now, as they disappear, and the historical competitive advantages of nearly every player in the world are in flux, both opportunity *and* risk are unbounded. In such an economy, trying to align your business decisions with the structure of a geographically defined industry is futile: The ground you stand on is disappearing beneath your feet. Ironically, trying to defend yourself in this way provides little control over the risks to which you are exposed.

The reality of a world economy that will increasingly operate without geographic boundaries means that the only safe harbor for a firm is to shape a competitive arena that is suited to its own unique assets and capabilities. Otherwise, the firm places its fate in the hands of the gods of chance. So the primary challenge for a company wanting to win the race for the world is to become skilled in proactive risk management. Otherwise, it will try to stand its ground and be run over by the forces at work.

This, in turn, means that firms must enable individual managers to manage business risks while the firm itself manages aggregate corporate risks. In most organizations, the individual manager has neither the incentives nor the capability to take the kinds of risks we are talking about. Risk-reward taking is too aggregated and too interdependent on the actions of others. Too many people find themselves on unfamiliar ground and because of "ambiguity aversion" retreat to taking actions where they feel comfortable. We believe the problem needs to be turned around. *Rather than thinking about how to make risk-reward decisions in a given organizing structure, we need to think about how to organize the corporation to make good risk-reward decisions, given the new transition economy.*

As we will describe in Chapter 11, it is the superior ability to manage the global risk-reward challenge at both the business and corporate levels that defines exceptional firms such as Coca-Cola, General Electric, SAP, Microsoft, Johnson & Johnson, and Intel. They create risk-return environments for their managers that enable individuals to make decisions with great confidence despite the unfamiliarity and uncertainty in the world economy. In effect, they load the dice and bet on business outcomes when they have high confidence they will succeed. By shaping the arenas in which they compete, they create businesses where they enjoy enormous advantages and thereby earn high returns on financial capital while rapidly growing earnings. Moreover, through corporate-wide management of their portfolio of businesses they gain collective strength.

Risk management is at the heart of what it will take to create extraordinary market capitalizations, create huge advantages in making acquisitions and partnering, and control your own destiny. It is possible for many firms—not just a few—to become proficient in risk-reward management. Successful risk-reward managers, be they managers of financial risks or business operating risks, rely on four proven risk management principles:

1. Disaggregate and structure risks so that decisions can be made on which risks to take.

2. Take risks only where you enjoy familiarity advantages and where the probabilities of favorable outcomes are high, and shed risks where others have comparative advantages or stronger preference for the risks.

3. Take advantage of portfolio theory to ensure overall results.

4. Use options to increase returns relative to risks and to overcome uncertainty.

Applying these principles—originally developed to manage financial risk-reward relationships—to managing operating risks can liberate the firm from internal constraints. Moreover, the payoff from using such techniques to make better operating decisions are actually *greater* than the payoffs from applying these techniques in financial markets. Business markets are far less "perfect" than financial markets. In global financial markets, participants are on a reasonably level playing field, given the degree to which the global financial market has integrated. In business markets, competitors have radically different competitive advantages and disadvantages because they are still in a transitional stage in which more and more participants with increasingly differentiated capabilities are entering the competitive arena. This makes the business markets less perfect (i.e., full of potential cross-geographic arbitrage and increasing returns opportunities). Eventually the forces at work will make these business markets more nearly perfect, but most markets for goods, services, and labor will remain imperfect for decades. It's a *transition* economy.

In this transition economy, participants are all establishing increasingly equivalent access to customers, suppliers, factor costs, and technologies as a more integrated global economic arena takes shape, and this equal access is making the successful strategies of the past based on privileged access extremely risky. On the other hand, the intangible assets they bring to that arena, out of a history of geographically segmented economic arenas, are highly individual. They bring to their competition unique knowledge, people, reputations, and relationships, and these intangibles can provide real advantages in risk taking. For example, the asymmetry between what a Chinese local company and what a French multinational brings, in terms of knowledge, is extreme.

Moreover, these differences are remarkably durable. A Chinese local company cannot easily acquire even a meaningful fraction of what the French multinational knows—and vice versa. This, in turn, means that the risks relative to the rewards of the participants making the same business decisions are quite different. The risks and rewards of a Chinese company hiring 100 skilled Chinese engineers are quite different than those of the French multinational hiring the same engineers.

The relative imperfection of business markets means that risk and return relationships are far less correlated than in financial markets. Thus, participants with intangible asset advantages have much better opportunities to find low-risk, high-return investments relative to participants in liquid financial markets, all of whom have relatively equivalent intangible assets (i.e., the same knowledge, the same kind of people making the investments, and so forth). There are simply far more opportunities to benefit from having superior knowledge, people, reputations, and relationships in business markets and thereby to earn superior returns.

Another major difference is that in liquid financial markets, individual decisions have an inconsequential impact on prices, given the size of the market relative to the decision and given that the decisions are passive decisions to buy or sell assets. In contrast, in business markets the participants are active agents. As they take action, they have considerable impact on the markets in which they operate, affecting market demand, capacity, prices, and the shape of the supply curve. Furthermore, the more tightly defined the business market and the fewer the participants, the greater the impact any one participant will have on the structure of that market.

The implications are that the variation in returns between business participants with equivalent objectives and risk preferences is wider than the variation in returns between equivalent investors in financial assets. Two financial participants can construct virtually identical portfolios with equivalent risks (e.g., through an index fund). In contrast, two participants in the same industry, with the same risk-reward objectives but different knowledge, skills, and access to information, are likely to have far more disparate outcomes. The trick is for each business participant to concentrate investment in arenas where the asymmetry of intangibles provides the participant with a risk-reward advantage.

Thus, the art of risk-return management, which has become a highly developed skill in financial management, is even more valuable in business management. Said differently, the relative returns in applying risk management skills to business markets in the transition economy are far greater than the relative returns in applying these skills in the increasingly "perfect" financial markets for which they were developed. In business markets, the use of risk-reward management techniques can have a far greater impact on future outcomes.

RUNNING THE RIGHT RACE

Taking better and smarter risks is not a matter of adding more analysts to your strategic planning function. The fundamental task is to understand the particular challenges and opportunities given your company's unique intangibles in the transition economy—and then to put this understanding in the context of other players in the industries in which you compete. Each participant must gain an in-depth understanding of how the industry in which it is competing is being restructured. Each participant must understand the company's relative position on the strategic control map for its industry. As the industry restructures, the underlying economics of each participant change rapidly, as do its options, value of assets, and market capitalization. These factors can quickly change the company's appetite for acquisitions or, conversely, suddenly make the company a takeover target.

First, it is critical to understand who you are and what your firm uniquely brings to the competitive arena. As the forces at work open up strategic degrees of freedom, there is an unlimited set of possible actions that can be taken. And we are more and more convinced that there are a large number of potential winning approaches and an equally large number of losing approaches. The challenge is in aligning and adapting the firm so it can capture the right global opportunities—by finding, in a universe of many possible winning strategies, the ones that are right for you. Of course, this is more easily said than done.

The opening of the world's economy has been relatively sudden, while the mindsets of companies have been remarkably durable. For many companies, the misalignments between how they think about the world and the requirements for global success are extreme. Without aligning the mindset of the firm to the global economy, the challenges cannot be met.

The essential first step is opening up the mind. When you look behind the success stories of high performers in the transition economy, you find institutions that have learned to think differently from the majority of other companies in the world. They adopt an open, global mindset—while remaining true to themselves. Their leadership teams have immersed themselves in understanding the effects of the new forces at work on their specific industries and business and, more generally, on the structure of the industries in which they compete. They have thought hard about how to increase access, become more specialized, or gain scale. They have opened their minds sufficiently to challenge conventional in-house wisdom about the appropriate definition of the industry, customer and market segmentations, and sources of sustainable value. In particular, they are willing to create options to recast the economics of the firm in light of a range of plausible restructuring scenarios.

Opening the firm is the essential act of leadership and intellectual honesty needed to trigger a chain reaction of development. Because they think differently, players with an open global mindset seek out different information, process the information they gather differently, and come to different conclusions and make different decisions than others with the same information. Where others see the transition economy as creating threats and complexity, they see opportunity. Where others see a barren landscape, they see an overabundance of choice.

Finding a way to win in an integrating world economy is not an impossible mission. If the leadership of a company has the will to run the race (a big if), there is an approach to winning that draws strength from the firm's unique capabilities (primarily its intangible assets) while simultaneously reducing the risks to which the firm is exposed. Think of this as an *inside-out approach to business strategy*. An inside-out approach allows you to draw strength from the firm's historical business legacy. It is also about pursuing opportunities that have very attractive risk-adjusted profiles—opportunities where the company has familiarity advantages drawn from having superior intangibles such as intellectual property or talent.

The inside-out approach has to be firmly grounded in an overall gameplan—a corporate strategy that defines what role the firm is going to play within the industries in which it competes as they are being restructured. The gameplan is about making real, discrete choices in a world of overabundant options. It is about accepting where the company will lose the advantages of geographic incumbency and anticipating decreasing return effects. It is about deciding to what extent the company wants to specialize, to integrate across geography, or to shape new industries. It is about thinking hard about how to gain virtuous cycles of geographic expansion, to earn increasing returns, and to capture cross-geographic arbitrage. It is about defining very high aspirations, particularly aspirations for earnings growth, return on equity, and market capitalization. It is about, most of all, thinking through the role the company will create for itself in the transition economy, which risks it will take, and which risks it won't take. Necessarily, the gameplan will have to evolve continually as industries continue to be restructured.

TISA: A SURPRISING RACER

Telefónica de España, Spain's telecom monopoly, is an unlikely company to have embraced the race for the world. And yet, like its compatriots Banco Santander and Banco Bilbao Vizcaya, it has developed an extraordinary presence in Latin America through an integrator strategy built on creating a virtuous cycle of geographic expansion and capturing cross-geographic arbitrage. Since 1990, through its subsidiary Telefónica Internacional SA (TISA), Telefónica has built a telecom-cellular-cable empire spanning most major Latin American nations. In 1997, international operations generated $2.9 billion in revenues and $232 million in net income. But more remarkable than these figures is the swift, generally asset-light way in which it has gone about building its empire.

Understanding unique competitive advantage

In 1990, Telefónica had hit a growth ceiling in the Spanish market. Contrary to conventional opportunity scans, management began its search for opportunities within by understanding Telefónica's unique strengths. A common language and cultural affinity made the Latin American markets a good personality fit with Telefónica. But these were not the only advantages. As one senior executive said, "We knew how to operate both analog and digital systems at the same time, and how to handle large volumes of investment in a short period of time, something American companies had no experience of."

Most other companies were fleeing Latin America in 1990. TISA, however, was willing to make equity investments in companies throughout the region. "We had confidence in Latin America because we have a Latin American culture . . . We made a bet that the region's economics would take off, and they did." They began to invest heavily in the region at the same time as the various governments decided to privatize their state-run monopolies. TISA benefited from first-mover advantages, not the least of which was a window of relatively low prices for attractive properties in the early 1990s.

Asset-light, relationship-intensive

TISA does not go into investments alone. Aware that the Latin American markets were in need of heavy investments in their installed telephone bases, TISA linked up with financial partners that provided some of the financing skills and access required, (for example, Citicorp in Argentina). Similarly, TISA often partnered with locals to access insider networks and knowledge required to bid and operate successfully. A recent example is the creation of Telefónica de Centroamérica (TELCA) in conjunction with the Mesoamerica Fund (a fund that groups together some of the most prominent business leaders in Central America). Working with partners not only allows TISA to manage the risks of these investments more effectively (by shedding many risks to comparatively advantaged partners) but also to spread its own capital across a larger number of high-return investments. Within four years of its first investment, the group had made minority investments in leading telecom operators throughout Latin America, including CTC of Chile, TASA in Argentina, Telefónica de Peru, and CANTV in Venezuela, and had generated over $200 million in net income. With these platforms secured, Telefónica has continued to expand its presence in those markets through a series of additional acquisitions in both the telecom arena and adjacent businesses (for example, its acquisition of

Startel, the cellular leader in Chile, or its entry into the Argentinean cable and media businesses).

Recently, Telefónica and its partners (Portugal Telecom, Iberdrola, NTT, Itochu, and RBS) paid over $6 billion for Telesp, the fixed-line operator in the state of São Paolo and the largest telecom company in South America, and Tele Sudeste Celular, the cellular company in Rio de Janeiro.[4] As Chairman Juan Villalonga explained, "We have acquired the crown jewels. Telefónica is today the undisputed leader in the Spanish- and Portuguese-speaking world."

In many of its investments, TISA also enters into a management agreement in which it provides management talent and technology on a fee basis. This encourages best-practice transfer from the parent company in Spain, making the operation more efficient (i.e., enabling the capture of cross-geographic arbitrage). In this way, TISA profits twice from the same intangible, enabling increased returns.

Today, TISA looks forward to an exciting future. With more than 19 million lines and a leadership position in most markets, it is now by far the largest and most dynamic telecom company in Latin America. It continuously adds new markets and products to its portfolio (e.g., cable TV, cellular telephony, paging, data transmission). TISA is starting to realize economies of scale as it begins the process of integrating its operations, as demonstrated in its plans to create a pan-Andean backbone carrier for Latin America.

TISA provides a compelling example of a company that, facing growth challenges at home, adopted an innovative, inside-out strategy. It started from within and built on its natural strengths and intangible assets to convert a Latin American global growth option into a significant profit stream over a very short period of time.

6

A STRATEGY FOR THE TRANSITION ECONOMY

IN THE TRANSITION ECONOMY, a strategist must think through the impact of the removal of geographic boundaries on market and industry structures in order to take best advantage of the resulting access, specialization, and scale opportunities. The goal is to create compelling value propositions that enable you to capture virtuous cycles of geographic expansion, increasing returns, and cross-geographic arbitrage. If you neglect these elements, the logic of the market-capitalization imperative will make you vulnerable to the loss of strategic control.

Because the transition economy provides an overabundance of new opportunities, companies must seek the strategy that is *exactly right* for them.[1] The disappearance of geographic boundaries creates a multitude of choices because it results in the simultaneous redefinition of value chains in the industry, the players, and their relative competitive positions. Matching a company's capabilities to the opportunities afforded by its industry is a constantly moving target. So achieving the goal requires pursuing an *inside-out* approach to strategy that uses the personality of the firm to bound the arenas in which the firm competes. This does not obviate the need, as a preliminary step, to take an *outside-in* look at the industry. But as we suggested in Chapter 5, a company's unique capabilities are the source of most of its opportunities and challenges in the transition economy. To succeed, the company must rigorously appraise its unique assets, primarily intangibles that the firm has developed through its history within its geographic base.

Strategists who master the inside-out approach will be able to shape their industries in the ways that are most advantageous to their firms, rather than endlessly reacting to the ever-shifting competitive environment.

CHOOSING WISELY

It follows that strategy in the transition economy must to a considerable extent be about deciding where *not* to compete. In a world in which geographically privileged access to customers, capital, labor, and technology is disappearing, companies must pick their battles carefully. Companies that diversified in the past or integrated across many business functions will grow their market capitalization faster if they take a more focused approach. Conversely, companies that fail to develop world-class capabilities, no matter where they choose to compete, place their entire enterprise at risk. In a geographically defined industry you have to compete only with players who are in one sense or another local. In a globally defined industry structure you are taking on the world. Anything less than world-class loses.

As industry structures change, many participants find that competitors with overwhelming advantages in access, specialization, and scale are encroaching on their historical core businesses. Sometimes the disadvantage this puts them at is so great that the only real option is to get out. This in turn frees up resources that can be invested where the firm does decide to compete.

The good news is that there is room for tens of thousands of global players in ever more specialized businesses as industry after industry is reinvented. As we have suggested, greater specialization will be appropriate in an industry with low interaction costs and a global industry structure, such as the electronics industry. Less specialization will be appropriate in an industry with high interaction costs and a still forming global industry structure, such as the funeral services industry.

New global microindustries are being created everywhere.[2] It is in these global microindustries that the real opportunities can be found. Through focus, a company can become the best in the world in a particular microindustry and can, in effect, erect durable barriers to competition by gaining overwhelming access, specialization, and scale advantages. If competitors gain such advantages in a microindustry, other participants must be prepared to restructure and then divest or eliminate those parts of the business that are experiencing decreasing return effects or otherwise acting as a constraint.

Companies must use the degrees of freedom provided by the removal of geographic barriers to shape a unique, enduring role for the company. The strategist uses the firm's intangible assets to gain access, specialization, and scale advantages. Rather than changing the company to exploit existing industry structures, the strategist is attempting to shape a new global microindustry structure around the firm's unique capabilities.

STRUCTURAL ADVANTAGE

Strategists should, therefore, search for structurally advantaged opportunities to shape global microindustries. What constitutes such a structurally advantaged opportunity? We believe these are industries or parts of an industry with at least some of the following characteristics—the more the better:

1. The opportunity is accessible to you, and you have the potential to create superior specialization and scale advantages.

2. The owners of the existing business are high-cost, low-productivity players with relatively low shares of the world market.

3. The opportunity has historically been embedded in industry value chains currently being restructured or not yet in existence in many geographies. There are as yet no participants with access, specialization, or scale advantages significantly better than your own.

4. No one has yet shaped the industry's global structure.

5. The transition process to global structures in the broader industry will take decades—so the opportunities to earn increasing returns and cross-geographic arbitrage in the global microindustry are durable.

6. The risks can be disaggregated, and players exist who are willing to take the risks in which you lack comparative advantage.

7. The principal assets needed to capture opportunities in the global microindustry are intangibles that you already have or can easily acquire.

In industries where enough of these conditions hold, there are enormous opportunities to create compelling value propositions through shaping how the industry structure evolves. As a firm leverages its unique intangibles, it can capture huge increasing returns effects in the global microindustry it is creating. The economic returns of taking advantage of cross-geographic arbitrage to deliver high-value goods and services at low cost can be spectacular. It is this shaping mindset that lies behind the success stories of the great global firms described throughout this book: General Electric, Coca-Cola, SCI, Enron, and others.

Most winning strategies will be a combination of specialization, integration, and shaping. All large companies, including integrators and geographic incumbents, have some areas of specialty strength on which to build. Specialists seeking to shape a microindustry globally will often need to act like integrators by acquiring other specialists in other geographies.

The measure of the success of any strategy will be the participant's ability to retain strategic control by achieving a world-class market capitalization. To dramatize the issues of corporate strategy, we have developed the case of First MidStates, a fictional U.S. regional bank. Our example comes from the financial services industry, but, as will be clear from the unfolding of First MidStates' situation—the dilemmas it faces and the resolutions it might select—there are parallels to the situation of many companies trying to respond to restructuring in industries as diverse as telecommunications, local media, the provision of health care, and retailing.

A STRATEGY FOR FIRST MIDSTATES

First MidStates is a U.S.–based superregional bank holding company with 1998 earnings of $2 billion, book equity of $12 billion, and market capitalization of $24 billion.[3] It has a large branch system on the East Coast of the United States, a large credit card business, a large mortgage business, a large domestic corporate banking business, a major international syndicated lending business, and a global capital markets business particularly strong in foreign exchange. However, with the exception of its capital markets and syndicated lending businesses, First MidStates has only a modest international presence. Its business mix was formed over the past decade by the acquisition of two banks and two nonbank financial companies in the credit card and mortgage businesses. First MidStates ranks among the top 35 banks in the world in terms of market capitalization. Taken together, First MidStates is a typical example of a large geographic incumbent.

The CEO has a fierce desire to remain independent and had, until recently, felt immune to the consolidation process. Now, however, he sees threatening change around him. It has become apparent that the banking industry has massive overcapacity. Many players are relatively weak geographic incumbents experiencing deteriorating economics. Accordingly, stronger players have been seeking share not by organic growth, but by taking over players in the same businesses.[4] Such acquisitions, in addition to realizing benefits from consolidating fixed costs, expand the acquirer's access to customers, provide sufficient business volume to allow building more specialized businesses, and give enough access to new opportunities to justify investments in everything from brands to new products to new technology platforms. These, in turn, have intangible scale effects. As a result, the banking industry is moving very rapidly from a fragmented situation in which thousands of participants have been protected by regulatory and other geographic barriers to a more consolidated but much more competitive industry.

In the U.S. banking industry, Chase, NationsBank–BankAmerica, First Union, and Bank One have all completed multiple major mergers. In terms of deposits, the share of the top 10 bank holding companies in the United States has gone from 21.3 to 38.5 percent in the past decade.[5] This is not merely a U.S. domestic phenomenon, as the mergers of ABN–AMRO, Bank of Tokyo–Mitsubishi, Lloyds–TSB, and UBS–SBC attest. Spanish banks have been active acquirers in Latin America. HSBC acquired Marine Midland in the United States and Midland in the United Kingdom, moved its headquarters to London, and has established or acquired major banking subsidiaries in a dozen countries.[6] The French insurance company AXA has acquired, in the United States alone, an investment bank (Donaldson, Lufkin & Jenrette), an asset manager (Alliance), and a life insurance company (Equitable). GE Capital has made dozens of acquisitions in financial services companies throughout Europe and Asia in the past several years.

In the financial services industry, then, the market-capitalization imperative is already an operating reality. First MidStates has good reason to fear being outflanked and losing strategic control. Unprepared to capture global opportunities, it finds itself unable to keep up with the bidding on domestic players as the price of acquisition for players of meaningful size has become very large.[7]

When First MidStates looks at the strategic control map, it doesn't like what it sees (Exhibit 6-1). It appears increasingly small compared to the largest global players in the industry. As we saw in Chapter 4, while the industry is dominated by geographic incumbents, there are a large number of players that have begun to pull away from the pack. Both geographic integrators (BankAmerica–NationsBank, Citigroup, Chase, and HSBC) and shapers (AIG) have developed enormous market capitalizations.

Against this competitive backdrop, First MidStates looks rather vulnerable, despite the relatively spectacular growth of its own market capitalization over the past several years. All of this suggests that, in setting its aspirations for the next five years, First MidStates must seek to *quadruple* its market capitalization to the $100 billion level. This is what it will take to be a viable player in the industry, to remain in the top 25, and to be reasonably sure of remaining in strategic control.[8]

Unfortunately, its business-as-usual forecast over five years would see earnings increase by 50 percent to $3 billion a year and give it book equity of $18 billion. With a constant market-to-book ratio of 2, it would have a market capitalization of about $36 billion—roughly 40 percent of what it estimates it needs. To achieve a $100 billion market capitalization by 2004, First MidStates needs to earn $6 billion a year on book equity of $18 billion. The aspiration, then, must be to increase earnings by 20 percent compounded, while increasing return on equity from 17 to 33 percent and achieving a market-to-book ratio of 5.5 (Exhibit 6-2).

These aspirations appear unrealistic. When First MidStates examines its business mix on a growth return matrix, it still doesn't like what it sees (Exhibit 6-3). The grid maps each business based on its underlying earnings growth and its return on equity. As we see from the exhibit, First MidStates' corporate

EXHIBIT 6-1   Strategic control map shows that First MidStates* is lagging behind industry leaders

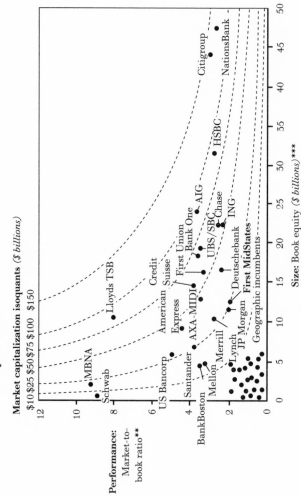

Performance:
Market-to-book ratio**

Market capitalization isoquants (*$ billions*)

Size: Book equity (*$ billions*)***

Sources: Data from Compustat; *Global Vantage;* Bloomberg.

*First MidStates is a fictional company.

**Market value calculated as price of common stock on March 31, 1998, times most recent available shares outstanding.

***Shareholders' equity as of March 31, 1998, or most recent previous reporting date.

lending and capital markets businesses are globally mature and therefore commoditized (i.e., low return on equity and low earnings growth), and First MidStates is an increasingly marginal player within them. Its branch-bank deposit business, although still profitable, is shrinking (i.e., negative earnings growth) and looking more and more obsolete in an increasingly electronic world. Its mortgage banking business is performing well, but is finding growth in the U.S. market increasingly difficult and currently has no international capability. Finally, the domestic credit card business, its main historical engine of growth, is slowing, so its deep data-mining capabilities are no longer driving profitable growth as much as they used to. First MidStates' recent attempts to take its credit card business into the UK through

EXHIBIT 6-2   First MidStates* aspires to reach a $100 billion market cap by 2004 *($ billions)*

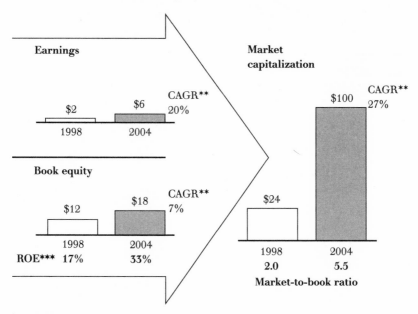

*First MidStates is a fictional company.

**CAGR = compound annual growth rate.

***ROE = return on equity.

direct entry (by issuing new cards) failed at a cost of over $100 million.

It's not that First MidStates has any shortage of ideas about what to do. The leader of the syndicated lending and capital markets businesses wants to acquire a regional investment bank. The regional consumer banking business wants to acquire and consolidate the last major in-market player. The mortgage business wants to finish building its national direct-channel business. The leader of the credit card business wants to expand its domestic cobranding businesses.

Unfortunately, these moves are too small to have any impact on First MidStates' relative position on the strategic control map;

EXHIBIT 6-3   **Growth return matrix shows First MidStates'* current business mix**

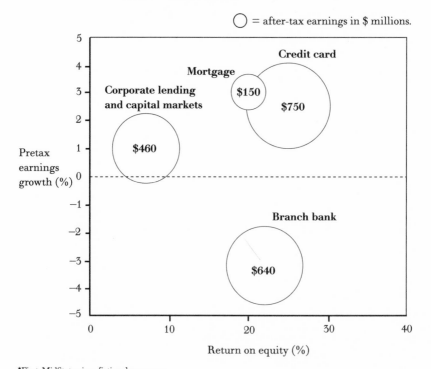

*First MidStates is a fictional company.

that is, none of them will have any real impact on First MidStates' market capitalization. At best, they will meet business-as-usual aspirations. First MidStates needs bigger ideas. It needs either to make far bigger moves domestically or to find opportunities outside the United States. Its mind is not yet engaged in a race for the world.

THE COMPETITIVE ARENA

By definition, the problem we all share is getting outside business-as-usual thinking. To do this, you must step back and take a dispassionate, *outside-in* look at the industry. Then the choices become clearer.

First MidStates competes in two very different business arenas. The wholesale financial services arena, where it has 40 percent of its capital but only 15 percent of its earnings, is an intensely competitive, rapidly maturing global business; historically fragmented, it is now consolidating quickly. The corporate lending business suffers from overcapacity and thin margins relative to the risks taken and is being displaced by various securitized forms of credit, including commercial paper, bonds, or the securitization of the loans themselves.

About a dozen large banks worldwide are beginning to dominate the relationship-based opportunities within this market, but First MidStates is not one of them. These banks are gaining access to customers throughout the world, building deep specialties in business after business, and enjoying major fixed-cost scale effects. First MidStates has strong relationships with perhaps 100 firms, but the bulk of its business is with companies where it mostly provides only credit. Some of the more specialized forms of credit extension such as leasing and project finance remain attractive, but First MidStates, like many banks in its size range, has no real position in these businesses.

In the securities and capital markets part of the business, First MidStates has an even weaker position. An elite group of players including Goldman Sachs, Merrill Lynch, Morgan Stanley Dean Witter, J. P. Morgan, Credit Suisse First Boston, UBS, and Deutsche Bank, have broken away from the rest of the industry. These banks are deep specialists in business after business, have huge intangible advantages in terms of talent, intellectual property, and brands, and are therefore gaining access to new customers. Almost all the UK merchant banks have been acquired and many U.S. players—among them Morgan Stanley Dean Witter, and Smith Barney/Travelers and Salomon Brothers—have merged. First MidStates' participation in this part of the industry is limited to bond trading and foreign exchange— perhaps the most perfect and therefore intensely price-competitive global markets in the world. The spreads earned on trading foreign exchange are much less than one basis point—much less, that is, than $100 for every million dollars traded.

Why, then, is First MidStates in these businesses at all? The answer is that these businesses are First MidStates' historical legacy. Its institutional identity is closely tied to the corporate lending and securities businesses. Although these businesses are both becoming structurally unattractive, top management's role in the local business communities it serves is derived from them. Leaving these businesses is almost unthinkable to the board of directors, many of whom represent some of the bank's best corporate customers. Yet to a dispassionate outside observer it is clear that if First MidStates stays in this business, it will never meet the market-capitalization imperative.

The second business arena in which First MidStates competes, personal financial services, is very different. This arena represents a global profit pool of some $300 billion that we expect to nearly double to about $600 billion by 2007. For the most part, this industry is still a national game. Over 95 percent of the available profit pool is being captured by nationally based competitors largely through branches and other forms of physical distribution, such as insurance agents and stockbrokers.

Personal financial services are, of necessity, consumed locally. It has been hard historically to compete as a nonlocal because the business has been such an insider's game. To succeed, you needed local scale, particularly in the physical distribution of services through branches. You also needed to be adept at working with local regulation and attuned to local cultural elements. Given the abundant physical distribution capacity of financial services players through the world, it has been very difficult for nonlocal players to gain a foothold even in the same country let alone across national borders. It is not surprising, then, that acquisitions have been the primary means of crossing geographic borders in banking. Even so, many cross-border acquisitions have failed largely because country differences make it difficult to capture synergies. Until recently, only a handful of players such as Citigroup, GE Capital, and AIG have had any real success building cross-border businesses in personal financial services.

Now, however, this business is beginning to integrate rapidly across previously separate geographic markets because players have found means of distributing financial services without relying as heavily on physical distribution. The leaders in this process are mostly specialized American nonbank financial institutions. Because of regulation, which has historically restricted U.S. banks to narrow geographic and product-line arenas, and because of the intensity of competition in the U.S. financial sector, the United States has become an incubator of powerful nonbank companies. As a result, as we pointed out in Chapter 3, U.S. companies such as GE Capital, AIG, Merrill Lynch, Schwab, and MBNA are now very skilled competitors. These institutions escaped the confines of bank regulation by funding themselves in the capital market and using innovation to overcome the physical distribution advantages of local banks through a variety of direct and indirect channels. Through partnering or acquiring local players to gain low-cost access to markets, these institutions are taking the same approach worldwide. Major accelerators in this process are the developments in electronic distribution and electronic commerce driven by the computing and communications revolution described in Chapter 1.

The essential skill of the nonbank is the ability to specialize. By disaggregation and focus, the nonbank can isolate a particular part of the business and focus on winning in that arena. Beginning with a single business such as credit cards, the nonbank disaggregates it into value-chain functions—issuance, merchant services, credit card processing, credit collection. Each of these functions, or microindustries, becomes a new business in its own right. This is the antithesis of universal or full-service banking.

These institutions do not try to compete with local players across the board. Instead, they offer customers a superior value proposition in their specialty. Having completed the process of moving across state lines in the United States, they have begun to shift their attention to crossing national boundaries. It is far easier to build capabilities in multiple nations if you are focusing on a narrowly defined sliver of the business. As you do so, and gain volume, you also gain increasing returns effects and are better able to get scale effects from intangible spending.

A PROBLEM OF PERSONALITY

First MidStates has a far better competitive position in the personal financial services businesses than in wholesale businesses, but it cannot realistically play the role of a geographic integrator. Given its size, it will never be able to outbid players such as BankAmerica–NationsBank, First Union, and Bank One in the market for bank acquisitions. Nevertheless, it can play a role in personal financial services. Its large, branch-based distribution system will become progressively more obsolete over the next decade as electronic distribution and electronic commerce become a reality. There are two arenas in which it has world-class skills and the potential to create a leadership role: credit cards and mortgages. If it has the will, First MidStates can take a specialized nonbank approach to capturing global opportunities in these businesses.

But it must first come to grips with who it is now. First MidStates, as a geographic incumbent, has an identity that reflects its history—an East Coast regional bank with close ties to the local corporate community. It has the mentality of a regulated entity. It defines itself, first of all, by the geography it serves, and has a history of serving all customers within that geography with a full range of financial services.

It has a culture in which corporate bankers and capital markets specialists are viewed as the elite and in which the heads of its best two businesses, credit card and mortgage, represent only two of the company's fifteen-person executive committee.

In other words, First MidStates has a corporate purpose that is implicitly focused on serving its geographic region, particularly corporations headquartered in that region. That corporate purpose is reinforced by the values, styles, and motivation of its leadership team and by its internal management processes and incentives.

First MidStates' identity fits perfectly with its historical strategy. Unfortunately, this identity does not fit a world economy in which geography no longer constrains competition. First MidStates assumes competitive advantages that no longer exist. What should First MidStates do to get its identity and a successful strategy back in alignment? It must first change its corporate strategy and then its identity.

A NEW VALUE PROPOSITION

First MidStates faces a fundamental choice. Where, given the transformation of the world economy and its own industry, should it *not* be trying to win the race because the race is already lost? Unfortunately, First MidStates' core business is structurally unattractive. Many companies, reluctant to seek profits elsewhere, search futilely for magic solutions to this problem. The real answer in many cases is to exit the business.

As time passes, the unmanaged outcome for companies and industries that do not reorient themselves to the realities of the transition economy will be stagnation, overcapacity, and decreasing returns. Waiting for some global oligopoly to replace the old national oligopolies may not be a wise application of patience. The sensible strategy is to accept the inevitable and seize the initiative while you still have choices. Sell, that is, while you can.

This is the choice we believe First MidStates should make—much easier intellectually than emotionally. In First MidStates' hands, its wholesale business and its branch-based businesses are wasting assets. It cannot afford the investment required to keep them, let alone to play the consolidator role in these businesses. This is why superregional after superregional has decided to sell out.

However, we do not believe First MidStates needs to sell everything. First MidStates should exit its wholesale businesses and its branch-based banking businesses, but should consider strategies to gain access, specialization, and scale effects in both the credit card and mortgage businesses.

Specifically, First MidStates should consider packaging its wholesale and branch-based businesses—its "bank"—and selling it to the highest bidder, thus becoming a nonbank specialist. The branch-based business is still profitable—and very valuable to a consolidator that can take out redundant cost and that has the electronic product capabilities to migrate customers to electronic distribution and electronic commerce. The wholesale business is similarly valuable to a consolidator who can retain the core corporate relationships and put more product through while eliminating redundant customer coverage costs and operating systems costs. A consolidator can also eliminate very considerable overhead costs. A megabank already active in both businesses—NationsBank–BankAmerica, Chase, or First Union—could probably extract the most value from these businesses and might well be able to convert a current 14 percent return on book equity to 20 percent or more, creating over $600 million in new earnings. It was such combinations that established these three megaplayers in the first place. They know how to consolidate a bank.

Although easy to describe, such decisions are incredibly difficult for CEOs and boards of directors who have grown up in these businesses. It is hard for a bank holding company to decide to get out of the banking business. But choosing where to compete requires deciding where *not* to compete and, in the short term, divesting low-return businesses will probably have a quicker impact on stock price than any other decision you can make.

How, then, should First MidStates proceed? One answer would be to sell the whole enterprise. Existing shareholders would get full value for the bank because the remaining geographic integrators would bid fiercely against one another for the opportunity to consolidate. A major problem with this approach, however, is that an acquirer would be unlikely to pay full value for the credit card and mortgage businesses. In particular, they would be unlikely to pay for the potential option to convert the opportunities to become a global specialist or global industry shaper in these businesses because they would have neither the desire nor the aptitude for such a transformation.

A better answer would be to sell the bank, but to have the existing shareholders keep the credit card and mortgage businesses. First MidStates' holding company would be acquired by a geographic integrator but the credit card and mortgage businesses would be spun off to First MidStates' shareholders. This new financial services company, let's call it First Global Credit, would pursue a global specialist strategy in the credit card and mortgage business. This approach provides First MidStates' original shareholders with full value for the bank while preserving the option value latent in the credit card and mortgage businesses.

However, First Global Credit would face two problems: Initially it would be smaller, in terms of market capitalization, than the old First MidStates and would therefore be vulnerable to acquisition. Additionally, while it would be competitive in the global credit card and mortgage businesses, it would not have any distinctive access, specialization, or scale advantages.

Here is an opportunity to do something "out of the box." Let's assume that it would be possible, instead of selling the bank to a geographic integrator, to exchange it and a 30 percent ownership stake in the new First Global Credit for the geographic integrator's own similarly sized credit card and mortgage businesses.[9] Let's assume also that First Global Credit and the acquiring geographic integrator were to set up a nonexclusive (to First Global) joint venture to distribute credit cards and mortgages to the geographic integrator's customers. From the integrator's point of view, this would provide them with 65 percent of the joint venture's profits (50 percent as a joint venture partner and, as a stockholder in First Global, 30 percent of First Global's 50 percent share of the profits—i.e., another 15 percent of the profits). The integrator would also have a 30 percent share in the option value of First Global Credit, becoming a leading global specialist in credit cards and mortgages.

From First Global Credit's point of view, it would now have greatly enhanced customer access advantages (through being able to market to the geographic integrator's customers), and the size to invest massively behind the intangibles needed to win as a global specialist in these businesses. It would have the base to launch a virtuous cycle of geographic expansion as well as the intangibles to provide opportunities to earn increasing returns. It would also have the scale to be able to focus on capturing internal and external cross-geographic arbitrage.

Assuming that First Global has also negotiated a five-year standstill agreement (preventing the geographic integrator from acquiring any more shares of First Global without First Global's agreement), First Global Credit would be in strategic control for at least five years, at which time, if it had been successful, its market capitalization and market-to-book ratio would likely be sufficiently high that any acquisition by the integrator would be prohibitively dilutive. Even if an acquisition were to be made in five years, First Global would have had the opportunity to capture its options to be a global specialist.

This new First Global Credit would emerge from this transaction with a real ability to focus on expansion in two core businesses, each of which meets many of the tests of structurally attractive global industries (because the opportunity is now accessible, existing players have no greater specialization or scale advantages, and the industry is not yet shaped globally). In combination, the estimated global profit pool available from these two businesses is roughly $66 billion.

The next step for First Global Credit is to capture a disproportionate share of this profit pool.

ACQUISITIONS:
A POTENTIAL SHAPER EMERGES

Determining the appropriate balance between organic growth and growth through acquisitions is one of the fundamental challenges of corporate strategy. In 1997, global mergers and acquisitions totaled $1.6 trillion, of which $433 billion were cross-border transactions.[10] Over 20,000 companies were bought out around the world. For the acquirer, acquisitions are a way to fast-forward a global strategy.

Many companies' first thought is to pursue domestic consolidation moves. But nondomestic acquisitions can also be a critical part of the arsenal of any company pursuing global opportunities, particularly in industries only now beginning to globalize.

First Global Credit has both domestic and global acquisition opportunities. In the United States, First Global Credit has specialization and scale advantages in the credit card and mortgage businesses that many domestic participants do not. Just as the old First MidStates was not the best owner of its own bank, many banks and other financial services companies are inappropriate owners of their credit card and mortgage businesses. Not surprisingly, many existing domestic U.S. owners of credit card businesses—and, increasingly, mortgage businesses as well—have reached the same conclusion and are selling their operations to the highest bidder. For example, in late 1997, AT&T agreed to sell its entire credit card business to Citibank for $3.5 billion. If a stronger player such as

Citibank or the new First Global Credit acquires a business of this sort from a smaller player, its superior specialized skill and scale advantages should generate far better returns. The acquirer also gains access to an expanded customer base it can cross-sell its other cards to. By making a large domestic acquisition in the card business, First Global Credit will be building up its scale advantages to compete globally and its total market capitalization (to keep control of its own destiny).

Outside the United States, First Global Credit may have even larger opportunities for acquisitions, particularly in mortgages. Because the credit card industry remains essentially a U.S.–dominated business, there are relatively few credit card businesses available for sale elsewhere. But there are hundreds of players of various sizes in the mortgage business worldwide. Because the mortgage business has barely started to globalize, First Global Credit has a potential first mover's advantage if it seeks the best available "beachhead" mortgage franchises to build a global mortgage business, just as GE Capital has been able to do in the leasing business. The fact that the equity markets are not yet integrated worldwide gives First Global Credit an advantage as an acquirer—there ought to be plenty of mortgage companies priced below their potential global value in the national equity markets because no one but First Global Credit is as yet very interested in creating a global mortgage industry.

No doubt this all seems radical. It is. But it should not be entirely a surprise that, when the rules of the game change, old strategies for success are liable to lead one astray. The central point bears repeating. *Business as usual will not be good enough.*

Of course, making the transition from a me-too superregional bank to a world-class global player in credit cards and mortgages involves more than simply having a corporate strategy based on divestitures. In fact, the real payoff would come if First Global Credit could emerge as a global shaper of these industries by building and executing superior *business* strategies. However, before we address how First Global Credit might do this, we need to lay the foundation in the next three chapters for the three components of the inside-out gameplan that must underpin such global business strategies: intangibles, global slivers, and cross-geographic arbitrage. Then, in Chapter 10, we will return to First Global Credit.

7

BUILDING INTANGIBLE CAPITAL

WE'VE ALREADY WRITTEN a fair amount about intangible assets—what they are and how they work. We suggested in Chapter 1 that intangibles were the scarce resource in the transition economy; that they would be the key determinants in gaining the access, specialization, and scale advantages that we believe will be central to success in the future; and that they would be key, also, in getting customers to pick your offerings as their ability to choose among suppliers increases. In Chapter 2 we discussed the way in which intangible assets are the core of building superior value propositions, providing opportunities to create virtuous cycles of geographic expansion and to earn increasing returns. In Chapter 3 we set out more generally the way in which intangible assets were critical for specialists, largely because they don't have the access that comes from size and are less able to capture internal cross-geographic arbitrage opportunities. We also described how intangibles lie at the core of any approach to shaping an industry. In Chapter 4 we described the increasing importance of intangible assets for the valuation of companies and the projects they undertake, as well as the way in which the market for strategic control will increasingly become a battle over acquiring intangibles. Finally, in Chapter 5, we discussed the centrality of unique intangible assets in gaining risk-reward management advantages and the relationship between intangible assets and the kind of "inside-out" strategies we recommend.

All of which amounts to a recommendation that companies find and develop their own intangible assets quickly as the only reliable way forward! Intangibles will lie at the center of any strategy to shape a role for yourself in an increasingly integrated global economy. But in order to build a strategy based on intangibles, companies must have a real understanding of precisely what intangible assets *are*, and how one goes about nurturing them into the intangible capital—and therefore the economic profit—so richly available today.[1] That is the burden of this chapter.

TRANSFORMING INTANGIBLE ASSETS INTO INTANGIBLE CAPITAL

Companies gain specific knowledge about how to apply a given technology to a particular business activity in order to gain labor and capital productivity advantages. They hire people with skill sets that can be leveraged to improve the company's operations. They build relationships with other companies, political leaders, and customers, and earn reputations through these interactions with customers and suppliers. The challenge is to manage most effectively the transformation of these intangible assets into the four kinds of intangible capital: *intellectual property, talent, networks, and brand* (Exhibit 7-1).[2] This is hard. But companies do not have to build intangible capital from scratch because the intangible assets from which they are made already exist as a by-product of doing business over the years. To a considerable extent, the raw material is free—making the challenge somewhat less burdensome.

Knowledge to intellectual property

Most companies have within them unique knowledge that can potentially provide competitive advantage over other companies in their industry. This knowledge might be in the form of a

EXHIBIT 7-1   Through directed investment and development, intangible assets can be converted into valuable intangible capital

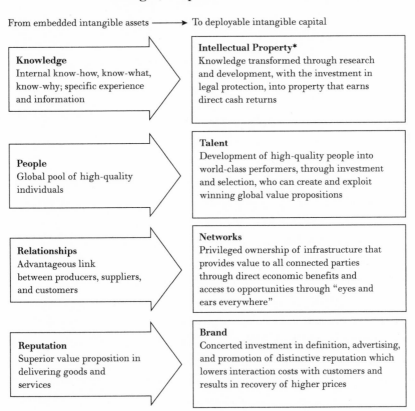

From embedded intangible assets ———▶ To deployable intangible capital

Knowledge
Internal know-how, know-what, know-why; specific experience and information

Intellectual Property*
Knowledge transformed through research and development, with the investment in legal protection, into property that earns direct cash returns

People
Global pool of high-quality individuals

Talent
Development of high-quality people into world-class performers, through investment and selection, who can create and exploit winning global value propositions

Relationships
Advantageous link between producers, suppliers, and customers

Networks
Privileged ownership of infrastructure that provides value to all connected parties through direct economic benefits and access to opportunities through "eyes and ears everywhere"

Reputation
Superior value proposition in delivering goods and services

Brand
Concerted investment in definition, advertising, and promotion of distinctive reputation which lowers interaction costs with customers and results in recovery of higher prices

*Patents, proprietary databases, trademarks, copyrights, computer software, trade secrets.

technological development, proficiency in a core business process, or simply information on or experience with a particular aspect of an industry's structure or type of customer behavior.

These assets have potential value, but they are highly "illiquid" in that they are embedded in the operations of the company and cannot easily be deployed to capture other opportunities. The challenge lies in the fact that knowledge comes in so many shapes and forms and is often deeply embedded within the organization. The task is further complicated within the global context by the sheer *volume* of knowledge available. Massive growth in connectedness through mechanisms such as the Internet has increased the transfer and integration of thinking and ideas not merely across different fields, but across countries and industries as well.

Much has been written on the topic of knowledge management and the conversion of knowledge to value-creating forms.[3] Few would disagree about the benefits to be accrued from institutionalized learning and knowledge sharing.

Of course, in many instances knowledge can be more easily transferred than companies would like. As any pharmaceutical or medical devices company can report, reverse-engineered and copycat products quickly reduce the period during which you can enjoy attractive margins from unique products. One of the challenges to competing and creating advantage through knowledge-based intangibles is in finding the balance between deploying them effectively to gain global access to markets while still maintaining proprietary control over them—a vital component of sustaining a competitive advantage.

Much of the most valuable knowledge resides inside people's heads; converting it into intangible capital is very difficult.[4] Indeed, as we heard time and again in interviews, even the simple transfer of knowledge across organizational boundaries—product groups, countries, functions—is challenging. The inside-out strategy for turning a company's existing knowledge into a global value proposition (described in Chapter 5) is one of the most important ways of gaining commercial value from a company's embedded knowledge. The talent team approach set forth in Chapter 10 is, we believe, the most effective mode of finding, mobilizing, and integrating an organization's knowledge and applying it against a specific opportunity. Hard though it may be, companies will find the effort worthwhile: Knowledge converted into commercially valuable world-class intangible capital provides the company with access to the world, reinforces the advantages of specialization, and has huge scale effects because the same knowledge is valuable everywhere.

When knowledge, an intangible asset, is converted to patentable and copyrightable designs and documents, it becomes proprietary intellectual property, a type of intangible capital. The conversion of knowledge to intellectual property is an increasingly important lever in the midst of the present technological boom, as the application of enormous, cheap computing power broadens our knowledge base and increases the rate of innovation exponentially.

With focused, directed effort many knowledge sources can be converted into proprietary intellectual property. Technical innovations, new production methods, and even ideas on organizational structure or industry analysis can be made proprietary through patenting or copyrighting. Effective leveraging of these patents or copyrights can shape an industry and give the owner a sustainable competitive advantage. In industries such as pharmaceuticals and software, this is the substance of the business.

Of course, knowledge-based competition is not always as simple as creating a few databases or patents. Often the key skill is transforming knowledge into a form that talented people within the company can use. One way or another, however, embedded industry information and experience can probably be converted into deployable intangible capital in almost any industry—whether it be via databases for data mining or cataloging a company's knowledge base or via software to facilitate operating processes such as product design or information management. Often, it is simply through ensuring that employees can obtain the information they need to make superior decisions on a timely basis, to engage in the creative development of ideas, or to overcome, quickly, unfamiliarity in a particular business activity.

People to talent

Talent lies at the heart of any successful business. Now, talent is more valuable than ever. As the world economy opens up, world-class talent has enormous scale effects as interaction costs fall because it can be leveraged across ever greater geography. It underlies most opportunities to specialize. It is the ultimate source of all intangible capital. It underpins all the other components of intangible capital necessary for global success. And, unfortunately, it is in short supply.

The *raw material* for talent, however—smart, motivated people—is becoming *more* available. As the world economy expands to take in the population of the entire world—at 5.7 billion, six times the 980 million in the developed world—the top 1 percent increases from 10 million to 57 million: a very considerable pool. Notwithstanding the fact that some of this 1 percent (e.g., much of the population in sub-Saharan Africa) is likely to remain beyond the reach of even the most aggressive companies, it would seem that the shortage of globally deployable talent in many companies is a recruiting and development failure and that there is no reason many more companies could not match the effectiveness of companies such as General Electric, SAP, and Johnson & Johnson that *have* developed a repository of powerful global talent.

Of course, it's not that easy. When people talk about talent, they mean a whole range of things—from individuals with strong intrinsic capabilities to general skills (project finance, marketing, supply chain logistics, etc.) to something as simple as the ability to get decisions made within a company. Broadly understood, therefore, talent has to do with the application of individuals with the right qualities, knowledge, and skills to convert a specific opportunity into a profit stream.

And herein lies the problem. The talent required to capture any particular opportunity is highly specific. It requires a specialized set of skills and knowledge to create value—how to operate within the context of the company, how to get work done, and how to get decisions made. Converting people into deployable talent is difficult, but it is at the heart of gaining specialization advantages.

Consider how one company quickly converted a pool of high-potential local recruits into deployable talent. In 1986, the "Big Bang" revolutionized London's financial system. Massively deregulated, the City would remain the domain of the local houses for only a few years more. It was the harbinger of a force that would sweep across the Continent several years later.

Like many major U.S. players, Goldman Sachs already had a UK presence in the mid-1980s. Unlike many counterparts faced with the prospect of capital market deregulation in Europe post-1992, however, the firm recognized the imperative to "go local"—the need to attract and develop a strong pool of Continental talent. Well ahead of deregulation, the firm began systematically to hire high-talent locals from the major European markets. It sought out skilled, young individuals from the various business schools, other local banks, consulting, and legal firms—raw material it hoped to develop into top investment bankers.

Local hires often suffer what is called the "cut flower" syndrome. Once out of their home markets, their value—local market knowledge and relationships—disappears. Far from flourishing, they wither away. Preventing this requires building up the locals' skill base. Thus, Goldman placed its new hires in London to build up their skill base—pan-European industry knowledge, exposure to professionals in other product areas, deep execution skills—while still being able to exploit their local knowledge and relationships thanks to the multiple airplane connections to their home markets.

But Goldman had another rationale for investing heavily in its local talent. In order to build a dominant position in the European capital markets, they would need to reshape the way in which transactions were executed by adapting techniques from the more competitive and sophisticated U.S. market. Local hires might already possess knowledge of their home markets, but they would also require world-class transactional skills. As a result, almost all new hires were sent for one to two years to the "New York machine" to learn global best practices, build internal networks, and develop cutting-edge execution skills. In this way they treated their talent like a strategic asset to be invested in, and subsequently to be managed as a source of value creation. They also effectively transformed knowledge gained from doing business in New York into intellectual property that could be deployed in Europe.

To begin the process of penetrating the local markets, Goldman sent many of its top performers from the United States to London, and subsequently to other continental markets to begin building local businesses. On their return to the European markets, these individuals mentored the younger locals until they were sufficiently senior to take over the country teams. Goldman designed its evaluation systems to measure cooperation across product groups and geographies, thereby facilitating the continuous, bilateral flow of knowledge. Finally, they provided considerable local autonomy and enormous rewards to leaders who succeeded.

Perhaps it sounds obvious, and yet we see few companies that will invest in new markets by sending their top people at many levels of the organization. Too often international assignments are a risk, not a reward or a requirement for success. Often no attractive position is available when the expatriate returns. Mentoring relationships have eroded. Not surprisingly, however, those companies that do invest carefully in mobility as a means of transferring and building intangible capital—Procter & Gamble, Caterpillar, Unilever—tend to dominate local markets more quickly than their counterparts.

Relationships to networks

What is the difference between a relationship and a network?[5] A relationship comprises an open line of communication for the exchange of information, ideas, or value. A good relationship develops into the "node" of a network when it becomes a source of privileged *access* to opportunities or other sources of intangible capital resulting in mutual economic gain. Access benefits can come in a variety of forms, ranging from early information that allows a company to be a first mover in an opening market, to an exclusive license for operating in a particular industry in a particular region, to lowered interaction costs.

Creating value from mutual-value–based relationships often necessitates their conversion into networks, a process that requires a significant investment of time and money. It's a worthwhile investment because, in today's global context, internal and external network-based strategies are becoming ever more important for accessing customers and suppliers, and for mobilizing and deploying knowledge.[6]

Opportunities to build networks are proliferating in the new economy. Most large companies need to manage hundreds of thousands of relationships—with business partners and customers, and internally among employees.[7] "Assets" of this sort can either be kept internal, in order to maintain some competitive operating advantage, or be made available through licensing alliances to partners, customers, or other suppliers.

A good early example of the value of networks is the Sabre system, developed in the 1960s by American Airlines. Originally designed to allow American Airlines to keep track of seats sold on its flights, the system has since developed into a universal reservations system connecting a network of more than 30,000 travel agencies, numerous companies, and three million on-line consumers worldwide. The system, which can book reservations on over 400 airlines, 50 car rental agencies, and 35,000 hotels, is backed by one of the world's largest privately owned computer networks. In 1997, the Sabre Group reported revenues of nearly $1.8 billion—fully 11 percent of American Airlines' revenues.[8]

Building and nurturing business relationships is more important in the new transition economy than it was in the old. As participants in different geographies seek to capture global opportunities, there are huge asymmetries in each player's intangible assets (particularly in knowledge and skills) allowing each player to accrue higher absolute profits through relationships. True as this may be for the developed world, it is truer still for the developing world, where relationships are the source of much necessary knowledge about how to operate successfully, how to translate the opaque into the transparent. The fact that the "own everything" approach (discussed later in this chapter) no longer allows a player to move quickly enough will only multiply the number of relationships a company has to manage.

Leading globalizers are becoming more and more adept at using a variety of relationships to capture both global and country-based opportunities. There are many types of partnering relationships representing different degrees of control and integration: *joint venture partners,* such as Banco Itaú's 50-50 joint venture with Bankers Trust in Brazil to provide asset management and investment banking, in which one party provides the customer access and the other the product capabilities; *captive distributors or suppliers,* such as Caterpillar's local partners who provide local distribution and after-sales service; *noncaptive suppliers,* in which, for example, automotive component suppliers serve the various automotive manufacturers; *contractual relationships with individuals,* such as Goldman Sachs' relationships with their country advisers; and *transaction-based relationships* such as Bechtel's project-based relationships with local construction companies.[9]

In thinking about different types of relationships, one useful way to classify them is as either *collusive* or *mutual value–based.* A collusive relationship is obstructive to market forces. Such relationships remain prevalent in the more closed markets in which governments or companies restrict the rights of access to a particular market or set of resources based on privileged insider relationships. While such relationships can be immensely profitable, market forces are making them increasingly hard to sustain.

A relationship based on mutual value is quite different. While it may still provide privileged access to opportunities or assets, it does so based on compelling economic logic. Partners in mutual value relationships act as counterparties in a trading transaction: The relationship remains in place while there is mutual trust and superior value is created. As soon as the value has been captured—or a better counterparty comes along—the relationship dissolves.

As geographic barriers between markets disappear and new global value chains start to form, competition for the most attractive partners or counterparties intensifies. In fact, while the focus on "slivers" that we recommend in pursuing global strategies (the subject of Chapter 8) simplifies the internal aspects of managing a company, it greatly complicates external aspects by multiplying the number and complexity of each company's external networks. Interviews suggested that managing these external networks effectively represented one of the most substantial impediments to success abroad. Developing the relationship skills for success becomes all the more important.

Indeed, insofar as it may be applied to relationships and networks in general, one aspect of network theory suggests that the successful management of a network will be a defining source of value generation. As each node becomes dependent on the network for its own effectiveness, the network owner gains influence over the network participants, sets the standards, and controls access. Owners of external networks can extract value in many ways, ranging from user charges to advertising. Owners of internal networks can make their employees more effective while simultaneously increasing the switching costs for employees thinking about leaving the firm. As discussed later in this chapter, it is relatively easy for owners of valuable networks to pursue "control, not own" strategies with network participants as long as they continue to provide value to all of the participants.

Adept "web masters" who own valuable networks include participants as diverse as Microsoft and many of the most successful
"overseas Chinese" families such as Li Ka Shing who operate
complex webs of businesses, relationships, and shareholdings
throughout the world.[10]

Reputation to brand

A *brand* is the intangible capital created from reputation. Most
people think of brands as purely product- or service-based: IBM,
Mickey Mouse, Colgate, Hilton. But a company can just as readily
be branded as a reliable provider of high-quality knowledge, or
a reliable partner, or responsive to customer requests.[11] The value
provided by a brand to the customer in this case is common
across all of these markets: trust, derived from repeated satisfac-
tion, results in lower interaction costs and lower risks associated
with purchase. As a result, the provider of the brand can extract
a price-premium and higher sales or usage.

As we move to a world in which supply constraints are
released and demand-based factors grow in importance (i.e.,
marketing becomes more important as customer choice increases), reputation becomes more and more critical. It will
become increasingly transparent to the end customer, worldwide,
where the sources of value are. Reputation, as a by-product of
doing business well, will grow in value.

Indeed, as risk becomes more manageable through risk management techniques, reputation risk will become more important
because it affects so many of a company's intangible assets—not
only its relationship with customers but also its ability to attract
partners, financial capital, talent, and so on. One need only look
at the effect of public relations nightmares such as the Shell-
Greenpeace conflict over offshore drilling, the "Nazi gold" difficulties of the Swiss banks, or the U.S. Justice Department's

pursuit of Microsoft for antitrust violations to realize the destructive potential of reputation risk.

To understand when a reputation becomes a brand, we need to be clear about what a brand is. Many believe that a name associated with a particular line of products or services is a brand. But simply knowing who you are and what you do won't earn you premium pricing or help you gain access to customers. A name becomes a brand when it satisfies two basic properties: (1) it is associated with a set of (real or perceived) tangible and intangible benefits that can be obtained through use of the products it represents, and (2) this association is strong enough to inspire loyalty in its customers, as well as a willingness to pay a price premium in return for the set of benefits.[12] A strong brand name can have a significant impact on a company's performance and on how it is viewed by the market.[13]

Companies such as Coca-Cola, Marlboro, Sony, Nike, and McDonald's have long recognized the power of branding to pry open markets and to further a global rather than an international model of their industries. Now, driven by increased penetration of global media, growing volumes of international travel, scale effects, and rising incomes worldwide, the model of brand-led globalization is spreading to new industries.[14] American Express, Merrill Lynch, and Fidelity are seeking to establish themselves as global brands; Citibank has already done so. Enron is investing in building a brand not simply with its investment community but also downstream with retail customers, in the talent markets, and with potential partners. Du Pont has achieved mass-market branding of Lycra, along the lines of Intel's "Intel inside" strategy. Nor are Western companies the only ones playing the global brand game. The Taiwanese PC company, Acer, has invested heavily in building its brand across all the major markets.

But if many companies have been successful in establishing a strong brand name in their local markets, most lack recognition outside their home base. This is the challenge that must be met by would-be players as they seek to create virtuous cycles of geographic expansion or to capture increasing returns from customers finding them.

Consider Nestlé. Nestlé's recognized willingness to commit to countries for the long term—to building the infrastructure and to being unfazed by market volatility—has assisted its establishment of locally valuable global brand names across many different types of markets.

Nestlé's strategy historically has been to establish a worldwide presence by catering to the specific conditions of numerous local markets. It has established a local brand hierarchy which ranges from about ten strategic global brand names to literally thousands of local brands in the markets they serve. Now, the challenge for Nestlé is to consolidate these thousands of local brands under the Nestlé umbrella in order to promote Nestlé itself as a leading global food brand. In order to do so, Nestlé has embarked on the selective incorporation of local brands close to its core—baby foods, milk products, chocolate, confections, and cereals. About 40 percent of their product turnover is carried directly by the Nestlé brand. Many of their other global and local subbrands are being carried with a "Nestlé Seal of Guarantee," which promotes the Nestlé name while preserving strength that the subbrands have already built. Brands incompatible with the image Nestlé wants to project (dog food, for instance) will remain under their own respective brand names.[15]

MOBILIZING AN INTEGRATED APPROACH

The greatest power from intangible capital comes when an integrated approach is taken, one that deploys a rich pool of intangibles that build off one other. Indeed, intangible capital often appreciates in value through use because new intangible assets are created in the process, thus creating increasing returns. Companies should seek to mobilize *all* their intangible assets into a compelling global value proposition.

Consider Citicorp. In the early nineties, after a particularly tough down-cycle in the U.S. banking sector, Citicorp's senior management recognized the value of their global franchise. Unlike their competitors, Citicorp had operated in various emerging markets for several decades, providing a formidable source of local intangible assets that could be converted into intangible capital. They began a significant push into the Asian retail banking markets.

Citicorp began with building superior *intellectual property* in marketing and in banking—their systems being both more advanced and more standardized than those of the geographic incumbents they were competing against. This they combined with local access and familiarity in many different countries, developed over decades of operating as a multilocal, to tailor the value proposition locally where necessary, while still leveraging global specialization and scale advantages. For instance, they could set in place standardized systems in certain processing functions while tailoring other pieces of their offering to recognize differences in customer behavior between branches in India and Poland.

Citicorp developed a reputation as an employer of choice in local markets, thanks in part to attractive training, mobility, and compensation packages, thus improving their access to smart recruits worldwide. They encouraged their people throughout the world to move to different offices, thus transferring best practice and innovation around the world (Citigold, for instance, originated in Asia) while simultaneously developing a global *talent pool.*

To build out their Asian and Latin American presence very quickly, they leveraged existing relationships with local governments and customers to create powerful pan-Asian, pan-American *networks.*

Finally, in combination with their marketing experience and high local name recognition, they built their reputation into a global *brand.* Along with Coca-Cola and Disney, Citibank now ranks in the top 10 in terms of brand awareness in Asia. Citigold, their affluent-customer banking service, is recognized as one of the elite clubs in Asia—a sign that an individual has made it in the world.

What has this pool of intangible capital provided Citicorp? Beyond its insider access in most markets, its extensive relationships, and its attractive customer group—formidable in themselves—it has begun to shape the various Asian and Latin American personal financial service markets to fit its unique strengths in electronic technology and customer service. They have converted their intangible assets into powerful intangible capital that makes it very difficult for others to compete. Their $2.2 billion 1997 net income from emerging markets (56 percent of their core business income) speaks for itself. Ultimately, it was Citicorp's global intangible capital that attracted Travelers to merge with it and why it made sense to retain *Citi* in the name of the new Citigroup.

CONTROL, NOT OWN

Citicorp has pursued a classic global integrator strategy in which it owns and controls most elements of the business system because it has been able to draw from intangible assets that arise from having been a multilocal operating around the world for nearly 100 years. However, many companies in the race for the world today have no such legacy. What should they do?

It is not actually necessary to own tangible assets everywhere to be able to compete everywhere. We believe many participants should center their strategies around a philosophical approach to assets captured in the mantra "control, not own." With ownership comes not only 100 percent of the returns, but also 100 percent of the financial risks. Given the volatility of the markets, such as the Asian turmoil in 1997 and 1998, the risks can be considerable. Lower capital investments mean lower risk of stranded assets as policies and market conditions change and as foreign exchange rates fluctuate. Moreover, owning everything is not only slow, it reduces flexibility. With superior intangibles, you can gain market access without owning local assets because local players want to partner with you. Speed increases, because it is easier to leverage intangibles across the world than to commission, design, build, and launch operations throughout the world.

It has been our theme throughout that, in the transition economy, the owners of intangible capital have the potential to capture much of the returns while making much less of a financial investment—and without taking much of the risk. On the other hand, we believe *control* is critical—particularly the control needed to protect your own intangible capital. If you control and leverage *intangible* capital in a way that avoids committing *financial* capital to investments where others are the natural owners, you can earn large returns, move quickly, maintain flexibility, and take little financial risk. As the old logic of corporate control through physical-asset ownership is challenged by the simultaneous explosion of opportunities and capital, we believe the "control, not own" mindset should be adopted by most companies as they expand geographically.

Legitimate and illegitimate ownership

Companies expanding geographically are not the long-term natural owners of the assets required to capture cross-geographic opportunities—particularly cross-border opportunities. As interaction costs fall, either specialists in managing those assets or local incumbents with superior local intangibles are potentially better owners. This is most obviously true of tangible, physical assets such as plants, distribution systems, and logistics systems. A foreign company always incurs operating risks that locals do not bear—and currency risks as well. Outside the developed world, there simply is no means of hedging against long-dated (e.g., two years) foreign exchange risk. Ownership can also be a problem because it reduces flexibility (it is hard to walk away from physical investments) and slows you down—a crucial issue as time and flexibility become increasingly critical.

But the "control, not own" issue is also true of many *intangible* assets—particularly intangible assets such as local knowledge. For example, take local country knowledge. It can take decades of living in a country to become thoroughly familiar with how to operate effectively there. Indeed, one may never become as effective as a local. Then there is the question of access to local labor pools, local relationships, and local reputation. Few Americans ever become leaders of companies in continental Europe, let alone China, India, Russia, or Brazil. And difficult as it may be for the individual, it is even more difficult for a company to acquire the specific knowledge needed to succeed in a particular local industry in a foreign country. Even countries with similar cultural heritage (say, the United States and the United Kingdom) have developed, over time, idiosyncrasies that make operating in each environment quite different. Acquiring the capabilities to operate seamlessly across *very* different countries (say, Indonesia and the United States) is even harder. Acquiring the country-specific knowledge across all aspects of the business system in the short term is literally a mission impossible. Even companies that have been operating as a multilocal in many countries for a long time may not have sufficient access to local knowledge to do this.

Different players know different things and are good at different things, so there are better and worse owners of different risks and pieces of the business. Much of the world's economy is still up for grabs in terms of natural ownership; however, local players are often the natural owners of the local customer base, so long as they move quickly and are able to satisfy their local needs at a world-class standard.

What should one avoid owning? Any part of the business system that promises little profit relative to the capital invested and the level of risk. In other words, almost any activity where you lack specialization advantages. You should be particularly wary of owning anything that reduces your flexibility and thereby narrows your strategic degrees of freedom. Sometimes, of course, a proprietary intangible asset simply cannot be separated from a tangible one; for example, much of Intel's knowledge-based intangible capital is inseparable from its manufacturing process.[16] In particular, separation sometimes can increase the risk of theft (or at least loss of proprietary assets) to unacceptable levels. You also need to be wary of giving others undue control over a critical part of an industry value chain. In most cases, however, with work and ingenuity, intangibles can be disentangled from much of the physical capital companies habitually hold on to. In particular, ideal partners to work with may be those with the intangibles you need, but who lack the skills to compete against you.

In general, then, one seeks to determine the *minimum* amount of tangible assets you have to own in order to operate an intangible business model most profitably and with the lowest risk of theft.[17]

Companies "travel light" by accessing the financial capital of others to fund investments in a variety of ways. They can raise principal investment funds to fund investments in new markets or technologies. They can coinvest with financial partners in large capital projects—as TISA has done with Citibank to fund the expansion of its installed-telephone base in Argentina,[18] and as many construction companies do with GE Capital. They can leverage other people's existing tangible assets; for example, Citibank uses the Japanese post offices as locations for its ATM network and for the sales and distribution of some of its products. They can put local entrepreneurs in business.[19]

Given the glut of equity capital available, there is no reason for companies to pour their own equity into low-return financial capital investments rather than intangible-rich investments. If you possess valuable intangibles, you can usually find someone lacking those intangibles to put up the needed capital so that they can earn higher returns than would otherwise be available to them. A number of firms have recognized this and retain many advantages of ownership—control, access to proprietary knowledge, relationships, talent—while owning relatively little. They are realizing far greater returns on invested capital while still growing earnings rapidly, thereby building superior market capitalization.

Keeping control

Most companies recognize that there is no capital constraint, but they have not realized its full ramifications. In general, companies we talked to were reluctant to replace control structures with different kinds of strategic relationships, even though they recognized their growing importance. They are more comfortable with using financial or physical capital investment to acquire access or physical scale advantages rather than using intangible capital to gain access or scale advantages.

There are good reasons for this. They find that partnering with local players or other market participants is complicated and that such relationships often fail to achieve benefits they were formed to capture. Cultural difficulties prevail. Many have been taken advantage of by past partners or have lost control of strategic, proprietary assets. Most companies find owning all the pieces of the business system less painful than forfeiting control.

Worrying about alliances failing is rational. Recent work on emerging market alliances suggests that less than half of all alliances meet their objectives.[20] This research also suggests, however, that the power in such alliances ultimately rests with the global players we call shapers; if the alliance or joint venture *does* collapse, the shaper is more likely to retain control because of disparities in capital, technology, brands, customer desire for global products, marketing know-how, and manufacturing process skills. This may be cold comfort for the smaller, emerging market participant—but it should encourage the developed-world multilocal in its global expansion.

But worry cannot be an excuse for inaction, for two reasons. First, getting in early is crucial: because there tend to be just a few attractive partners as each market opens up, the race really *is* to the swift. Second, it is *governance*—what we have called *control*—that counts, not ownership.

How, then, does one go about making this work? We believe there are three ways to structure a strategic alliance. The first is through a global *captive structure* in which, typically, the local player is a captive distributor or supplier for the larger, global player. Coca-Cola, Hilton, McDonald's, and Caterpillar all use variations of this approach. The second is through a *counterparty structure* based on a mutual, symbiotic relationship. Here the structure is, by definition, less formal and lasts for as long as there is mutual value to be created. The third approach is a *local dominant* approach.

In a *captive structure*, the dominant player retains control by creating value that would not otherwise exist for its local partner and by structuring win-win agreements that will persuade the local player to give up considerable autonomy. This structure evolves when the business system necessary to deliver the good or service can be divided easily between the two players, when it is in neither party's interest to own the other's intangible assets, and when the value provided by the global player is sufficiently great to confer bargaining power over the local player. This is often the model of choice for global players owning truly valuable intangible capital.

A *counterparty structure* is based on a mutual relationship in which both parties pursue "control, not own" strategies. Both parties reduce investment costs by leveraging each others' intangible and tangible assets, largely through contracts rather than formal alliances. These structures often evolve when neither party has bargaining power over the other and when there are several alternative parties with relatively equal capabilities.

A *local dominant* approach evolves where the number of desirable local partners is limited and a large number of global players with equivalent capabilities want to work with them.

This situation typically arises when local governments restrict market access to privileged local players. Chinese government offices frequently help favored local companies negotiate relationships of this kind. Despite the relative disadvantage *within* the relationship, successfully negotiating such an arrangement with a dominant local player gives a company real advantages over other global players. Over time, of course, the forces opening up the world economy will reduce the ability of local participants to maintain the privileged access needed to negotiate and protect these arrangements.

From a global player's point of view, any of these three structures is appropriate, provided it can protect its proprietary intangible assets. Over time, however, we believe that the *counterparty structure* will dominate as markets integrate. Such a structure is already widespread in capital markets businesses and is becoming so in industries such as electronics and automotive, in which distributors, suppliers, and manufacturers increasingly work together through contracts rather than alliances or as captives.

MANY WAYS TO GLOBALIZE INTANGIBLES

It is not always necessary to enter into an alliance or partnership in the traditional sense. Any arrangement that preserves for you key *decision-making rights over the asset* and your right to the appropriate part of the cash flows will suffice.

Licensing, far from a new way to access global opportunities, has taken off across more and more industries. Any sort of intellectual property that can be legally protected and then licensed out represents a control strategy. For years, players in the pharmaceuticals, chemicals, semiconductor, consumer electronics, and engineering industries have licensed out their intellectual property as a way of gaining market access. (As an alternative to royalty-based licensing, many companies are acquiring equity stakes in exchange for contributing their intellectual property to ventures.)

Indeed, we believe we are observing a fundamental shift in mindset toward licensing intellectual property as companies learn from the competitive errors of the past and set clearer strategic and financial objectives for their technology-licensing activities. From liquor and clothing to the hi-tech arena, companies in more and more industries are obtaining value from patent and brand portfolios to achieving global reach while keeping ownership at a minimum.[21]

The *franchise model,* long associated with retailing and fast-food industries, has begun to spread into de facto franchising agreements in disaggregated pieces of other industries. The Marriott hotel chain is a global franchise: the parent, Marriott Corporation, owns very little of the overseas real estate, instead earning considerable low-risk returns by providing management services and global marketing. British Airways is experimenting with a franchise approach. Their small European feeder airlines operate under a franchise model in which British Airways owns and operates no planes, but concentrates on managing schedule integration, code-sharing protocols, service quality assurance, and marketing and purchasing.

As we noted earlier, *electronic delivery* has already begun to revolutionize the economics of many intangible-heavy industries, enabling access to customers without physical distribution. Hence, the emergence on the Web of companies such as Amazon.com in books and music, Columbia House in music and video, or any of a host of Internet-based information or financial service providers, who have the potential to build a global distribution network at very low cost.

Successfully setting a *global standard* represents perhaps the ultimate "control, not own" strategy, enabling a company to reap near-monopoly profits because it actually directs industry evolution without owning any other parts of the business. As the world's economy opens up, a battle of standards is being waged in industry after industry, and a small number of companies are creating powerful positions as architects of global webs. Netscape (Internet), Microsoft/Intel (PCs), Incyte and Genset (genomics), Ericsson (mobile telephony), Schlumberger/IBM (smart cards), Visa (credit cards), TI (semiconductors), and Roche (diagnostics) reap or will likely reap huge returns from globalizing through intangibles.

Nevertheless, those unfortunate enough not to have developed the Windows operating system or the Intel microprocessor also have to expand their reach into new markets. We close this chapter with three examples from industries ranging from traditionally asset intensive to naturally asset light in which leading players have reduced their asset exposure to a remarkable degree.

THREE INTANGIBLE-HEAVY, CONTROL-NOT-OWN STRATEGISTS: SARA LEE, BANCO ITAÚ, CATERPILLAR

Sara Lee: A traditional company goes asset light

By almost all measures, Sara Lee is one of the world's leading apparel and food companies. Its multitude of brands ranges from Kiwi in shoe care, Hanes in knitwear and hosiery, Champion in sportswear, Coach in luxury goods, and Playtex in bras, to Douwe Egberts in coffee. Sara Lee has enjoyed consistently strong performance; in fiscal year 1997 it generated $1 billion in profits, over half of which came from non–U.S. markets.

How has it achieved this success across so many of its businesses for so many years? Through a combination of highly decentralized management and very strong performance incentives.[22]

But, because of its decentralized culture, Sara Lee has experienced some difficulty in encouraging its business units to leverage its intangible assets globally, particularly when it comes to entering emerging markets or even to building regional brands and businesses. As a result, many of its intangible assets have remained underexploited, the profit opportunities only partially realized.

Recognizing the value of many of its brands and their earnings potential if truly leveraged globally, Sara Lee's management also recognized the unattractiveness of owning the manufacturing base to produce many of its products. Despite its past initiatives to move the manufacturing base to lower-labor-cost nations, the management was concerned about the low returns from which manufacturing activities traditionally suffer. A number of Sara Lee's back-end activities were becoming commodities, available broadly at good quality levels.

Sara Lee saw another, more attractive alternative. In September 1997 Sara Lee announced a radical restructuring plan, one that would enable the company to shed the low returning pieces of its business system and to focus on the high returning facets. Instead of owning and running the manufacturing operations associated with its food and clothing businesses, Sara Lee announced its intention to concentrate on the highest-value-added part—the building and marketing of its world-famous brands.

The company is outsourcing its manufacturing to specialist third-party vendors, allowing Sara Lee to enjoy most of the advantages of low-cost production without the ownership. It also plans to sell selected noncore businesses as opportunities present themselves.

All in all, the restructuring is expected to generate incremental cash flow of $3 billion over the next three years, as well as substantial after-tax savings. Predictably, investors reacted positively to the announced restructuring, driving the stock price up 14 percent in one day. In order to boost shareholder returns further, Sara Lee plans to use the cash from the restructuring to buy back at least $3 billion worth of stock over the next three years.

Thus, Sara Lee has disaggregated its previously integrated ownership approach and replaced it with an asset-light strategy that should generate far higher returns and enable it to globalize its intangible assets more effectively.

Banco Itaú's double play

A global player is comparatively advantaged in owning the pieces of the business system endowed with intangibles that can be leveraged worldwide. But somebody has to own the tangible pieces of the value chain, and it is typically the local player for whom it makes sense to do so. The presence of the global player generally leads to higher cash flow than the local player would otherwise capture from its assets.

Banco Itaú is the third largest retail bank in Brazil, with $600 million in profits and a market capitalization of $6 billion. It has 2,000 branches, 9,000 ATMs, and (after significant cost-cutting) 30,000 employees. In the face of heightened pressure from deregulation, Itaú consolidated its position by buying three other local banks, BEMGE, BFB, and Banerj, to fill out its client base. Not exactly an asset-light play.

Because there are few distribution channels in Brazil outside the national banks, Itaú's branch network earns attractive returns—not least by virtue of the bargaining power it provides with foreign partners. Itaú has a joint venture with Bankers Trust in asset management and investment banking; if the alliance works, they will generate significantly higher returns together than they would be able to generate independently.

In the face of deregulation, however, more and more emerging market players are having to set their sights beyond their borders in order to retain control over their destiny. Here Itaú faces all the same capital and resource constraints as a global player when it seeks to expand—except more intensely because of its relatively small size. It, too, then, must go asset light and build an entry through intangible capital.

During the hyperinflationary era in Brazil, Itaú had developed truly world-class technology-based processing skills, allowing it to create that much-talked-of concept, the paperless branch. Studying the South American scene, Itaú determined that it could enter Argentina, a significantly less-productive, higher-cost market than Brazil, in which the mass market is currently served by local banks with expensive branch networks, high fees, low-to-no interest, and poor service.

Banco Itaú's bank-without-a-back-office—a radical advance even over the hi-tech U.S. model—allowed it to leapfrog local incumbents, setting up branches manned by only one employee. New customers quickly flocked to Itaú's distinctive value proposition—account opening in one day versus seven for the nearest competitor, and 30 to 50 percent lower fees. Today, Itaú has 30 branches in Argentina and should expand into an extraordinary position with economics that are likely to be unassailable for many years to come.

Caterpillar: Leveraging locals

Caterpillar's yellow mechanical earthmovers are a familiar sight worldwide. With 40 to 50 percent of the market, Caterpillar is the world's largest manufacturer of such equipment. It has built and maintained this position by using captive distributors to obtain and retain customer access, in a way that allows the company itself to focus on its own areas of strength. Caterpillar was in fact thrust into the global marketplace by the exigencies of World War II, during which years its equipment was used around the world, and the fact that the United States dominated construction worldwide during the period that followed. In order to maintain this customer access, Caterpillar built a global network of independent, exclusive dealers to sell and service its equipment. Currently, about 190 dealers run over 1,100 stores worldwide. The combined net worth of these dealers is $5 billion—about 40 percent of Caterpillar's current market capitalization.

The sale of earthmoving equipment creates a ten- to twenty-year service and parts relationship. These expensive machines normally run between twelve and twenty-four hours a day in tough, remote environments; thus, after-sales service and repair is difficult but critical. And because the machines last ten to twenty years, they require constant maintenance. Not surprisingly, service is highly localized.

Recognizing not only the significant long-term relationship and service implicit in its product but also the complications of owning the required global distribution capability, Caterpillar established a network of exclusive distributors. This allows the company to respond to customer needs far more effectively. It also allows Caterpillar to pass on local risks to its local partners to manage—far more appropriate owners of those risks.

By staying out of the service business, the company also sheds complexity, enhancing its ability to focus where it can extract returns with manageable levels of risk—research and development, sourcing, and manufacturing.

But owning those parts of its value chain where it has relative competitive advantage is only part of the Caterpillar story. Also highly distinctive is the extraordinary level of support Caterpillar provides to its dealer network. The company regards its dealer network as long-term strategic partners. It almost never sells direct—when the Alaskan Pipeline consortium insisted on direct purchasing, the company refused. It repurchases parts a dealer cannot sell, and, in 1982 to 1984, when a strong dollar made its machines uncompetitive, Caterpillar cut profit margins significantly to protect the dealers—losing $1 million per day for nearly three years. It strives to structure win-win agreements and keep its dealerships family-owned, profitable, and independent. It educates dealers' children and sends them to management training courses so they can take over from their parents. Not surprisingly, the loyalty of their dealers is legendary.

8

WINNING THE WORLD THROUGH SLIVERS

TWENTY YEARS FROM NOW, some $50 trillion of globally integrated economic activity will permit an extraordinary degree of specialization. An economy of this size could easily be disaggregated into 5,000 global business arenas, each representing $10 billion of production. Or perhaps, 50,000 "global microbusiness arenas," each of which would represent $1 billion of production. Or, more likely still, 5,000,000 tightly defined "global nanostructures" representing $10 million of production each.

SLIVERS AND MICROINDUSTRIES

This is specialization to a different degree and business on a different scale than that which occurs in local, regional, and even national economies. For example, it is accurate to say that the dry cleaner down the street offers a specialized service to the neighborhood. We are talking about something else entirely. A *sliver* is a specialized product or service that is economically viable at the global level. In the investment banking business, a sliver can be a hot new financing technique. In the software business, a sliver can be a "killer app."

The ability of any individual participant to deliver a sliver profitably is limited by its access to a sufficient volume of customers and the scale effects—particularly the intangible scale effects—of delivering that product. The advantages of delivering specialized output must be balanced against the costs: both the costs of acquiring access to customers and the related ability to spread fixed costs over as much volume as possible.

Companies that succeed in delivering slivers to an ever-widening market do so by developing infrastructures specifically geared to the task. These microindustry structures are significantly different from the industry structures, even the global ones, familiar to most of us. Traditional industry structures were built by integrated companies that controlled or owned every aspect of the value chain. "Microindustry" structures are complex webs of alliances, counterparty agreements, standards, and protocols that allow companies to participate in a discrete element of the value chain without owning the whole thing.

The transition economy is dynamic. Geographic barriers erode in different places, at different times, at different rates. This makes it easier to find customers across geographic markets, which makes it possible for companies to establish the scale to specialize. Interaction costs fall. This lowers the costs of specializing and the minimum efficient size of production. But customers become more demanding. Competitors enter established industries from unpredictable directions. The pace of technological innovation increases. Companies must tailor and retailor their offerings—always balancing customer needs with the scale effects—to suit these ever-changing conditions.

Issues of access, specialization, and scale exist, of course, in every economy. But these issues are of particular importance in the transition economy because of the sheer size of the opportunities and the speed at which companies must move to capture them. The transition economy can provide enormous scale benefits to extremely specialized products. But the *pace* at which these scale-versus-specialization trade-offs change can be very rapid. In this volatile situation, timing is everything. Being in the right place at the right time with the right sliver creates the opportunity to shape new microindustry structures. This is the way to win the race for the world.

A sliver is thus a product or service, based on specialization, that is economically viable within the limits permitted by the existing structure of an emerging microindustry at a given moment in time. Slivers therefore all have a limited life span; they expire as the limits permitting increased specialization are continually relaxed, enabling new slivers to be created. Companies cannot, therefore, rely on one sliver to sustain them.

We believe the most successful sliver strategies are highly correlated with an intangible-based strategy. The highest value slivers are intangible rich—typically based around distinctive intellectual property, distinctive talent, brands, or networks. By taking full advantage of the access to customers and corresponding scale effects provided by a global market, a company can afford to make significant investments in intangibles. This is what is required to fill the pipeline with slivers that are so distinctive that they literally overwhelm offerings by less specialized, less scale-effective competitors who may be drawing only on the resources of local or national markets. In other words, competitors pursuing global sliver strategies gain overwhelming specialization and intangible scale advantages.

As we suggested in Chapter 2, the ultimate end state of this process is one in which customers will be able to select from the entire world's offerings, all of which are world class, and get exactly what they want, when they want it, at the best possible price. To us, then, a sliver is an offering that delivers a value proposition that is as close to this end state as is possible given the *existing* geographic structure of a market and an industry *at a given moment in time*.

In some local industries, such as personal financial services or food, that are still geographically organized, the ability to do this is presently limited. Walking into a bank in China and asking for a mortgage is a different experience than using Homeshark on the Internet to find the best mortgage available in the United States. In contrast, a company based in Hong Kong ordering 100 personal computers from Compaq has essentially the same choices, allowing for differences in transportation and transaction cost, as does a company based in Austin, Texas. No global slivers are yet possible in mortgages because the market and industry structures do not permit it. In contrast, producers like Dell and Compaq are continually delivering new slivers to the global market. Because of continually declining interaction and transaction costs, microindustry structures can deliver ever-more-customized offerings. Indeed in many markets, thanks to electronic delivery, the notion is ultimately to deliver offerings tailored to a global segment-of-one customer.

Until global market and microindustry structures form, it is difficult to deliver global slivers. This is a "chicken and egg" problem. Which comes first? The answer, of course, is that markets, microindustry structures, and slivers are created through an interactive process.

SLIVERS IN FINANCIAL SERVICES

Slivers often emerge from specialization in a particular local or national market. Let's look at an example of the process at work in the distribution of financial services in the United States.

In the mid-1960s, both large corporate customers and retail customers were largely served out of the same physical full-service bank branch. Throughout the United States, partly due to regulation, and partly to other barriers to cross-geographic service, it made economic sense to locate banking services centrally in a large branch to which all customers would come. Over the last thirty years, particularly in the last ten, technology and weakening regulatory forces have lowered the cost of distributing and tailoring products to meet specific customer needs. Transaction and access costs have fallen as well. The result has been a great increase in specialization.

Corporate customers today have specialists, often based thousands of miles away, calling on them to offer products and services in nearly every conceivable area— from payroll services to derivatives, to retirement plans for their employees, to mergers and acquisitions. Direct distribution electronic channels are appearing for everything from credit approval to leasing services to executing foreign exchange transactions. At the retail level, multiple separate channels have been created for credit cards, mutual funds, payment services, and an enormous range of other services. For example, distribution channels for mortgage products alone include not only the traditional physical bank branches but also phone, mail, real estate brokers, home builders, and— increasingly—electronics channels. Simultaneously, the service offerings have become steadily more specialized as it becomes cost-effective to offer customers their choice over the amount of the mortgage, the percentage of down payment required, the nature and timing of the repayment program, and so on. Some mortgage providers have literally developed 3,000 different offerings tailored to tiny variations in customer preferences.

In other words, as geographic barriers such as regulation fall away, players who used to be able to sell their products and services only in a restricted geographic area are now free to sell anywhere. This also means that new, nontraditional players can enter the market as well. It used to be that if you wanted a mortgage, you went to a bank. Now you can go to your real estate broker or to Homeshark. Everyone's ability to do this in a cost-effective way has been greatly enhanced by the digital innovations that make it physically possible to do business at a great distance. Consequently, purchasers of mortgages are increasingly able to buy the best product—and by best we mean the product that is most closely tailored to the exact needs of the customer. In such a world, cross-geographic specialists focusing on those exact needs are far better at meeting those needs than the commercial banks that are trying to trade off serving different customer needs within a specific geography.

Unfortunately for the specialists, the banks at the moment have the customers and the infrastructure to integrate across geography. But the battle between the nonbank specialists and the banks in the United States is well under way and it is unclear as yet who will win. At this time, however, most specialists in personal financial services cannot get the scale effects they need to take the next step, which is to use slivers to enter markets outside the United States.

FROM LOCAL SPECIALTY TO GLOBAL SLIVER

Companies that are the best local or national specialists, if they are able to manage the risks and if there are sufficient degrees of freedom in their industry, can initiate a virtuous cycle of geographic expansion leading to the creation of a new global microindustry.

With the exception of a few "born global" businesses, industries come into being as local phenomena. Like the mortgage business just described, they grow within the national economies of countries, each of which has its own distinctive character. The value chain is defined geographically, regionally, or nationally. Size is typically achieved through vertical integration and diversification into multiple businesses. That is, the scale benefits of sharing costs to deliver goods and services (distribution, overhead, etc.) are achieved not through expanding volume in a narrow area (which the geographic limitations will not allow), but through expanding the business scope of the enterprise throughout the relevant geography—with resulting compromises in delivering more specialized services. Specialists who can cross geography can have it all: increased volume, scale benefits, and highly specialized offerings.

This is happening in the contract catering industry, tradition-ally a fragmented and predominantly local business. Typically, most of the activity in this $1.7 trillion worldwide industry has been performed by contract caterers that provide relatively undifferentiated service to all the institutions they serve, from businesses to hospitals to prisons to educational institutions. Op-erating profits are slim at 2 to 3 percent of sales ($30 billion to $50 billion) and the main competition has been in-house or government provision.

However, this is changing. Thanks to purchasing scale effects and outsourcing economies, the sector has begun to consolidate and open up to specialist contractors. In Great Britain today, the four leading companies account for over three-quarters, and in the United States for almost half, of total industry revenues. These consolidated players are positioning their service delivery around targeted customer segments, providing differentiated ser-vices to businesses, hospitals, prisons, and educational institutions.

The next step is to serve these markets on a global basis. For example, triggered by global companies' demand for one-stop shopping for catering services, a few players are beginning to take their best practices abroad. IBM uses the services of Eurest, a division of Compass, in seventy sites across the United States, Europe, and South America. Other companies like Sodexho and Aramark are also building out their European and U.S. operations.

As this takes place, specialists are created that have developed "best-in-world" skills or productivity in what, in the context of a national economy, might be an impossibly narrow specialty. Realizing their competitive advantage, these specialists explore moving beyond their home geography insofar as distribution channels and interaction costs allow. Frequently, the specialist goes into a new local market when its piece of the business system, product, or customer segment is being poorly served by the local players. Specialists will go, that is, wherever they see customers being taken advantage of.

UK—based Compass was among the first to move into foreign markets, predominantly through acquisitions. Compass has built a valuable portfolio of intangible assets in managing tailored food delivery, purchasing, and logistics, which it has leveraged worldwide. Its strategy entails building a brand in the particular segment—Chartwell in education, Bateman in health care, Roux in executive fine dining, and Canteen Correctional in prison services—which, together with tailored, branded service offerings, it has used to win long-term contracts in multiple countries.

Compass, in its global microindustry, is also able to use its expanded purchasing power to find suppliers willing to give it better prices, thus improving margins (currently, Lehman Brothers estimates its margin in the United Kingdom is 4.9 percent which is 1.5 percent higher than the industry average). The increased profits are then used to launch ever more specialized offerings and to build the brands, enabling the company to win more bids and encourage primary demand. This cycle of increasing returns gives Compass a considerable advantage over later entrants who do not enjoy the same cost advantages and reputation, and who are locked out of the more lucrative contracts—most of which are long term. It also helps Compass to afford the investment to enter new geographic markets, thus fueling its virtuous cycle of geographic expansion.

The results have been remarkable. In just five years, Compass has grown from a company that had 99 percent of annual sales of £350 million ($560 million) in the United Kingdom in 1992 into a company with operations in forty countries and annual sales over £3.5 billion ($5.6 billion), less than 20 percent of which comes from the United Kingdom. In the process, Compass is redefining UK contract catering into a global microindustry with discrete value propositions aimed at distinct global customer segments.

MAKING STRUCTURES MICRO

As this process unfolds and other competitors adopt similar strategies, national value chains are atomized into discrete businesses and global microindustry structures, which in turn makes it easier for global specialists to deploy their specialty in the various national catering industries. At first, before these structures form, the work of accommodating the requirements of each national value chain has to be performed by individual participants, like Compass, who enter the market because the local industries are not organized to meet the needs of global specialists.

In contract catering, for example, the caterers entering new markets find the need to source from local suppliers whose practices vary from market to market. Over time, though, they find food suppliers who gear their operations to the global contract caterer's needs. In the future some of them go global themselves to better serve the contract caterers. Eventually standards emerge, counterparty relationships form, and a new value chain is created. In the new value chain, each of the global customer segments is served by specialized contract caterers contracting, in turn, with different suppliers who, in turn, provide caterers with food, labor, and so forth, geared to the discrete needs of the customer segments being served. (Prisoners get different food than hospital patients, who get different food than business executives.)

Companies that succeed in delivering the best slivers to the largest possible market, given the existing structure of a market or a microindustry, earn the opportunity to shape new global microindustries. At the same time as the producer is gaining access to more markets and interaction costs are continuing to fall, customers from different markets search for the producer— drawn by the reputation that inevitably accrues to those who offer the market world-class value propositions. As a result, the volume in the sliver grows rapidly, providing the company with increasing return effects. This, in turn, provides the resources to build more of the infrastructure needed to create a global microindustry, as well as the resources to invest in developing the next sliver designed to leverage the specialization permitted in the future structure of the market and the industry.

As sliver after sliver is created, and increasing returns are earned, the distance between the company and other competitors in that industry grows. The company in the lead can out-invest its competitors, particularly in intangibles. Due to the remarkable scale effects of intangibles, the company then gains the opportunity to shape, and dominate, the new global microindustry. However, if the company fails to invest continually to produce new slivers, it makes itself vulnerable to a competitor emerging from another industry or another geography. Remember, slivers have a short life span because, as the economy continues to integrate, new opportunities emerge to create slivers that represent even better value propositions.

Slivers in industries with existing global structures

This process does not just apply to local industries that are beginning to globalize. It also applies to industries with already existing global structures. The experience of the integrated oil majors—an early globalizing industry—is salutary. Effectively, Exxon, Shell, Texaco, British Petroleum–Amoco, Mobil, and Chevron, acting as geographic integrators, globalized the entire value chain at once by owning every aspect of the business. They did everything from exploring and producing the crude oil to shipping it around the world to refining it into petroleum products such as gasoline, and wound up distributing it to the end user. And, for over fifty years, the major integrated oil producers have been enormously successful because they built distinctive skills in managing across functions and geography, deployed vast amounts of capital, leveraged the latest technology, and fully utilized the access, specialization, and scale advantages from being global over smaller participants worldwide. However in the United States, and increasingly abroad, a new trend is emerging—the "atomization of big oil."[1] Tightly focused, specialized players are now entering the field.

The combination of a more open playing field due to industry deregulation and technology commoditization, world-class intangibles among the new specialized competitors including state of the art functional skills (e.g., risk management, logistics), and the removal of capital constraints on the growth of smaller players have created fundamentally new competitive conditions. Together, these forces have eliminated many of the traditional advantages derived from scale and scope. And so players like Huntsman in styrene and polystyrene (petrochemical by-products of refining oil), Tosco in refining, and Koch in logistics and trading have found competitive advantage in developing and leveraging world-class skills within increasingly global microindustries.

For example, Tosco operated its Avon refinery in northern California in a traditional manner (focusing on production of petroleum products such as gasoline) for over a decade. During this period, Tosco used its position as a platform to assemble critical operating capabilities and gain credibility within the industry as an owner-operator. Afterward, Tosco was able to initiate an acquisition strategy that transformed it from a $1.9 billion company with a single refinery in 1992 to a $13.3 billion company with eight refineries and an extensive retail distribution network in 1997.

Tosco was able to grow at such a pace by exploiting an anomaly in the market. It used emerging futures markets in crude oil to help minimize purchase price risks as it capitalized on the rush by many traditional players to exit the low-margin refining business. Using the expertise gained over the previous decade, it then transformed the operations at newly acquired refineries and drastically reduced costs. In the process it developed new ways of competing and new intangible assets (skills such as deal structuring and risk management). This is what enabled Tosco to build on its successful purchase of the Bayway refinery in 1993 from Exxon and subsequently acquire BP's Ferndale and Marcus Hook refineries, Circle K, and Unocal's refining and marketing business. The stock market rewarded Tosco with a $540 million increase in market capitalization when it announced in 1996 the purchase of Unocal's West Coast refining and marketing (R&M) assets for $1.4 billion.

As a result, the big global oil players are watching as large specialized players, who grow by focusing on slivers of the business, are becoming increasingly skillful at extracting value formerly being captured by integrated producers. Given that the global law of one price applies for crude oil and all refined petroleum products, integrated majors who are less effective than the specialists either wind up providing a price umbrella or, if prices fall, earning lower returns than they would have otherwise. Eventually, as this process continues, the integrated major, unless it becomes world class in each area of specialty, either has to drop out of activities where it has inferior skills or cross-subsidize the specialties where it is weak with areas where it is strong.

From slivers to global industry structures

The process of becoming continually more specialized is even at work in an industry that was born specialized: the personal computer business. In this industry, for structural reasons, many of the specialists have been able to use slivers to shape new global microindustries that they have been able to dominate. The computer industry has, of course, been highly influenced by the pace of technological innovation. Even apart from the semiconductor industry, innovation is rapid and creates substantial intangible assets for the innovator. Another key aspect is the heightened returns expected from the installed base, which creates sufficient "stickiness" to impart a reinforcing advantage to incumbents with a large market share.

The computer industry started with integrated players dominating the landscape. From the fifties through the seventies, the industry was nascent, and few standards had evolved. While the pace of change was moderately fast, it was mostly dominated by large players who set the tone for the industry. IBM came to dominate the mainframe-based computer industry globally through heavy investment in intangible assets, superior marketing, and relationship management skills, an early lead, and—

subsequently—global scale advantage. It dominated all aspects of the value chain: hardware, operating systems, utilities, application software, and services, in mainframes, the primary computer market.

Over time, technical innovation and other industry forces led to the creation of slivers. Digital Equipment Corporation (DEC) was created from the vision of an MIT professor, Ken Olsen, that minicomputers, not mainframes, would bridge the gap between corporate data–centric and business use of computing. DEC was highly successful in the late seventies and early eighties with its VAX series of minicomputers.

The pace of change has accelerated in the computer industry over the past couple of decades, most particularly in the PC industry, which changed the face of computing in the eighties. The PC industry saw the rapid emergence of global specialists such as processor manufacturers, operating system developers, and application developers. Relatively low barriers to entry in most parts of the value chain (except processors and, to a lesser extent, operating systems) caused a proliferation of players and further balkanization of the already divided value chain. Global specialists emerged very quickly in motherboards, disk drives, memory, displays, printers, and other accessories. Better known, because they touch the consumer more closely, are the specialists in system utilities (e.g., Norton), applications (e.g., Lotus), and development software (e.g., Borland). In particular, the hardware specialists quickly went global to exploit intangible scale effects and to capture cross-geographic arbitrage opportunities to access low-cost labor pools in other countries (e.g., motherboard manufacturing in Taiwan) and government subsidies.

The facilitating factor of this change was the largely open standards on which the PC industry was based. Apple was the exception to this rule. For legacy reasons, Apple was largely an integrated player that insisted on owning all parts of the value chain. It resisted specialization by independent producers in hardware manufacturing. It attempted cross-geographic arbitrage, but only through internal means. In contrast, the rest of the players in the PC industry largely adopted first IBM standards and later Intel-Microsoft standards, and were able to benefit from the external web of participants in the value chain. The natural owners of each part of the business were able to align their comparative advantages in risk taking and intangibles with appropriate parts of the value chain. This created a low-cost, high-performing external web that was best positioned to capture both internal and external cross-geographic arbitrage.

Many specialists did and continue to do very well from the globally standardized business system that emerged. The true winners in this race, however, were not just specialists, but rather those who became shapers, continually increasing the gap between themselves and the competition. Microsoft capitalized on an early breakthrough in operating systems.[2] An interesting example is the joint development project with IBM on the next-generation operating system. Having anticipated the value of a graphical user interface (GUI) in stimulating usage of PCs, Microsoft pulled out of the joint venture and concentrated its efforts on a GUI–based operating system. Through early introduction of such functionality, however incomplete, it was able to consolidate its already comfortable position in the market. It is interesting that Microsoft was not the innovator in GUI–based PCs—Apple was. For quite some time, market share of Apple's Mac was comparable to that of Windows-based PCs. Eventually, however, a more efficient external web in the PC industry beat out an integrated business model employed by Apple. From a position of strength, Microsoft has used its superior access to capital to create mainly alliance-based options in the rapidly converging world of computing, multimedia, and telecommunications.

The importance of agility in this fast-paced industry cannot be overemphasized. Because the PC industry has been global for years, proprietary cross-geographic arbitrage opportunities are harder and harder to find (because they are available to all participants). However, fundamental technological changes—the convergence of communication, computing, and multimedia—

have opened new opportunities and made obsolete business models that were relevant only a few years earlier. As the history of this volatile industry shows, those who ignore these changes do so at their own peril. Consider DEC, which thought it could ignore PCs in the eighties and subsequently struggled through most of the late eighties and nineties (to be eventually acquired by Compaq).[3]

One company that has made the most of the opportunities available in the personal computing transition economy is Dell, whose odyssey we discussed earlier. Dell started as a low-end PC assembler. However, instead of using intermediaries, it adopted a direct sales approach (large, established competitors like HP, Compaq, IBM were using resellers). Dell (along with Gateway 2000) recognized early on that a direct sales model, if executed well, would be superior to the traditional approach. The emergence of relatively informed, technically savvy customers, particularly the high-margin corporate customer, meant that customers did not need resellers to guide their purchasing decisions; they were willing and able to search out and negotiate directly with the supplier. Because of the high rate of obsolescence in the PC industry (1 percent per month, and even higher for newly released models), assemblers like Dell could not afford to carry inventory. By establishing superior assembly methods, Dell was able to manufacture a PC to exact customer specifications *after* the PC was ordered. Traditionally, assemblers concentrated on forecasting demand and managing inventory based on information from the reseller network—information that was one important step removed from the source, the customer. The direct model obviates the need for detailed demand forecasts for combinations of components that go into a PC, substantially decreasing exposure to obsolescence and forecast errors.

To deliver on its direct sales model, Dell has elevated supply-chain management into an art form. It works with a few suppliers on a global scale, integrating their supply chains with its own information systems. Having fine-tuned its processes, Dell actually ends up with a negative level of working capital! It buys components on credit and receives payment from its customers when the order is placed—so its customers and its suppliers finance its operations. Its sales staff is focused on partnering with customers, particularly large corporate buyers, to play a consulting role in their purchase decisions. It leverages its customized assembly process to deliver significant value-added services such as custom software installation and asset management (by adding custom bar codes) at small incremental cost. Decreased interaction cost from on-line ordering further enhances the appeal of direct sales. Dell has been wildly successful with its business model, its market capitalization rising from $356 million in 1990 to $93 billion as of December 31, 1998. In the short term, it has been successful in expanding its model overseas despite infrastructure and other inadequacies. Whether Dell can continue as a shaper as its industry evolves remains to be seen. While other players in the value chain have not been as successful as Dell, the unique structure of this industry has led to its explosive growth, and by implication a larger profit pool for *all* its participants.

SLIVERS IN THE MEDICAL DEVICES BUSINESS

When we look at the medical devices industry, we see a series of global microindustries that deliver slivers to what appears to be multiple local markets—the world's health care providers. While state ownership and regulation have kept most aspects of patient care local, the knowledge of medical practice itself is measurably global. Discovery lies at the heart of medicine, and any new procedure is spread rapidly—around the developed world at least—through seminars, conferences, electronics, and training. The most global aspects of health care delivery are pharmaceuticals and medical devices.

The medical devices industry already comprises many global microindustries and hundreds of global slivers—heart valves, arthroscopic instruments, contact lenses, and pacemakers to name a few. Each of these slivers is part of a distinct medical devices product family, each a global microindustry. These microindustries are dominated worldwide by a few companies (in many cases only one) due to their technological superiority (often supported by a patent), premier reputation, strong physician relationships, or other intangible assets. These companies, although specialists, tend to be fully integrated producers (i.e., the product itself is the sliver). This approach may become more asset light in the future as new specialists emerge.

While the medical devices industry shares certain characteristics with the pharmaceutical industry, many of the market characteristics are quite different. Drugs are consumed on multiple occasions, whereas most devices are used for procedures that occur no more than once in a patient's life. As a result, even the largest national market for any one medical device is relatively small—which makes the economics for developing global microindustries compelling (although even these global micromarkets are often not large). For example, the largest medical devices market in the world in 1995 was the global imaging market, at an estimated $10 billion in sales. Cardiological devices were estimated at $7.3 billion, and even the widespread intravenous–vascular access market was only $2.5 billion.

Technological complexity and an accelerating pace of change and innovation have also expanded the industry's horizons globally. R&D expenses are high and product life cycles can be brief due to new advances, parallel R&D programs, and reverse engineering. Specialized products, or slivers, are often rapidly overtaken. As a result, medical devices companies tend to take their products global quickly to cover their high development costs and maximize profits during the typically short time before a new and better product appears. Fortunately, the medical devices industry serves a specific global customer base—doctors, surgeons, and other health care providers. Highly networked and well informed about the latest developments in science and technology, this population makes the global adoption of new products relatively rapid—something facilitated by the fact that most devices can be sold around the developed world with only minor customization to different markets.

Another driver of globalization in medical devices is the fact that product-based disaggregation occurred early on in the industry's development. Companies that tried to fulfill all the needs of a particular customer base typically failed. Medtronic attempted to provide all the devices associated with heart management, but it never attracted as many customers for its angioplasty catheter business as it did for its pacemakers (nor did anyone else in the industry, for that matter). Others have tried to bundle the devices and procedures associated with ophthalmology in a common kit and similarly failed to build substantial sales. These failures were, in fact, classical demonstrations of a basic fact about globalization: It is extremely hard for any one company to guarantee the best value across several product groups. As a result, many medical companies tend to specialize in a particular device technology to ensure that they have the best product.

The device players had yet a further inducement to specialize. They found that specialization around global microindustries led to the accumulation of competitively valuable intangible assets—relationships with a specialty group of physicians and scientists, knowledge in a particular branch of research, a sales force with deep knowledge and skills in a particular device area, and a reputation among physicians as the best provider of a specific device. All these sources of intangibles helped provide ways to create and sustain predominance in a global sliver.

Given these forces, it is not difficult to see why the medical devices industry disaggregated itself from the larger health care industry early in its development and why product-based specialization and globalization also occurred very quickly. The existence of what was effectively a single market, in the developed world at least, populated by highly trained professionals effectively operating on a global standard—the tenets of Western medicine—led to the swift and near-universal adoption of technologically superior U.S.–made goods. In fact, many products, such as Johnson & Johnson's stents or Baxter's newest heart valves, were first sold in Europe, where the regulatory barriers for approval were lower than in the United States. In addition, international prices have tended to be much higher than in the United States, mainly due to reimbursement differences in the medical systems.

Let's consider one sliver in the medical devices industry: surgical sutures. How did this sliver come to dominate a microindustry? Johnson & Johnson's Ethicon division was the first company in the industry to develop a global presence in surgical sutures based on a patentable technical innovation used in wound closure after surgery or trauma. It is a good example of how a company has been able to turn a sliver into an opportunity to dominate a global microindustry continuously. Today it controls about 80 percent of the U.S. market and approximately 70 percent of the European market, despite attempts by various competitors to erode its leadership. To succeed, J&J had to displace a variety of alternative ways of closing wounds using different national practitioners. Part of J&J's success can be attributed to the fact that, as the first entrant in the global arena, and to gain from a virtuous cycle of geographic expansion, it was able to shape the sutures market to suit its product and become the one company able to capture increasing returns effects as it became the product of choice worldwide. However, the company's ability to hold on to its leadership position owes much to its commitment, from the very beginning, to surgeon and nurse training.

Even the introduction of fairly simple medical devices like sutures requires that practitioners receive training to acquaint them with the new technology. Once doctors become comfortable with a particular product, it becomes more difficult to break into the market with a new one (unless it is clearly superior). In other words, switching costs are high. J&J's training programs enabled the company to forge close relationships with its customers and ensured loyalty to its products. Because there have been no radical advances in sutures to render J&J's products obsolete, its customer relationships have served as an effective entry barrier to potential entrants, solidifying J&J's dominance. J&J has further bolstered this loyalty with a series of modest, but important, enhancements in its product line.

VALUE CHAIN SLIVERS

As technology advances, more and more product-based slivers will emerge based on innovation by companies specializing in different global microindustries. However, we also expect to see other forms of disaggregation take hold around value chain roles.

To make this point, let's return to the medical devices industry. While most of today's successful devices companies concentrate on narrow product slivers, most are still integrators. At the global microindustry level, the largest companies (J&J, BMS, Baxter, Becton-Dickinson) perform everything from R&D to product sales in-house. Their labs employ hundreds of scientists, they own and operate large manufacturing facilities, and they market and sell their final products through their own sales forces. However, as interaction costs continue to fall and as the economy continues to integrate, the degree of specialization permitted by the existing industry structure rises.

We are already seeing the first signs of the disaggregation of these individual global microindustries into more specialized business systems—global "nano" industries. Hundreds of small medical companies, focusing primarily on the R&D of new products, have appeared over the last ten to fifteen years (particularly in the United States, where venture capital is more readily available to fund these start-ups) to run in the race to build patentable intangible capital. Most of these boutiques simply cannot afford to build the distribution networks required to have access to the global market, so those with successful, marketable products have either allied with or sold out to the larger players in order to utilize their sales capability. A few independent players such as US Surgical have built direct sales forces abroad, but even relatively large companies such as Boston Scientific and St. Jude use the third-party distributors in second-tier markets.

It may be that further disaggregation of global microindustries in medical devices will ultimately be limited in terms of the sales and marketing function. Selling a medical device demands more sophistication than selling most other products; indeed, it typically requires training a surgeon in a new procedure. Sales forces that can do this are not fungible; it takes significant investment to train a sales force in a new device.

There remains, however, a rationale for specialized distribution companies, not dissimilar to the "rent-a-rep" companies that have emerged for pharmaceutical products, to focus on customer-rather than product-based slivers. Instead of each producer separately targeting, say, cardiologists, to sell its narrow range of products, the specialist distributor could reduce costs by selling the complementary products of a number of companies.

In the manufacturing function, the obstacles to specialization are smaller. Contract manufacturing has already begun to appear among simpler devices, in such areas as injection molding. Some companies have even outsourced the production of certain important elements of their product, as did St. Jude—a key component of its mechanical heart valves is produced by Carbomedics. We expect that subcontracting in manufacturing will become more common because it will enable players to benefit from the economies of scale generated by large-scale manufacturers located in nations with low factor costs. More complex devices, of course, require greater skill to manufacture, and are likely to disaggregate less quickly. Even for some fairly simple products, such as sutures, a company can achieve a competitive advantage through know-how related to the production process, rather than the product itself. In these cases, outsourcing is unlikely to be justified because manufacturing requires unique intangibles.

COMMODITIZATION AT THE END OF THE ROAD

In the final stage of globalization, commoditization appears. Parts of the medical devices industry are beginning to show some early signs. Over the past five years, prices have come under pressure and in some markets have begun to converge, as health care systems everywhere become increasingly cost-conscious. Not surprisingly, commoditization is appearing first in the simplest products, such as needles and catheters, which are sold around the world at effectively the same price. For many more complex medical devices, commoditization is still far in the future, held in check by the rapid rate of technological innovation.

Another hindrance to full globalization is, of course, the fact that the market for many devices is largely contained within Europe, North America, and Japan, as developing countries are often too poor to afford even the most basic elements of health care. The few countries outside the developed world that can afford Western health care standards have to pay much higher prices for the privilege. This too will change soon, as a fast-growing middle class emerges in many of these markets. This will create strong incentives for Western companies to build cheaper, stripped-down versions of their current products— which would nevertheless still be far superior to alternative local treatment methods. If they do not, enterprising local companies surely will. Inventive ways of providing certain procedures will also expand the market, such as the mobile video imaging units for laparoscopic surgery used in poorer and less densely populated rural areas where doctors cannot afford their own machines.

CREATING VALUE FROM SLIVERS

Sliver strategies depend on the structure of the industry. In industries with nascent global structures, such as the beer industry, there is no real opportunity to roll out slivers because there is no pathway to the market. The global microindustry must be created first. Still, it is easier and faster to create a global microindustry, as in the contract catering industry, than to create a whole industry structure, as was done historically through a classic integrator approach.

Slivers create value for a customer by delivering better service, better quality, better product features, or lower prices. Sliver players can capture value in one of three ways: utilizing first-mover advantages, owning unique assets, or owning an industry standard.

Value can derive simply from first-mover advantages; that is, by being the first to apply intangible assets to create a new global microindustry, even if the assets are not unique. In a given industry, there are often many players around the world with roughly equivalent intangible assets developed through parallel industry evolution (e.g., telecommunications, banking, electric, and utilities). In this instance, the global microindustry is difficult to dominate unless the player is the first mover. But there are possibilities. For example, a company can generate high consumer loyalty, as did J&J in sutures. It can lock up the best local partners or build strong, lasting relationships with its partners, as Caterpillar has so successfully done (see Chapter 7). By focusing on a global microindustry early, it learns more, which enables it to further deepen its specialization advantages relative to latecomers. If you are the only player with a pathway to the global micromarket you want to serve, it is easier to create slivers.

The second way to capture value is by owning unique assets. Here, value is derived from the ability to exert bargaining power over the rest of the business system. Coca-Cola is an obvious example: Their unique asset—the brand—captures significant value worldwide. However, its value is essentially limited to its own industry.

The third way to capture value through slivers is by owning an industry standard that the rest of the world has adopted. This sort of position is envied because it spawns so many valuable intangible assets: strong customer relationships, brands, networks of best-in-class partners, top talent, exceptional intellectual property rights. This is not to say it is an impenetrable position—as the current battle between Netscape and Microsoft demonstrates—but it is a pathway to riches.

THE CUSTOMER AS KING

Over time, we believe it is the customer-based segment that will become the most potent form of global sliver, because the transfer of power from producers to markets described in Chapter 1 ultimately puts power in the hands of the customer. Globalization will eventually belong to customers, not to companies, as their ability to choose among suppliers increases.

As with geographies, today's relatively limited access to customers will open up. It will become easier to reach customers who have hitherto been offered only limited choice. Likewise, it will be easier to reaggregate globally around customer-based segments by serving the purposes of the customer rather than those of the producer.

In a world economy composed of billions of diverse people, millions of diverse small businesses, and thousands of very diverse large enterprises, the opportunities to build specialized businesses by delivering discrete global value propositions tailored to distinct global customer segments is enormous. In the past, relatively few players in each market controlled access to customers, determining what customers could see—epitomized, in one incarnation, by the battle for shelf space. Now, that control is being wrested from them by digitization. Customer relationships are being built through "narrowcast" rather than broadcast models, making it easier for the customer to find the players offering truly distinctive value, even in the absence of a physical channel. And so customer-based slivers will become more and more prevalent. Historically, to the extent global customer segments did exist, they centered around large business markets or the high-end private customer—both very mobile, very visible, global customer segments. The spending power of these segments afforded the cost flexibility to overcome expensive interaction barriers.

Now, however, economically viable global customer segments are emerging well below the very high end. As transaction and interaction costs plummet, many more types of global customer segments are possible. Thus, we see the likes of CNN and the Four Seasons hotel group serving the global business traveler, Intuit serving the PC banking needs of the active PC owner, and MTV serving the world's teenagers. Specialists are beginning to develop to serve the borrowing needs of low-income customers and small businesses. Thanks to electronics, scale in highly specialized customer segments will be readily achievable for even local players. A business built around serving, say, 10,000 master craftspeople around the world who need highly specialized English, Japanese, and American tools to build handmade fine furniture becomes a viable enterprise.

It is the possibility of creating literally millions of different customer microsegments that leads us to the conclusion that this is where so many of the world's global slivers will emerge. And, given the accessibility of today's markets, it is not too early for a pioneer to begin creating and shaping these global slivers, particularly where products can be delivered electronically such as in the financial services or media businesses.

PORTFOLIOS OF GLOBAL MICROINDUSTRIES

While dominating one or two global microindustries that you can shape is a powerful position, an even more powerful position is dominating a portfolio of related global microindustries.

Consider General Electric. GE is in fact the composite of hundreds of global microindustries. It owes much of its success to its ability to derive value from being a leader in multiple, interrelated businesses. For example, GE has been able to derive advantage both from manufacturing equipment and financing that equipment through its subsidiary GE Capital. Over its twenty-year history, GE Capital has migrated from being a relatively mundane sales finance arm for GE (financing consumer appliances and so forth) to one of the greatest financial institutions in the world. GE Capital, like GE itself, is made up of dozens of individual businesses competing in dozens of global microindustries.

Let's look at how GE Capital has dominated one global microindustry—the aircraft and aircraft-engine leasing business. GE Capital Aviation Services got its start through financing the sale of GE–manufactured aircraft engines. It now provides operating and financial leases not just for new GE–produced engines, which helps sell the engines, but also for the engines of other vendors' used engines, such as Pratt & Whitney.

As part of its value proposition, GE Capital offers its customers different types of leases, including some that provide engine maintenance. When the aircraft engine comes off lease, GE Capital restores the engine and uses its market-making capabilities to sell "good as new" engines while arbitraging global price and availability differences. If GE Capital executives feel the price of the engines or aircraft coming off lease is too low, they have the option of leasing airplanes to airlines or running charter services until prices improve.

In some ways, each of these businesses is a global microindustry. GE is a world leader in selling and financing its own engines, in financing the sales of aircraft, in maintaining aircraft and aircraft engines, in restoring used engines, in making global markets in used equipment, and in financing the sale of used aircraft and aircraft engines. What holds this business portfolio together is the power it gives GE Capital to create new generations of slivers that help customers finance aircraft and aircraft engines in infinite creative ways.

GE Capital's big advantage is its intellectual property. It knows more about the key uncertainties in financing aircraft engines and aircraft—the terminal value of the equipment and the different duration of engine and airframe life—than anyone else. Moreover, it has put in place a business system enabling it to get the best price for used equipment. This, in turn, enables the company to offer better terms and conditions to airlines, transaction by transaction, than anyone else. In this industry, where each sales transaction is valued at $50 million or more, each transaction is practically a sliver of its own.

GE Capital takes such a global microindustry and sliver approach to every business it is in, from financing and owning commercial real estate, to financing container cars, to processing credit card receivables, to providing mortgage insurance. Over a twenty-year period it has transformed itself from a small consumer and commercial finance company in the backwater of its industry to become the second-largest financial institution in the world.[4]

SLIVER-BASED VALUE PROPOSITIONS

The challenge, as global market and industry structures mature, is to avoid participating in a globally commoditized industry. In a globally commoditized industry, the law of one price begins to apply, and players compete primarily on price. Unless you have come to dominate the global microindustry in which you are now competing, opportunities are limited when the microindustry structure matures. The new industry structures delivering the global value chains have been set. It is essential, therefore, to shape an industry structure around your own unique intangible assets. To avoid commoditization and to make the most of opportunities within a fully globalized industry, such as aerospace, a company must have either overwhelming physical and intangible scale advantages (such as Boeing in airframes) or the ability to add new functionality and service dimensions to the product (such as GE in aircraft engine maintenance and leasing).

Once a business is globally mature, the process in a sense comes full circle. Usually the globalization process has completed itself around only a portion of a broad-based value chain or for a certain set of customers within it, and some other area with more local or national structure begins to undergo the process. In even the most globalized of industries, it is usually possible to find and create ever more specialized, disaggregated nanoindustry structures, enabling the creation of new value propositions that are sufficiently differentiated to avoid commoditization.

However, most industries have yet to globalize; even largely global industries such as petroleum or automotive are undergoing wholesale market and industry restructuring. So most companies still have the chance to prepare for, and shape, the transition.

It is not easy to say whether the challenges facing smaller, more specialized companies taking on the world through slivers are more daunting than the challenges facing large, integrated companies that must restructure themselves to be competitive as new global value chains are being created. Either way, developing and exploiting global slivers will lie at the core of almost every successful strategy. However, to capture the benefits of the transition economy fully, participants will also need to become proficient at the capture of cross-geographic arbitrage, the subject of the next chapter.

9

CROSS-GEOGRAPHIC ARBITRAGE

T HE TRANSITION ECONOMY offers opportunities to transfer labor and productivity advantages developed in one geography to another. A company can lower its production costs while living under the price umbrellas of producers with lower productivity or higher factor costs. Multilocal and classic global companies have long done this through internal integration. But now, as we described in Chapter 3, it is possible to capture these opportunities by means of external agreements with other players. Counterparty agreements give companies the flexibility necessary to take advantage of these opportunities without making large capital investments.

It is becoming imperative for companies to capture these opportunities systematically, just as traders in the financial markets must always search for financial arbitrage opportunities. The successful arbitrageur should always be trading off the benefits, risks, and costs of capturing arbitrage internally versus capturing it externally through counterparties. In particular, getting the timing right by understanding the dynamics is critical because these opportunities are volatile, not just due to the rapid change in foreign exchange rates but because of the overall volatility of the transition economy.

Cross-geographic arbitrage will grow in importance because the opportunities now becoming available are both large and abundant. Capturing these opportunities can separate winners from losers.

What about timing? On the one hand, it will take a very long time for the world's markets to integrate fully, thereby eliminating the potential for arbitrage. This is good news because it implies that if means can be found to capture arbitrage, the value will prove to be durable. On the other hand, relative to historical experience, the lowering of geographic barriers is happening rapidly. Those who do not move now to take advantage of these opportunities will find themselves on the sidelines as the pace of economic integration accelerates.

The continuing reduction of transaction costs, the increase in access to new markets (including the markets for highly skilled labor), the inclusion in the global economy of emerging nations with radically lower factor costs, the adoption of common standards and protocols, and the increasing availability of counterparties all serve to both lower the barriers to capturing cross-geographic arbitrage opportunities and to increase their potential value. This is creating real opportunities for all players, be they specialists, geographic integrators, or shapers.

ARBITRAGE IN CAPITAL MARKETS

In this chapter, we look at arbitrage between markets in the real economy, particularly in relation to cross-geographic differences in productivity and factor costs. But before we do that, it is worthwhile reflecting on how arbitrage has been captured in the global capital markets, where the practice is the most advanced.

The art of arbitrage in the financial markets evolved over a twenty-year period. Like many of the opportunities in the transition economy, it started with a change in regulation. In the mid-1970s, foreign exchange rates were allowed to float. Large banks and corporations quickly discovered they could take advantage of these floating prices. They could borrow money in one currency at a given rate, convert the money into another currency, and lend it to another institution in another country at a higher rate, since money market interest rates varied from country to country. At the same time, they could neutralize foreign exchange risk with a foreign exchange contract. In effect, they shared the guaranteed profit on the differences between the countries' interest rates with their counterparty in the foreign exchange contract.[1] The only risks were that the borrowing institution would default on the loan or that the foreign exchange counterparty would default on the exchange rate contract.

Arbitrage opportunities were relatively easy to find in the foreign exchange market because the necessary information—exchange rates and lending rates—was readily available. It was relatively easy to estimate the potential value of the arbitrage, the transaction costs, and the risks. It was also relatively easy to acquire the skills to capture the arbitrage—hiring away a few traders enabled relatively unskilled participants to gain the core skills needed to capture simple arbitrage opportunities.

In the mid-1970s, such arbitrage transactions were undertaken by highly skilled investment bankers who took rates quoted to them by brokers over the phone and did the math with slide rules or calculators. The transactions were cumbersome and expensive to complete. It might cost several thousand dollars to make such a transaction but, at the time, arbitrage spreads were sufficient to absorb these costs. In some markets, spreads were initially as large as 1 percent of the volume traded. The daily volume of foreign exchange traded was perhaps forty to fifty billion dollars a day. Naturally, many participants quickly moved in to capture the foreign exchange arbitrage. As they did so, they served as counterparties to each other, thereby splitting up the arbitrage opportunity while enabling volume and profits to soar.

Today, traders use computers and global information systems to find arbitrage opportunities. Twenty years of technological innovation and regulatory change have eliminated most of the physical and regulatory barriers that used to preserve different prices. The transactions now require relatively little skill and are easy and cheap to complete.

As the global foreign exchange markets have become more tightly integrated and the law of one price increasingly applies, arbitrage profit spreads have become microscopic (i.e., far less than one-hundredth of a percent of the volume traded). However, arbitrage of foreign exchange remains profitable because computer systems have slashed marginal transaction costs even more rapidly and volume levels have become astronomical. (The volume of foreign exchange traded daily often exceeds $2 trillion.)

The profitability of foreign exchange arbitrage, in terms of returns on capital invested and returns on expenses, probably peaked in the late 1970s and early 1980s. Today, it is the ultimate commodity business, where volume and efficiency drives profitability.

As the global financial markets have matured, it has become possible to undertake ever more complex arbitrage transactions and to arbitrage a wider variety of instruments. Derivative instruments enable counterparties to exchange specific risks, for a price, in foreign exchange, interest rates, equities, and commodities such as oil and gas futures. Specialists have emerged to arbitrage differentials in every conceivable category of financial instruments in both the cash and the derivative markets. The only real risks to much of this trading are counterparty risks (i.e., the risks of default).

Over the last twenty or so years, the systematic capture of trading arbitrage opportunities has funded much, if not most, of the investment in the technology platform and infrastructure needed to globalize the capital markets of the world. Players such as Goldman Sachs, Morgan Stanley, Merrill Lynch, and J. P. Morgan have come to dominate the global capital markets businesses significantly because they are skilled in the art of arbitrage.

ARBITRAGE IN THE REAL ECONOMY

The evolution of arbitrage in the financial markets illustrates how the use of counterparty agreements increases access to arbitrage opportunities while simultaneously reducing inherent risks. It shows how players become more specialized over time, how volume increases as transaction costs and risks fall, and how prices thereby converge. The end result is an integrated global financial marketplace in which the practice of arbitrage largely ensures that the law of one price rules for most financial instruments everywhere at all times. And it shows that relative success in capturing arbitrage can help fund long-term roles and positions in global industries.

We are moving toward a time in which arbitrage practices will increasingly spread into the real economy, where the potential for arbitrage is far larger—but far more difficult to capture. Fortunately, once captured, these arbitrage opportunities will be more durable than those in the financial economy. Capturing them will provide the funding to make the investments required in the race for the world.

Arbitrage in the financial markets deals with tradable instruments denominated in different currencies; arbitrage in the real economy is about arbitraging differences in the costs of production arising from the geographic separation of markets and industry structures.

Players in the PC industry have for years been reaping the benefits of cross-geographic arbitrage through an extensive web of external counterparty agreements. Open standards, adopted early on, and the existence of efficient means of global transport made it possible for specialized component manufacturers to capture the factor cost and productivity advantages the world economies had to offer. The lack of vertical integration in the industry testifies to the enduring advantage of an external network in capturing cross-geographic arbitrage.

Most of the PC industry's component manufacturers are spread over North America and the Far East. Components with high technical sophistication and proprietary knowledge advantage are concentrated in North America, the traditional engine for innovation in the industry. A good example is the microprocessor industry; almost all leading manufacturers (Intel, IBM, Motorola, DEC, etc.) are based in the United States. Components such as monitors and liquid crystal display (LCD) panels have traditionally been located in the Far East. Japan, a leader in the consumer electronics industry, was ideally suited to cost-effective manufacture of monitors. The storage industry (disk drives, CD-ROMs, etc.) moved to Southeast Asia very early as manufacturers pressed by low margins sought to take advantage of inexpensive skilled labor. Memory chips (particularly DRAMs) have become commoditized, and scale advantage is significant. Micron, a U.S.–based manufacturer, has used this to its advantage and remains a highly specialized player in the semiconductor industry. Other leading players in South Korea have sought to take advantage of access to lower factor costs (capital and labor) to become strong players in the memory market. Even in the sophisticated and capital-intensive microprocessor industry, Intel relies on lower labor costs in Asia to mount and encase the chips it produces, as do the DRAM manufacturers.

The impact of this efficient, low-cost, external web on the PC industry has been enormous. Without this global advantage, the cost of a typical PC manufactured entirely from U.S.–manufactured parts would be significantly higher.[2] More important, however, is the stimulus this cost reduction has provided to PC penetration. Arguably, the industry has returned a large part of the surplus created from capturing cross-geographic arbitrage to the user, kicking into motion a virtuous cycle that has spurred demand much beyond early estimates. It can be argued that the slower penetration of PCs in the late eighties and early nineties in European and Japanese markets can be attributed, in part, to the relatively high cost arising from vertically integrated, local players dominating the industry. Most of these players have either given way to more nimble, world-class players or have significantly transformed the focus of their business.

ANTICIPATING THE TRANSITION POINT

In terms of arbitrage opportunities, the financial markets differ from the real economy in one important way. In the financial markets, arbitrage became profitable as soon as foreign exchange rates were allowed to float. When that happened, the value of the potential arbitrage available greatly exceeded the costs and risks of capturing it. In other words, there was no period of time when the costs and risks exceeded the value.

In the real economy, this is not the case. For every arbitrage opportunity, there is a transition point after which, for a certain period, the value of the arbitrage exceeds the costs and risks of capturing it. Moving too early will only incur losses and moving too late will cede most of the opportunity to early movers. Eventually, of course, as more and more producers seek out and capture the arbitrage, the value will fall off rapidly (it will be *arbitraged away*) until it disappears. As with many of the opportunities described in this book, getting the pace right is critical. For every arbitrage opportunity, there will be a *transition point*, the moment when the arbitrage becomes profitable. A first mover who is ready to act will capture enormous arbitrage profits before competitors can move in. Cross-geographic arbitrage capture in the real economy is a highly skilled activity requiring use of superior intangible assets and specialized skills.

This is the underlying reason why arbitrage opportunities are durable. If arbitrage were easy to capture, it would quickly disappear and soon the price of everything from haircuts to cars would converge globally, as would the wages earned by an engineer in Beijing and an engineer in Chicago. But capturing cross-geographic arbitrage is difficult, and it will take a long time to integrate the world's markets.

The first mover has an opportunity not only to capture enormous profits, of course, but to shape their industry as well. The excess profitability from arbitrage can be used to out-invest competitors in building intangible capital or to share profits with partners to get them to do your bidding. The lion's share of this potential arbitrage is between the emerging markets and developed world markets because of the huge differences in factor costs, capital productivity, and labor productivity.

Strategies built off cross-geographic arbitrage can provide lucrative, enduring specialization and scale advantages over slower-moving geographic incumbents living under the constraints of local or national value chains.

There are three major difficulties in capturing cross-geographic arbitrage. First, the opportunities are generally opaque and require a significant amount of work to identify. Second, players may be able to identify an opportunity, but often don't have the skill or the will to pursue it. Third, players who identify the opportunity and are willing and able to pursue it often conclude that the transaction costs and risks involved outweigh the potential yield. Frequently they do not understand how quickly the dynamics can change and when the transition point to profitable arbitrage capture will be reached.

IDENTIFYING AN ARBITRAGE OPPORTUNITY

The identification of a cross-geographic arbitrage opportunity involves understanding four dynamic variables: (1) the potential value of the arbitrage; (2) the duration of the arbitrage; (3) the transaction costs to complete the arbitrage; and (4) the risks inherent in capturing the arbitrage. An attractive cross-geographic arbitrage has a large value, lasts for years, has low transaction costs, and involves you in little risk.

Potential value

In a financial arbitrage transaction, the potential value of the opportunity can be determined through analysis of prices provided by global information services, such as Reuters or Bloomberg, and direct quotes from dealers. Its value is relatively transparent. In the real economy, the information necessary to analyze the opportunity is not easy to come by. Therefore, the search costs of identifying a specific arbitrage opportunity can be high.

For example, to estimate the arbitrage opportunities between just two countries in producing a single product you must identify local factor cost differences (labor rates for each skill category, rent, taxes, regulatory costs, etc.). That's the easy part. It is more difficult to understand differences in quality. It is harder still to understand productivity differences because you must compare your own productivity to world-class benchmarks and to local players—usually some reverse engineering and some intelligent estimating is necessary. The process becomes even more difficult when you consider multiple countries and multiple products.

Nevertheless, given the sheer magnitude of the potential arbitrage available, it is usually possible to develop reasonable hypotheses, relatively quickly, as to whether there is a sufficiently large opportunity available to justify further exploration.

Duration

Another critical variable is how long the discontinuities creating the arbitrage are sustainable. Will the opportunity disappear before you can recover your transaction costs? Answering this question can be complicated. Unlike a typical financial arbitrage opportunity, in the real economy there may be many different kinds of cost involved in the arbitrage, and the duration of each cost element may be different. However, many productivity differences can be eliminated quickly through the simple transfer of technology.

Sometimes, this transfer of technology can create anomalous, profitable situations. Consider telecommunications equipment. In the early 1990s, through technology transfer, the telecommunications industries of several Latin American countries boosted their capital productivity levels significantly above that of the United States.[3] However, because local regulators effectively prevented competition (from new entrants and between existing participants), the companies that achieved these productivity improvements have been able to pocket much of the resulting savings. Here, the arbitrage proved to be durable despite the ease with which the telecom companies captured it. Of course, in relatively open, competitive telecommunications markets like the United States, arbitrage based simply on purchased technology quickly disappears.

The most durable form of arbitrage springs from productivity differences based on proprietary production processes or intellectual property. The Japanese automotive manufacturers, particularly Toyota, have been able to maintain productivity advantages in the production of cars for over twenty years. While many of their production processes are not strictly proprietary, they are so deeply ingrained in the fabric of Toyota's organization—that is, its personality—that they are not readily reproduced.

The durability of factor cost differentials also varies enormously. Differentials in the labor rates for world-class talent (e.g., concert pianists) rapidly disappear; at the other extreme, differentials in low-skilled labor persist for decades due to its abundance and lack of mobility.

Generally, we have found that it is more important to be able to estimate duration roughly rather than to strive for an overly precise answer.

Transaction costs

Cross-geographic arbitrage opportunities persist because of the transaction and interaction costs that must be incurred to capture them. In financial markets, marginal transaction costs are approaching zero; thus, the volume of transactions increases exponentially as it becomes possible to arbitrage smaller and smaller differences in the prices. But in the real economy, transaction costs can be very high. However, when the arbitrage opportunities are large enough, significant transaction costs can be comfortably absorbed.

Assume labor rates in India are 10 percent of rates in Germany, and that labor productivity (given skill differences) is 50 percent of German levels. The potential arbitrage opportunity suggests a reduction in labor costs of 80 percent.[4] The choice, then, would appear to be between spending $100 million on labor in Germany or $20 million in India. The issue is whether the transaction costs—hiring, training, managing, and quality-controlling the labor—and the interaction costs—integrating the product of the labor incurred in this activity in India with the products of other labor incurred in different but related activities in Germany or elsewhere—together exceed $80 million. If not, there is value to be claimed.

In reality, the decisions will be more complex because capital costs may be incurred to enable the low-cost labor to be 50 percent as productive. So the duration of the returns to capital must also be taken into account. This, in turn, means understanding the pace at which labor rates converge relative to the pace that productivity improves, and the pace at which price levels for output change relative to the cost of raising and deploying the capital invested.

Obviously, when transaction costs approach the magnitude of the arbitrage opportunity, the opportunity becomes less attractive. But because interaction and transaction costs are falling rapidly, there is an enormous array of attractive arbitrage opportunities becoming available.

Risks

At the center of the decision to undertake cross-geographic arbitrage in the real economy is the question, "How do you manage the risks?" In financial markets, it is often possible to capture arbitrage opportunities without taking any real risk—usually through the use of derivative contracts. An interest rate swap can be used to convert a floating rate risk to a fixed rate risk if a participant wants to be protected from rising interest rates. With such contracts, the principal remaining risk is that a counterparty might default—a relatively rare occurrence.

Undertaking cross-geographic arbitrage in the real economy involves taking real risks. These risks include operating risks, reputation risks, and financial risks. It is difficult to estimate what productivity and quality level can be achieved through using labor drawn from an unfamiliar source. The potential to underdeliver against expectations for quality or service levels creates huge reputation risks. Committing the capital to produce locally, particularly in emerging markets, can create huge financial risks related to foreign exchange movements or political risks such as expropriation. For example, there is, at present, no real opportunity to hedge long-dated foreign exchange risks in most emerging countries. This can be a real problem if your currency depreciates by 50 percent or more against your home currency—as happened to the South Korean, Thailand, Indonesian, and Malaysian currencies in late 1997.

On the other hand, cross-geographic arbitrage can also provide you with greater flexibility in managing foreign exchange risk, particularly if you pursue approaches that rely on local counterparties and partners. If you have multiple countries to source from, you can move marginal production to whichever currency becomes cheaper as a result of exchange rate movements. If you operate in two countries with equal productivity and factor costs, an exchange rate move between them of 30 percent can generate for you a 30 percent cost advantage over a competitor who has only the option of producing in the country with the stronger currency.

INVADING NATIONAL VALUE CHAINS:
A CASE STUDY IN AUTOMOBILES

The challenges of cross-geographic arbitrage go beyond quantifying the potential opportunity. Many potential arbitrageurs lack the skills needed—skills that go far beyond simply hiring a few people. But perhaps the greatest challenge of all lies in overcoming the underlying structure of the industries themselves. Because most industries in the world have been built around national value chains, the arbitrage opportunities are embedded in value chains that are interconnected and interdependent at the local and national levels. There may be a massive opportunity to leverage low-cost assembly labor, but that opportunity is very difficult to capture if you can't bring together the parts to be assembled at high enough quality, and in a cost-effective manner, on a timely basis.

Let's look at the specific challenges and strategic opportunities to capture cross-geographic arbitrage in the automotive industry. The industry has established significant cross-geographic arbitrage processes in the developed world. It is now making massive investments to capture them in the emerging markets. Arbitrage opportunities are migrating from the internal capture of arbitrage by geographic integrators to the external capture of arbitrage through specialized counterparties.

From 1945 to the mid-1970s, the car manufacturing industry worldwide was organized around national value chains. In the United States, explosive domestic demand and oligopolistic competition among the Big Three North American manufacturers created a relatively complacent atmosphere. Similar conditions existed in Europe, although the relatively small size of each national market led to a more fragmented market.

In Japan, however, local competition was more intense so car makers developed superior car-building productivity compared to U.S. and European manufacturers. Moreover, Japan's dependence on imported oil had led Japanese automobile manufacturers to produce fuel-efficient cars.

After the OPEC crisis in the mid-1970s, Japanese cars became more popular outside Japan, particularly in the United States. Japanese manufacturers first captured demand primarily through exports. By the early 1980s, aided by a weak yen, Japanese manufacturers had a $1,700 cost advantage per car, which exceeded the per car contribution margin of U.S. manufacturers on most of the equivalent cars. Much of this cost advantage was due to lower Japanese labor rates (at the time about half of U.S. rates) and higher Japanese labor productivity (at the time about 30 percent higher than in the United States).

Through the early 1980s, Japanese automotive manufacturers were able to capture the labor rate and productivity differentials simply by exporting cars. However, as they began to take market share, and American jobs were lost, an enormous political backlash developed in the United States. Responding to political pressure and the related political risk, Japanese manufacturers began to transplant production into the United States, even though the cost of labor in the United States was much higher. (In 1981, an auto worker in the U.S. earned $17 per hour as compared to $8 in Japan.) Between 1982 and 1992, the number of Asian transplant and truck assembly plants in North America rose from one to twelve, reaching a production capacity of 1.3 million cars a year (25 percent of total U.S. production, and greater than the total production of cars in France). Japanese manufacturers using U.S. labor were able to achieve 90 percent of the productivity of Japanese workers. They increasingly standardized parts and subassemblies so that these parts were fungible with cars assembled in either the United States or Japan. As a result, despite the enormous increase in labor costs, Japanese transplants were able to maintain major cost advantages through arbitraging productivity differentials; that is, transferring best practices from Japan to improve the productivity of their U.S. operations thereby providing a large cost advantage over the U.S. players.

As the wages of Japanese auto workers rose in Japan, and as the yen's value increased relative to the dollar, the gap in effective labor rates between the United States and Japan narrowed considerably. By 1992, the Japanese labor rates were about $19 an hour versus about $25 an hour in the United States. When the advantages of lower transportation and transaction costs are considered, Japanese manufacturers were able, by the early 1990s, to produce cars in the United States about as cheaply as they could in Japan, but with far less political risk.

Developed world arbitrage

By the early 1990s, the Japanese automotive manufacturers found themselves with potentially large, ongoing arbitrage opportunities between Japan and the U.S. markets through their own internal operations. Although it had not been the original intent of their decision to transplant production, by the 1990s Japanese manufacturers realized they had the ability to shift production back and forth between Japan and the United States. When labor rates, foreign exchange, or market demand changed, Japanese manufacturers could respond. U.S. manufacturers, at a productivity disadvantage and lacking major production capabilities in Japan, had no equivalent opportunity. When the dollar began to appreciate rapidly against the yen in 1996, 1997, and 1998, Japanese manufacturers could shift marginal production back to Japan. Given what it took to put the infrastructure in place, this advantage is likely to be durable for Japanese manufacturers.

Of course, it is not just the Japanese automotive manufacturers who have learned to play this game. General Motors' Opel subsidiary has also been able to exploit productivity advantages relative to German manufacturers by making transplants into Germany. Together with Ford, they have over a 30 percent share of the domestic German market.

In the 1990s, German automotive manufacturers, by reverse engineering and benchmarking best practices from Japan and America, have been able to make major improvements to their own labor and capital productivity. As German labor rates have passed U.S. rates, producers such as Daimler-Benz have begun to leverage lower U.S. factor costs for labor, rent, and taxes while saving transportation costs by shifting production to the United States.[5] In theory, the Daimler-Benz–Chrysler merger will create even greater arbitrage opportunities for Daimler-Benz.

As discussed in Chapter 3, there are many benefits to the Daimler–Chrysler merger.[6] One feature is that it provides each party with access to the other's factor costs and techniques of production. North America is already the low-cost luxury car manufacturing center of the world, and Daimler's plant in Alabama produces its successful high-end sports utility vehicles. Other opportunities abound and complementary geographic presence will eventually allow the new company to capture these.

From the early 1980s to the mid-1990s, then, the automotive industry moved from producing cars through national value chains to value chains that spanned the developed world as a direct result of the world's automotive producers' learning the skills necessary to capture cross-geographic arbitrage. The capture of potential arbitrage in the developed world is reasonably advanced. Consequently, the arbitrage opportunities going forward in the automotive industry will appear in emerging markets, where productivity and factor cost differentials are much larger and potentially more sustainable.

Emerging market arbitrage

McKinsey's automotive experts estimate that the emerging markets will form 50 percent of the world automotive unit share (versus 20 percent in 1985) and 30 percent of value produced by 2015.

At first, it would seem difficult for U.S. manufacturers, which spend about $9,500 producing a conventional small car, to compete with products such as the Maruti, which sells in India for $4,000. In fact, research suggests that the theoretical cost of producing a car could be less than $2,000 in India. Of course, this would involve significant "de-contenting," but it would remain superior to the local product. Some $1,000 per car of these savings comes from simplifying the design. $1,500 can be saved by optimizing the purchasing process (e.g., outsourcing for maximum efficiency), and a further $2,500 could be saved through relocation of production to the lowest relevant factor cost countries. Finally, up to $3,000 could be saved by selling cars directly from the factory, eliminating distribution costs.

Savings to this extent are, of course, still theoretical. However, many of the levers just described are already being pulled. For example, the "Asia car" of Toyota and others has implemented extreme simplification of design and, in part, factor cost and distribution savings. The extreme differences in factor costs create the potential to redefine the manufacturing process to make it less capital intensive and more labor intensive—just the opposite of the developed world, where labor is expensive and capital is cheap. Moreover, there are far more opportunities from outsourcing to leverage factor cost advantages along the entire value chain, while simultaneously placing quality risk with local producers who are more adept at employing local labor.

General Motors' Opel subsidiary has found that it can successfully replicate small-scale factories in different locations (due partly to its making a simple car). Its new plant in Eisenach, Germany, the second most productive in Europe after Nissan Sunderland, is now being replicated in Gliwice, Poland. When the company recognized the logic of expanding into eastern Europe to capture growth in the region and to take advantage of lower local labor costs (amounting to a savings of 10 percent of total costs), they designated the Eisenach plant as their template for new operations. The new plant in Gliwice cost approximately $200 million, using a modular construction approach that allows the initial capacity of 70,000 units to be expanded to 130,000. Two hundred team leaders in the new plant were trained in Eisenach and then sent to Poland.

As yet, no one is shipping components made in the emerging markets in volume back into the United States or Europe for assembly into locally produced cars. But it is only a matter of time. The Malaysian Proton (a joint venture between Mitsubishi and the Malaysian federal government) has significant sales in the United Kingdom (over 9,000 cars per year) despite a nonexistent brand. (The Proton costs £9,000 versus a VW Golf that starts at over £11,000.)

The potential for leveraging labor costs through arbitrage is enormous in the automotive industry. Toyota's plant in Thailand achieves 68 percent of the labor productivity of its average plant in Japan (roughly equivalent to the productivity of the average European automotive manufacturer) with labor at 15 percent of Japanese levels.[7]

How attractive are the potential emerging market arbitrage opportunities in the automotive industry?

Let's revisit the four variables for assessing a cross-geographic arbitrage opportunity. The potential value is apparent. Moreover, the duration of the arbitrage is likely to be great because of the large supply of skilled and semi-skilled labor that is becoming available as the developing world emerges and because the high labor costs in the developed world will continue to provide a price umbrella.

The real issues are the transaction costs and the risks. Some of the transaction cost issues are critical. Take, for example, transportation costs. It costs only $200 to ship an entire car from Nagoya, Japan to the U.S. West Coast, but $300 to ship a single car seat from Thailand to China. Given the need to integrate subassemblies, transportation costs can make it very expensive to assemble a car with parts produced in different emerging nations. The risks can also be considerable. Successful cross-geographic arbitrage often requires managing the elusive balance between local considerations such as tailoring products and business systems to local markets and global considerations such as gaining global scale economies.

Companies like Coca-Cola avoid this by making their products *the* product worldwide. But cars differ between markets: No one has yet quite pulled off that elusive goal, the "world car." In tailoring to local market needs and conditions, companies sometimes inadvertently concentrate so much energy in doing so that they sacrifice some of their core strengths. Many companies have embarked on major investments, sinking hundreds of millions of dollars into local plants *before* they established a stable market position.

It would certainly be easy to conclude that cross-geographic arbitrage in the automotive industry is not worth the bother. In this industry, the number of participants competing to capture the opportunities is as daunting as the challenges they face. This would be a mistake: The capture of cross-geographic arbitrage will be one of the distinguishing characteristics between winners and losers, not just in the automotive industry but in many others as well. But effective cross-geographic arbitrage doesn't take place until the conditions are right. Up until now the conditions have not been right in many industries, including the automotive industry, in the emerging world. However, the forces at work in the world economy are rapidly putting in place the conditions that will make it far easier for arbitrage capture, not just in the automotive industry but in all industries. Transaction costs and risks are falling rapidly; the value of the arbitrage—once available—will be large, and the duration of the arbitrage, while dependent on industry structure, could be quite long. Industry after industry, we believe, is approaching the transition point at which arbitrage profits will be a major source of profits and competitive advantage.

WHO WILL CAPTURE ARBITRAGE OPPORTUNITIES?

The critical issue is whether arbitrage opportunities will be captured internally by geographic integrators or externally by specialists working together as counterparties in a global value chain. We think the answer is clear. Ultimately, the advantage in capturing arbitrage will go to specialists working together. Industries organized for external contracting can capture far more of the potential arbitrage than can individual companies working by themselves. Moreover, counterparty structures provide everyone involved with greater flexibility and abilities to manage risk. But this will be truest as industries develop global structures. In industries that are today largely local or national in structure, there will be continuing opportunities to capture arbitrage internally; in fact, absent potential counterparties, the only way to capture arbitrage is internally, by establishing your own global protocols and standards as Coca-Cola, Caterpillar, and McDonald's have done.

The critical constraint in the emerging markets has been the lack of a local supplier infrastructure. Capturing cross-geographic arbitrage beyond one's own borders requires the transplanting of the techniques of production. However, in the automotive industry, the costs of doing everything yourself in the emerging markets are prohibitive, as are the financial risks given the magnitude of the required capital investment. Moreover, there are considerable specialization effects in that component suppliers are often far better at producing their component parts than an integrated assembler and at tailoring the output for an emerging market country. This makes the core issue for an automotive assembler wanting to capture arbitrage in the emerging markets the lack of an adequate supplier base.

Transferring one's own best practice is challenging enough, but raising the quality levels and productivity of an entire national value chain poses considerable difficulties. When the Japanese started manufacturing in the United States, they found that they had to ship steel and paint from Japan. Building a supplier network is not easy, as the example of Volkswagen (VW) in Shanghai shows. After huge expenditures in supplier development and eleven years of effort, they have achieved a very high local content rate but have not succeeded in transforming the Chinese base into a part of their global supply network. New original equipment manufacturers (OEMs) coming to India have also found the lack of a world-class supply base to be one of their biggest impediments.

The most important shortcomings are (1) low levels of technology and quality from suppliers accustomed to protected local markets, (2) absence of sufficient investment capital for local firms, and (3) a lack of standards. Another shortcoming is the challenge of often unpredictable political and regulatory changes. For example, Chrysler's Beijing Jeep was faced with long investment approval lead times and regulatory tangles because of local politics.

The answer to the challenge is to unbundle the problem. The OEMs need to provide real incentives for suppliers acting as counterparties to commit to producing at high standards and high quality in emerging markets, and suppliers need to globalize around their specialties and to capture the resulting "simplified" arbitrage transactions. And, where appropriate, OEMs should consider acting as a component manufacturer themselves when they have a real existing skill in producing a particular component.

One example of this vision can be seen some 100 miles north of Rio de Janeiro, in the town of Resende, where Volkswagen is piloting a factory of the future that appears to have resolved many of these problems. It has a capacity of 30,000 units per year, produces both trucks and buses, and is operated by 400 employees who all wear the same uniforms and get the same wages and benefits package. It does not, on the face of it, appear unusual.

But the factory is a revolutionary, modular facility; one of the revolutionary things about it is that the factory's eight suppliers pay up to $50 million apiece for the modules. Their employees work in the factory assembling cars, but instead of the traditional assembly line, the plan runs subassembly lines parallel to the main line, so that the suppliers assemble their components simultaneously. VW workers do no assembly; they handle only product engineering, quality control, and distribution. The suppliers, including Rockwell, Cummins/MAN, Eisenmann, and Iochpe–Maxion, are responsible for order processing, model quality control, wages, and labor relations. VW pays suppliers only when the vehicles are completed and pass inspection.

This asset-light approach has greatly limited the capital VW had to put up to build the factory—$250 million versus over $600 million. Complexity is greatly reduced because the number of suppliers is reduced to 8 from the normal 400. In the words of Paulo Butori, president of the Brazilian automobile parts association, Sindipecas, "By being free to focus only on vehicle design and how to sell it, you get the most lucrative parts of the business and pass on the onus of production to the suppliers." It should be noted that the Resende plant is a pilot experiment, and the ultimate success of the approach will be known only over time once it has undergone the same refinement traditional auto assembly methods have gone through over the past decade.

In this model, all of the participants, even Volkswagen, are specialists working through counterparty arrangements. It is a relatively small conceptual leap from using this approach to build cars for one country, such as Brazil, to using such an approach to produce standardized parts for export to the developed world. Component parts are easier to standardize across countries than are whole cars. They are also easier to ship around the world. It is easier for a component parts specialist to transplant particular productivity techniques and to leverage intangible strengths. In fact, by focusing on just a sliver of a value chain, the specialist gains increasing returns advantages from the capture of cross-geographic arbitrage in the area of specialty. The better the specialist gets at capturing cross-geographic arbitrage, the more intellectual property it creates, the more talent it builds, and the more its reputation as a reliable counterparty grows, which in turn makes it a supplier of choice.

Going forward, we believe the future of capturing cross-geographic arbitrage in the automotive industry will be through components parts manufacturing in the emerging markets.

Let's look at how this could work in a nation like China. Components manufacturers worldwide, including OEMs, should be considering going to China to focus on producing components in which they have real skill—whether it is brake pads, batteries, engine blocks, or wiper blades—not only for the local Chinese market but also for the world. The demand for passenger cars in China has been growing quickly, albeit from a small base. The compound growth rate between 1990 and 1995 was 25 percent. Between 1995 and 2001 it is estimated to be 13 percent— for a total increase over the decade of 2¼ million vehicles per year. Major Chinese automotive industry groups (including Western partners) have all taken steps in building their own parts supply bases, leading to enormous increases in the growth of the local automotive parts industry. Nevertheless, many important parts for which future demand will be strong are barely produced today in China. No electric engine control units, antilock brake systems, or airbags were being produced until recently. Estimates of demand for the year 2000 are for one, one, and three million units, respectively. At present, Chinese parts makers are far behind in terms of scale and, crucially, quality. Even for the leading Chinese suppliers, automotive parts labor productivity stands at about 20 percent of U.S. levels. Other suppliers have much smaller scale and poorer asset utilization.

Component suppliers are mostly state-owned, captive suppliers to state-owned or regulated assembly plants. This fragmented and protected market fails to achieve economies of scale. Low capital investment over the years has resulted in outdated technology processes.

Now, however, the Chinese government has seen the problem and is deploying an aggressive plan to reshape the auto component sector. At present, 180 subscale auto assembly plants are fed by 5,000 to 7,000 suppliers. The government is targeting a future of less than 10 assemblers, fed by fewer than 2,000 suppliers. The transition is to be achieved by a process of "natural selection" that will heavily favor approved Chinese-foreign joint ventures (JVs). Accordingly, the government is also encouraging foreign participation in a big but controlled way.

All of this suggests that there is a near-term opportunity in many components to attempt to become a utility for as many of the assemblers as is possible—that is, to act as a reliable, high-quality counterparty for as many producers as possible, not just in China, but for the world.

Not surprisingly, in response to the government's vision, many auto component JVs between Chinese and foreign firms have formed. We have identified fifty-seven JVs, spread among thirty-six partners from developed countries. For example, Bosch is engaged in a $2.5 billion partnership for fuel injectors, pressure regulators, control panels, sensors, ignition systems, and oil pumps with five local partners. GM-Delphi has deployed ten JVs in compressors, wiring harnesses, engine management systems, driveshafts, electrical systems, and spark plugs. The market they pursue includes both the expanding local one and export targets worldwide.

So, the window of opportunity in making parts is considerable. The market is immature, but local players are fragmented and all elements of the business system offer possibilities. On the other hand, the race is to the swift: Even now, the Chinese government is applying higher barriers to latecomers. In fact, to avoid redundant investment and to force development in some weak areas, the government may tell latecomers either to invest in second-choice product areas with second-choice partners or not to come at all.

Further, good local partner candidates are few and being snapped up. One major player, Shanghai Automotive, now has partnerships with OEMs VW, GM, and Honda, and suppliers including Koito, ITT, Valeo, and ZF. Even when JVs are formed, it can take years to make the match work, mostly because of different fundamental assumptions in the partners' respective business cultures. Global players expect to invest up front to establish and maintain a brand, seek expansion, strive to avoid conflicts in sales territories; want to consolidate JVs as production centers; and seek a competitive cost base. Local partners typically resist investing in marketing and channel development, avoid expansion due to lack of capital and fear of equity dilution, will happily sell to anyone everywhere, want to retain the JV as a profit center, and oppose personnel cuts.

Participants who master the art of working effectively with JV partners will have huge advantages. Working with such partners is just one of many skills needed to capture cross-geographic arbitrage.

CROSS-GEOGRAPHIC ARBITRAGE AS THE CORE OF A VALUE PROPOSITION

Given the challenges of capturing arbitrage opportunities in the automotive industry, winning in this game will require great skill. However, it seems clear that any of the major global automotive assemblers or components manufacturers that do not become adept at cross-geographic arbitrage between the developed and the emerging world will be unable to remain competitive in the long term. Given the players and the resources they are committing, capturing arbitrage from the emerging markets will become an element in survival.

The integrated manufacturers with the greatest global reach in production, the greatest ability to assemble cars where factor costs are the lowest, the least loss of quality while maintaining productivity at world-class levels, the lowest investment of their own capital, and the greatest flexibility to shift production volume from country to country will have enormous ongoing advantages over players locked into production in a few countries. Simultaneously, those suppliers that specialize in providing high-quality parts in the emerging markets with the greatest labor and capital productivity, that can also master transportation and logistics in the emerging world, will have almost unlimited demand from the global integrated manufacturers as well as from local producers. They will become the counterparties of choice.

Over time, the global automotive industry will be reshaped. While integrated assemblers will still be vital as geographic integrators, component parts manufacturers that learn how to dominate global slivers through the capture of cross-geographic arbitrage will become increasingly their equal. Over time, an assembler who does not use the best global components parts specialists will wind up at a competitive disadvantage relative to other assemblers. This will drive volume, and the resulting increasing returns and geographic arbitrage advantages, to the best suppliers. To some extent, this process is already well under way.

In 1992, there were just sixteen component suppliers with greater than $2 billion in sales. In 1997, thanks to mergers and global expansion, there were forty-seven large suppliers.

At present, there are no global industry shapers in the automotive industry, although Daimler–Chrysler, Ford, and Toyota are certainly candidates. Going forward, it is an open question whether specialists will emerge as shapers in various microindustries or whether some of the integrated assemblers will discover that by focusing on the intangible heavy parts of the business system (e.g., car design, marketing, quality control) they can retain much of the profits while shedding most of the capital.

Each industry is different, of course. In between the most global industries such as capital markets and electronics and the most local such as personal financial services and health care delivery, industries are at various stages of readiness to capture cross-geographic arbitrage. What they all have in common is that it will become much more important.

As the transition economy unfolds and as specialist counterparties emerge, a disproportionate share of the cross-geographic arbitrage being created will fall into the hands of players with the ability to see the opportunity, who have built the skills to capture it, and who have the will to be a first mover. In turn, the resulting financial gains will provide the support for investments in the intangible capital needed to win in the specialist game, as well as investments in reach and scale. To win, we must all become arbitrageurs.

10

STRATEGY ONCE MORE

BUILDING GLOBAL VALUE
PROPOSITIONS

WHAT, IN ALL THIS, of our hypothetical financial services company, First Global Credit? In Chapter 6 we discussed the challenges that might lead the bank to divest itself of its traditional banking businesses, and, through an *outside-in* perspective on the universe of possibilities, to focus on the credit card and mortgage business arenas. At that point, we held off, because determining the specific businesses First Global Credit would turn to requires an *inside-out* look at the world based on an understanding of the company's intangible assets, and the opportunities they provide to pursue slivers and arbitrage strategies. Now that we have a better understanding of these strategies, we can return to First Global's situation and the value propositions it should develop.

CREATING A GLOBAL VALUE PROPOSITION

Earlier, in Chapter 1, we briefly defined how we are using the term "value proposition." A *value proposition* offers a clear articulation of what value customers get, what value you provide, what value your partners (if any) provide, why the resulting offering provides more value than competitive offerings, how the risk-reward trade-offs will be managed, and how the economics work.[1] The first step in creating a global value proposition is a working hypothesis, which is then refined and adapted as knowledge is acquired and as uncertainty is resolved.

Using an outside-in approach at the level of slivers—rather than at the level of general business areas in which a company might compete—doesn't work. This is where we find many companies get themselves into trouble. Most people still see the world as a series of national economies, so the first reaction of most business strategists is to undertake worldwide studies to find opportunities. The problem is that the world's economy is so big, so complex, and so dynamic, country economies are so different from one another, and the forces at work are changing conditions so rapidly, that even a serious attempt to study the world produces only superficial insights. Even if you are already an insider in many countries, it is very difficult to mobilize and integrate the right information. By the time you have completed your analysis, your major conclusions are that the potential market opportunity is large and that different countries represent different opportunities and challenges—all of which you knew before you started. And by the time you are prepared to act, the world has changed so much that much of your original work is useless, and you have lost ground to other players.

Finding a specific global value proposition by scanning outside-in is like trying to break the combination of a ten-tumbler combination lock without knowing any of the numbers. Get any one number wrong and the lock won't open. A better approach is to start with a combination lock where you already know eight of the ten numbers and then do the hard work to discover the last two numbers. How do you do that?

Once you've determined that a business is structurally attractive to you, as First Global Credit did with credit cards and mortgages, you start from within. There are a world of global opportunities inside a company—first and foremost the intangible assets embedded in its people, plants, laboratories, databases, customer base, relationships with distributors, and so on. By delving into its own intangible assets and personality, a company can create reasonable hypotheses about how to take advantage of the forces at work to create potentially attractive global value propositions. By brainstorming how to deploy and leverage its unique assets, a company can obtain enough focus to be able to find the last two numbers of the combination lock.

We are not saying that one should ignore input from the outside as you build sliver strategies. To the contrary, we believe having eyes and ears everywhere is essential to discovering new opportunities. But because of the overwhelming input you can receive from the outside, you have to find a way to improve the signal-to-noise ratio of that input. And the starting point is a good hypothesis. You can then focus on converting the raw idea into a real opportunity through rigorously gathering specific outside knowledge.

One reliable method for doing this is to create entrepreneurial units, or talent teams, and task them with finding the unique knowledge needed to craft a winning global value proposition.

IDENTIFYING CORE BUSINESS STRATEGIES WITH GLOBAL TALENT TEAMS

Most companies use *project teams* or *task forces* to do many different kinds of work. But we use the term global talent teams very specifically. *Global talent teams* are the primary vehicles for converting the intangible assets of the firm into intangible capital. They create not just intellectual property but also the talent and other intangible assets needed to gain familiarity advantages in their area of focus. At companies such as GE, Enron, AIG, J&J, and SAP, top management or their designates sponsor an individual or small team to convert a possible global opportunity into a reality. These efforts are often also cosponsored by a line business, but the resources and expense dollars used and the risks taken are usually not commingled with the line business's results. Rather, they are retained at the corporate level.

What does a talent team look like? The principles are straightforward. An accountable manager is assigned responsibility for assembling a team that operates across geographic and organizational boundaries to convert an investment hypothesis into a specific investment proposal. Often the individual leading the team is an ex-line manager, ex-consultant, or other expert with a good starting knowledge of the business being explored.

In addition to this leader, one or two others are often committed to the effort. This small team is accountable for developing an investment proposal and often for executing it if approved. The team is empowered to scour the rest of the organization (and the world) to access the knowledge and relationships required to determine the best proposal and overcome any unfamiliarity associated with the opportunity. In this way, the team is able to mobilize the intangible assets embedded throughout the organization and apply them against a specific opportunity without unnecessarily disrupting the frontline. Given the go-ahead, the team will then harness these intangibles and resources to capture the opportunity.

The team has a high likelihood of succeeding: The individual heading it is often betting his or her career on the outcome, and frontline managers have every reason to cooperate because top management is sponsoring the team. The success or failure of these teams often depends on the creativity and problem-solving skills they bring to finding ways to make money, while minimizing the need for large outlays of financial capital and high risk by disaggregating and structuring risks. They often discover "foothold" acquisition opportunities and major alliance opportunities. However, they are encouraged to find ways to invest capital, even very large amounts of capital involving major acquisitions, if they can build a compelling case that the returns will be high relative to the risks taken.

Because talent teams have an expense budget but are not given much financial capital, they represent limited financial risks. They earn the right to capital by demonstrating the value of the investment. If after exhaustive search no compelling strategy and value proposition can be found, the team will have failed. In other words, while the corporation may view the talent team as pursuing an option, the team itself must play a championing role. At some of the organizations that use an approach like the one described here, failure often means that the head of the team leaves the company and the unit is disbanded. On the other hand, the talent team has an opportunity to grow with few limits, provided it can continue to demonstrate high returns for the risks taken.[2] If it succeeds, the talent team is well compensated, like an entrepreneurial team starting a new business.[3]

Talent teams become vehicles for establishing accountability for capturing discrete opportunities rather than placing that accountability on line managers overwhelmed with responsibility for running day-to-day operations. The burden of overcoming all the internal and external obstacles such as mobilizing the required knowledge, acquiring or developing the talent, or finding the right local partners is placed on the talent team itself.

We should be clear that projects of this sort are not minor undertakings: acquiring the intellectual property and talent needed to establish whether an idea is genuinely attractive typically involves large financial commitments. Large companies can easily spend $10 to $20 million or more in expenses simply to determine if an idea is worthy of significant investment.

This alone is enough reason to create a special team. Few down-the-line business managers can create room for such spending on their budgets. Top management judgment will be required to get such funding. Although these ideas often have the highest return on spending in the medium to long term, in the absence of a top-management mandate, line managers accountable for results simply will not spend money on them for fear of hurting current earnings.

Of course, if the opportunity is the right global sliver, the potential business profits being forgone may be hundreds of millions of dollars, as well as the loss of creating an increasing returns cycle and the opportunity to dominate a global microindustry. This is the reason it is essential to have a corporate strategy as described in Chapter 5, and why the inside-out approach is essential. The approach starts out by providing the company some familiarity advantages and therefore increases the odds that overcoming unfamiliarity is likely to have high returns.

We began this section by saying that global talent teams are a company's primary vehicle for converting its intangible assets into intangible capital. But not only do they lead to the deployment of the firm's existing tangible and intangible capital, they also can be—through the intellectual property, talent, networks, and reputation they build—one of the primary means of growing the immediate stock of intangible capital available to the corporation as a whole.

UNLEASHING ENTREPRENEURIAL ENERGY

One important feature of the talent team approach is that it replicates internally the entrepreneurial energy being unleashed around the world—something companies need to generate if they want to compete.[4] *Talent teams do not undertake studies; they build businesses.* The reward for success, just as for real entrepreneurs, is the opportunity to run the business. To make this model work, the entrepreneurial units need to be balanced by the same discipline real entrepreneurs face. Companies need to re-create this discipline internally by maintaining a *global principal investor's* mindset.

Companies with a global principal investor mindset never feel capital constrained, even in pursuing opportunities in developing countries. But they believe that their *own* tangible and intangible capital is scarce and expensive. Beyond seed capital they avoid investing much capital initially, because they believe the best return lies in creating the opportunity and getting others to put up financial capital as needed. They want to control, rather than own, tangible assets. By traveling light they can move quickly and preserve flexibility. They avoid making low-return, high-risk investments by locating others with different comparative advantages, opportunities, and capabilities who find these same investments attractive. (If they find *high*-return, *low*-risk investments, they fund them themselves.) By taking this approach, they are able to focus their attention on the higher-return segments of the marketplace and the business system and invest in many more opportunities while taking less financial risk than they would by using only their own financial capital.

On the other hand, while they are slow to commit capital, they are quite willing to spend expense dollars to find and create high-return opportunities. This is a fundamentally different environment from what exists in most companies today, where capital is plentiful but expense dollars are scarce.

By adopting a principal investor mindset, these companies put an increasing focus on developing a pipeline of opportunities, some of which are always maturing into high-return options for investment. Almost all companies can create such a pipeline. The starting point is to be able to develop an internal environment where a flow of new ideas is constantly being generated.

The challenge, of course, is not simply in coming up with the ideas. It is the way in which ideas and thinking are nurtured that distinguishes companies such as J&J and AIG from their competitors. It is critical to avoid either killing or committing to ideas prematurely. Companies must learn to suspend judgment until it is possible to acquire the knowledge needed to determine whether ideas are viable.

For many companies a common sticking point has been developing good raw ideas for business strategies—sound hypotheses about potentially attractive global value propositions that fit their personalities. It is a key first step. Because once you have a sound idea, the work needed to prove or disprove the hypothesis—or to improve it—becomes much clearer.

Brainstorming around leveraging intangibles, creating and dominating slivers, and exploiting cross-geographic arbitrage lies at the center of developing sound hypotheses. All three of these approaches point the company toward the requirements for success in a transition economy because they are all based on developing durable cost and value advantages through leveraging specialization and intangible scale effects that can be used to claim territory (i.e., gain access) while preserving flexibility. They lend themselves to capturing opportunities while maintaining high returns on financial capital, taking little real risk and deferring major investments until the returns can be seen, while creating the value propositions that can launch virtuous cycles of geographic expansion or increasing returns. The power of the talent teams approach can be illustrated by the transformation at Monsanto.[5] A few years ago Monsanto, then a U.S. chemical, pharmaceuticals, and life sciences group, undertook an ambitious project in which the organization was encouraged to generate growth initiatives. This effort resulted in many lucrative opportunities, particularly in pharmaceuticals and life sciences. Many of them fit well with Monsanto's existing businesses and were pursued by the appropriate business units. Several opportunities, however, were quite different. In order to explore the possibility of undertaking those projects—which may not have received proper attention in existing business units—CEO Bob Shapiro put together a separate arm of the organization, Monsanto Growth Enterprises, headed by one of the management board members. This group, reporting through a steering committee to the management board and CEO, was charged with finding ways to convert these opportunities into actual business ventures.

After three months, several projects were approved and provided with some start-up funds, a mixture of expense dollars and capital. Several hundred individuals joined the new unit to pursue the opportunities, ranging from developing new products to entering new countries. Eventually many of the new growth ideas became part of the core business. This whole effort was a critical part of transforming Monsanto into a bioagricultural company.

The benefits of having a separate arm to pursue new business initiatives through talent teams are increased transparency and the tailoring of accountabilities, performance metrics, and time horizons for measurement to the individual project. Additionally, if information on the distribution of expenses between the offline and line organizations is made transparent to the stock market, it can help the market distinguish between day-to-day operations and investment in intangible assets, helping to put separate values on each.[6]

With this framework in mind, let's return again to First Global Credit and some of the value propositions it might develop in the two business arenas on which it has chosen to focus: credit cards and mortgages.[7]

Credit cards

The credit card business (including credit cards, debit cards, and travel and entertainment cards) is a significantly global business that continues to become more global in both reach and structure. It is now a very mature business in the United States, where there is an average of seven cards per household. It is widely present in Europe, albeit at a far lower rate of penetration (one card per household). And it is accessible in most of the emerging markets, primarily to wealthy people who travel internationally. The cards can be used in almost every international city in the world; in the developed world there is almost universal acceptance.

The global talent team that First Global Credit has unleashed on the credit card question will quickly discover that, in its maturity, the card business has disaggregated into issuance, credit extension, customer servicing, clearing and settlement, merchant processing and merchant acquisition, each of which is becoming a global business. Companies such as Citibank, MBNA, and American Express are focusing on global issuance and credit extension; VISA, Mastercard, American Express, and Japanese Credit Bureau (JCB) on clearing and settlements, merchant networks, and merchant acquisition; and GE Capital and First Data Merchant Services on customer processing. Many national players are active in clearing and settlement, which is still a local business. Citibank and American Express are the most integrated participants across the entire business system.

Where does this leave First Global Credit? The talent team knows that it is looking for a sliver that leverages the most attractive aspects of intangibles and cross-border arbitrage—an intangible-rich sliver based around distinctive advantages First Global possesses in intellectual property, talent, networks, and brands. It quickly comes to the conclusion that the company has no global role to play in merchant services, merchant acquisitions, clearing and settlement, or customer servicing—indeed, it largely outsources these functions in the United States. This leaves it with issuance. But First Global realizes it has little access to customers outside the United States, and lacks the reputation, information, and willingness to extend credit needed to take a direct approach. Indeed, it has just experienced a painful experience in this area in the United Kingdom, as we recall from Chapter 6.

On the other hand, First Global Credit *does* believe it has one essential world-class skill: data mining.[8] *Data mining* involves using computer models to analyze the information available from processing customer transactions to identify attractive product-market segments. By helping you understand how different customer groups respond to different direct marketing approaches (i.e., what credit balances, interest charges, payment charges, and credit losses result), data mining enables you to identify which customers show the best risk-return prospects, which product features and terms will most appeal to them, and which marketing and servicing approaches work best. This then enables you to craft tailored value propositions and marketing approaches that appeal to discrete customer segments. For example, should you find that people who windsurf are an attractive micromarket in Spain, you can develop a cobranded product with the P.B.A.E., the Spanish windsurfing association, to craft a marketing program tailored to its members. Then, as you learn from experience how members use the cards, you can continuously refine your offerings. Use of these techniques has propelled card companies such as MBNA and First USA to the forefront in the United States over the last several years, where skilled players have discovered thousands of attractive micromarkets. But they have barely penetrated markets outside the United States.

The talent team recognizes that developing a specialty in data mining meets all the requirements of an ideal transition economy opportunity. It manifests all seven of the elements of structural advantage we identified in Chapter 6: (1) the opportunity is accessible, and First Global has the potential to create specialization and scale advantages; (2) the owners of the existing business are high-cost, low-productivity players (because data mining either doesn't exist or is very unsophisticated in the markets First Global will be going into); (3) the opportunity has historically been embedded in industry value chains; (4) no one has shaped the industry's global structure; (5) the transition will take decades; (6) the risks can be disaggregated, and the ones First Global doesn't care to take can be passed off to counterparties; and (7) the principal assets are intangibles that First Global possesses.

What is First Global's hypothesis? The company will seek to shape a data mining specialty by partnering with the leading bank issuers of credit cards around the world. These banks, while leaders in their countries, are all geographic incumbents.

Partnering with First Global can help them stay in the race. By working with First Global, these banks will be able to offer their customers better credit availability at better rates, while simultaneously capturing market share and earning higher returns with fewer loan losses. This is possible because data mining will enable First Global's local partners to cherry-pick their other local competitors. Their local competitors will be adversely selected—just as competitors of First USA and MBNA have been in the United States. First Global's objective is to shape, and dominate, a new global microindustry—global credit card data mining.

First Global's value proposition to local partners would be to cobrand with only one bank per country. It would maintain proprietary control over the computer models and would be paid through a 1.5 percent per year royalty on credit outstanding, out of which it would also absorb 10 percent of any credit losses. The local bank partner would retain customer relationships, absorb 90 percent of credit losses, fund any credit extension, and be responsible for all other aspects of the business system.

Effectively, First Global is *exchanging its intangible capital for privileged access*. Recall that success in banking businesses everywhere—but especially outside the United States—has required, historically, local scale, adeptness at working with local regulation, and being attuned to local cultural elements. We noted earlier that the abundant physical distribution capacity of financial services players throughout the world made it difficult for nonlocal players to get a foothold across national borders and that few players have had any real success even through acquisitions.

First Global solves these problems by restricting its involvement to the single area—the sliver—in which it is completely advantaged. By offering unbeatable intellectual property (data mining is in fact a textbook case of "information on a type of customer behavior," one of our examples of classic intangible assets)[9] along with the experts necessary to deploy it in each country, First Global is trading the first two kinds of intangible assets—knowledge and people—for the other two—relationships and reputation. The latter are contributed by the local geographic incumbent, in a fashion similar to the 50-50 joint venture Banco Itaú has set up with Bankers Trust.[10]

The hypothesis also meets three other ideal conditions for transition economy opportunities. First, it takes advantage of the fact, noted above, that players in different geographies—and particularly in the developing world, where relationships are key—have enormous asymmetries in intangible assets. Second, it will allow First Global to integrate its intangible assets in a classic "control, not own" strategy. Finally, it will be working with ideal partners, those who have the intangibles it needs but will almost certainly lack the skills ever to compete against First Global.

This is the basic hypothesis. First Global Credit can now begin to acquire the specific knowledge needed to enhance the value proposition and can then move quickly to piloting the concept in a couple of countries. It wants to be the first player to gain global access to the market through data mining and the first to gain specialization and scale effects *in* data mining. It wants to establish virtuous cycles of global expansion while earning increasing returns. It wants to shape a global microindustry, global data mining, that it will dominate.

Mortgages

Unlike credit cards, the mortgage business is still primarily a local business. Within the United States, thanks to the existence of Fannie Mae and Freddie Mac, which provide credit guarantees and ensure standardization of terms and documentation, a highly disaggregated securitized business system has evolved, comprising mortgage origination, credit enhancement, mortgage servicing and securities structuring, and securities issuance. This business system is highly efficient and can provide mortgages to almost any household in the country. As a result, the United

States has the highest ownership of houses as a percentage of the population in the world. Moreover, terms and conditions are highly flexible with regard to method of payment (i.e., floating versus fixed), duration, and amortization schedule.

Outside the United States, however, banks or savings banks in most countries both originate and hold the resulting mortgages. Each provider has the freedom to set its own terms. Often these terms are effectively set by a local oligopoly that dictates pricing, terms, and conditions. In some countries, mortgages are readily available to the wealthy and to few others. In other countries they are indirectly or directly subsidized. Sometimes they are available only in floating-rate form; sometimes only in fixed-rate form. In many countries they are hardly available at all. The ability to enforce mortgages through foreclosure varies enormously from country to country. In other words, the market is extremely local.

Other than Citibank, few players originate mortgages outside their home country. Despite its higher efficiency and capital productivity, securitization has not been widely embraced outside the United States for a variety of reasons, including the lack of a Fannie Mae or Freddie Mac, local bank dominance over liquidity, the small size of underlying national mortgage markets (making it difficult to assemble mortgage portfolios sufficiently large to be pooled into securities), and the willingness of banks to accept low returns on mortgages (given both the shortage of other assets and a lack of performance pressure from the local equity markets). For example, the mortgage assets securitized in Europe total less than $200 billion. If mortgages were securitized in proportion to U.S. securitization levels, that figure would be $1.3 trillion.

However, the securitized mortgage system is now beginning to spread outside the United States, particularly in Canada and the United Kingdom. And as the global equity market puts increased return-on-capital pressure on European banks to securitize low-return assets, and the Continent moves to a common currency—which creates opportunities to assemble mortgages into larger pools—mortgage securitization seems likely to take off. At the same time, in the emerging markets, rising incomes are likely to create demand for the conventional, on-balance-sheet mortgage product at attractive interest rate spreads.

First Global Credit develops a hypothesis that there is an opportunity to play a shaping role in the global mortgage business. Again, however, First Global does not consider moving lock, stock, and barrel—or anything like it—into the mortgage business in any given country. Recall that the specialist is looking for a local market where that piece of the business system at which it is most advantaged is being poorly served by the local players. Specifically, First Global thinks it has superior skills in mortgage issuance and in mortgage servicing. Moreover, because it specializes in customized "jumbo" mortgages, it feels it is adept at serving the specialized needs of the wealthy, who represent very different risk characteristics than the general population.

First Global then develops two distinct hypotheses for global value propositions it wants to explore in the mortgage market and sets up talent teams to explore each. In Europe, First Global establishes a talent team to explore becoming a world-class mortgage servicer (as FDC and GE Capital are doing in credit cards), anticipating as it does that a common currency will create a market for an efficient servicer and make obsolete existing local approaches. First Global wants to be the outsource mortgage servicer of choice, offering local European banks these capabilities far more cheaply and far better than they can provide them for themselves.

In this case, although First Global will be open to partnerships if they are necessary to gain a particular bank's business, it would prefer to own the operation itself because it believes that it can better arbitrage its labor productivity and capital productivity advantages. Moreover, by locating the mortgage servicing centers in lower-cost areas such as Ireland or eastern Europe, First Global believes it can arbitrage factor costs (i.e., rent, labor rates, taxes) while living under the price umbrella of European banks operating in high-cost locations. Labor laws that require overqualified, full-time employees bar most European banks from using the low-cost part-time labor that helps make servicing profitable. First Global further hypothesizes that once it has become proficient at servicing European mortgages, it will be well positioned in the direct mortgage origination business should the mortgage market in Europe move to a more securitized approach. It will also have the option to pursue a global servicing strategy.

First Global Credit has a second hypothesis for a new value proposition it wishes to explore—originating and holding large mortgages for wealthy customers worldwide. Here, First Global will be focusing on a customer segment rather than simply on a product. As we have suggested, in a world where the customer is or will be king, this may be the most durable of sliver strategies. Its approach will be to identify the three or four most attractive countries in the world—including both developed world markets and emerging markets—in terms of market accessibility, availability of local acquisitions, credit spreads available, skill levels of competitors, and ability to foreclose.

Consider, for example, a country such as Argentina. Since 1991, economic reform has led to rapidly rising incomes. Successful stabilization of interest rates and inflation has reduced credit risk and has led to a reemergence of consumer credit (which had almost disappeared). A 1995 law on housing finance greatly enabled foreclosures and creditor recourse. Mortgage lending spreads are a full 10 percent—1,000 basis points—compared to 1 to 2 percent in the U.S. market. And mortgage penetration is extraordinarily low. In Argentina, mortgages equal only 3 percent of GDP, as against 50 percent in the United States.

By focusing on this specialized business in specific countries, First Global believes it can leverage the intangible assets it has developed as a leader in large mortgage loans to wealthy United States residents, and can offer mortgages to these new market segments with far better availability, service, and pricing than local competitors. First Global also believes there is less credit risk in this segment than in others. Once it has tested this concept in three or four countries, First Global would then roll it out worldwide. Becoming proficient in this one segment will also represent acquiring options to go down-market in these countries later.

As First Global Credit uses talent teams to convert these three potential global value propositions—credit card data mining, mortgage servicing, and direct mortgage origination to wealthy customers—into real global opportunities, it will learn much that will lead it to refine and rethink these hypotheses. It will be turning ideas into slivers—compelling value propositions that will take the world by storm. Acquisition candidates will emerge. New options will surface. Microindustries will form.

What will not change are the high aspirations set out by First Global in its strategy for maintaining strategic control. Therefore, in addition to these three potential value propositions, it will be exploring many others as well. The path First Global takes may vary from the original plan; the destination remains constant.

First Global Credit is attempting to transform itself into a specialized player in the global credit card and mortgage businesses with deep anchor strengths in the U.S. market. Indeed, it seeks to play a shaping role by defining the future structure of microindustries in global credit card data mining, global mortgage servicing, and global origination of mortgages for wealthy customers. It wants not only access to profit pools but also capture of increasing returns and cross-geographic arbitrage effects. Its ability to succeed in shaping these microindustry structures will depend on whether it is able to create compelling, global value propositions in each business that others will not easily be able to imitate. To win, First Global will need to produce sliver after sliver, as falling interaction costs and an evolving global industry structure permit more and more specialized value propositions. The measure of the success of these strategies as a portfolio will be whether or not, in aggregate, they provide First Global Credit with sufficient earnings and returns on capital to enable it to remain in control of its own destiny.

A DYNAMIC ALIGNMENT OF STRATEGY AND CAPABILITIES

We return to where we began in Chapter 6. There, we suggested strategy has become more about where *not* to compete and about using the freedom provided by the forces at work to shape a unique, enduring role for the company in the transition economy that others will not easily imitate. Such an approach, we suggested, aims at creating compelling value propositions that draw strength from the forces driving the integration of the world's economy and bring into dynamic alignment *what* a company wants to be with the capabilities it possesses. Because the intangible assets used to construct value propositions are unique to a company and because talent teams will be pursuing strategies that build new capabilities unique to a company, the strategy is hard for competitors to replicate.

In the process, the history and experience gained, the culture of the company, the people attracted, retained, and developed, and the leadership of the company become aligned with the purposes and strategies of the company. The company is, in effect, drawing energy from the transition economy and building durable competitive advantages. In contrast, companies that try to compete through traditional geographic approaches that rely on privileged geographic access are building their strategies on sand.

11

SHAPING THE FUTURE

S HAPING THE FUTURE" sounds like hubris. Let us be
clear: shaping the future is not about *determining* the
future. In a highly uncertain world, any particular outcome is always in doubt. No participant, given the forces at work
in the world economy, has sufficient control to determine the
future. Rather, shaping the future means taking advantage of
the degrees of freedom present in the transition to a global
economy to achieve highly desirable outcomes given your own
capabilities and aspirations—*despite* the confusion, complexity,
and uncertainty over what will happen.

An analogy may help. A participant in the world economy
has no more ability to control the forces at work than a shipbuilder has in controlling the weather in the Pacific. However,
by careful engineering and construction and by taking advantage
of weather patterns, charts, maps, and navigational aids, the

shipbuilder can build a ship that can with reasonable certainty be sailed from one Pacific port to another on a predictable schedule.

As it happens, this analogy does not provide the full perspective of the management challenge because there is one challenge at the business level and another at the corporate level. Moreover, a firm has not only to deal with the forces at work but also with competitors with unknown capabilities and plans. So a better analogy is the problem of trying to move supplies and troops by ships across the Pacific during World War II—when getting across meant dealing not only with weather but also enemy submarines, other ships, and air attacks. The answer was not to build single ships, but to deploy whole convoys, with a mix of aircraft carriers, battleships, destroyers, escorts, troop ships, and supply ships. The convoys increased the ability of each individual ship to cross the ocean and, crucially, helped to ensure through "portfolio effects" that sufficient supplies made it across the ocean even when any given ship or ships did not.

You cannot determine where battles will occur, or which ships will be lost to the enemy action. But you can increase the *probability of success* for each individual ship and for the mission as a whole.

So shaping the future has very different implications at the business (ship) level than at the corporate (convoy) level. At the business level, shaping the future is about building a business with the best possible chance of succeeding on its own by trying to shape the competitive arena for the business. At the corporate level, shaping the future is about helping individual businesses prosper while using portfolio effects to ensure that a sufficient number of businesses will succeed to enable the firm to maintain control of its own destiny. At each level, shaping is about creating high probabilities of desirable outcomes.

There is, of course, a management discipline devoted to ensuring as far as possible that outcomes are desirable. It is called risk management, or, more accurately, risk-reward management.

RISK-REWARD MANAGEMENT

We suggested in Chapter 5 that risk-reward management is the essential skill needed to overcome internal constraints to action and unleash a firm's potential. Companies and individuals are naturally reluctant to take risks with which they are unfamiliar. Pursuing opportunities in the transition economy is full of overcoming confusion (lack of necessary knowledge), complexity (unknown interdependencies), and uncertainty (unknowable future events). Unwise risk taking can be fatal, particularly in a market for strategic control, where a stumble can make you vulnerable to acquisition.

Risk-reward management is about taking actions where you have some control over the outcome and where the probability of a favorable outcome is high, while avoiding actions where you lack sufficient control to affect the outcome or where the probability of a favorable outcome is low. Much progress has been made in risk-reward management, particularly in the last two decades, but almost all of it has been connected to applications in financial markets and the taking of financial risks. Few companies have learned to apply these skills to nonfinancial business or operating risk. The principal exceptions are the companies described in this book as shapers—companies such as Coca-Cola, General Electric, Enron, Johnson & Johnson, SAP, Microsoft, and Monsanto. They are adept risk-reward managers almost by definition, because shaping their respective industry allows them to limit their own area of action to one in which they have some control over the outcome and in which the probabilities of favorable outcomes are high.

In Chapter 5 we summarized the four principles that successful risk-reward managers rely on: (1) disaggregating and structuring risk so that decisions can be made on which risks to take and which risks not to take; (2) taking risks where you enjoy familiarity advantages and where the probabilities of favorable outcomes are therefore high—and shedding risks where others have comparative advantages; (3) applying portfolio theory to optimize overall results; and (4) using options to increase risk-reward by managing uncertainty. Now, let's take them one by one.

Disaggregating and structuring business operating risks

Disaggregating and structuring risks is about reducing the confusion and complexity of decision making to better enable effective risk-reward assessment.

Most business decisions begin as an aggregated bundle of risk-reward relationships.[1] A decision to produce cars in Brazil is really a decision to take on a whole conglomeration of risk-reward relationships. The decision embraces reputation risks, legal and contractual risks, counterparty risks, and a host of microeconomic risks having to do with customer behavior, competition, and labor and price issues. It also embraces Brazil-specific economic and political risks, as well as financial risks such as currency, interest rate, and illiquidity risks. Trying to make a good decision on the bundle *as a whole* is hard because the risk-reward trade-offs are nearly impossible to estimate. Not surprisingly, the common responses are to avoid taking action, to put such constraints on action as to limit any hope of success, or to take a "leap of faith." None of these approaches is wise. The better approach is to *unbundle*, or *disaggregate*, the risk-reward relationship into its component parts. This clarifies the risks actually being incurred, reducing confusion, and enables the unbundling of interdependencies, reducing complexity and systemic risk—the risk that the entire "system" will fail because one piece of it fails.

Once risks are disaggregated, they can be structured. Structuring risk is a process used by financial engineers such as investment bankers to determine which risks are taken and which are not taken. It usually involves use of contracts or legal entity structures that determine who will bear what risks, for what returns, under what conditions. Derivative contracts, for instance, are risk structuring instruments, as are special-purpose vehicles used to turn mortgages into securities—vehicles that determine who will be paid the principal and the interest on the mortgage under what conditions and thereby who will bear the related credit risks and interest rate risks.

Let's return to the challenge of producing cars in Brazil. In Chapter 9, we described how Volkswagen is approaching this challenge by building a modular facility using eight different suppliers in Resende. Another way of describing this approach is to say that Volkswagen is disaggregating and structuring its risks by working with eight subassemblers—contractual counterparties. These suppliers are each responsible for the risks inherent in their respective components for quality assurance, labor rates, and labor productivity and, more generally, for much of the Brazilian political and financial risk.

Volkswagen is not, of course, without risk itself. Although the suppliers bear "first loss" reputational risk for defects, Volkswagen, by putting its name on the car, "reinsures" reputational risks. As with arbitrage, counterparty risk is Volkswagen's primary risk in this undertaking, other than the risks it retains for vehicle design and sales. However, given the quality of its partners, this counterparty risk is low. Moreover, if a single counterparty were to default—due to, say, a labor strike—neutralizing that risk would require VW to find a replacement for only a single subcontractor rather than for all operations in the plant. In contrast, an integrated producer like GM in the United States has little flexibility when a wildcat strike at one of its own plants can shut down multiple assembly plants elsewhere.

As we suggested, the jury is still out on whether this innovative model of producing cars designed by VW through contractual counterparties will work. Certainly, there have been some challenges in achieving the hoped-for productivity and quality of output. Even here, however, one sees the power of the risk-reward management approach. By structuring and placing the risks with counterparties, VW has the opportunity to gain enormous learning benefits from this experiment without exposing the firm itself to significant financial risks. If the experiment does not work out, the learning gained from it can help build a more effective approach in the future.

Taking risks where you have familiarity advantages

The key to this risk approach lies in the fact that different participants have radically different comparative advantages in taking different risks. This is particularly true in a world economy bringing together participants long separated by geographic barriers because there are huge asymmetries in the risk-taking capacity of participants from different geographic home bases; that is, the probabilities of gain and loss are very different for different participants taking the exact same risks.

Many people believe that risk simply exists, that someone has to take the risk, that the whole process is a zero-sum game, and that for every winner there has to be a loser. In fact, risk is often in the eye of the beholder. For not only do different participants have different risk preferences, they have different skills in assessing risks and different abilities to absorb the losses.

The concept that risk takers have different risk preferences was first developed by Daniel Bernoulli in the eighteenth century. Bernoulli developed the concept of "utility," observing that an individual's propensity to take risk is directly proportionate to the size of the reward relative to the individual's existing wealth. What is new today is not the concept, but the combination of the breakdown in geographic barriers—which brings together participants with very different risk-preference profiles—with new, contract-based techniques for enabling the effective exchange of those risks.

This reality is what has enabled the market in derivatives to grow to its current enormous volume from a tiny base twenty years ago. In the derivatives markets, different participants, for a known price, take risks compatible with their different preferences and comparative advantages. In their day-to-day operations, global commercial banks are exposed to large aggregations of credit risks, interest rate risks, liquidity risks, and currency risks, among others. The derivatives market allows sophisticated global banks not only to neutralize their risks but actually to profit from reducing them. For example, a commercial bank with a large, natural exposure to floating-rate interest risks can offset that risk by writing interest rate swaps, earning a "bid" and "ask" spread where one of the customers is the bank's own balance sheet.

In principle, such risk-reward exchanges can be made, not just for financial risks, but for business operating risks, through partnering, particularly in industries where counterparty relationships have developed. By placing and structuring risks, participants can strive to take only risk-reward opportunities they believe will offer them high returns for the risks taken. Many of these opportunities arise because of the asymmetry of ownership of intangible assets, allowing individual participants to take unfair advantage of their comparative advantage in intangibles. A simple example can help show the advantages intangibles can provide.

Consider two runners racing on a narrow path at night. The path is strewn with rocks and trees, and crossed by streams and other obstacles. If one of the runners is able to practice in the daytime and at night, while the other is allowed no practice time and doesn't even get to see the course in advance, the runner with the superior intangibles—here, knowledge of the course—will win, even if the runner lacking the intangibles is faster.

In today's transition economy, there is an opportunity to run only those races where you have intangible advantages.

Portfolio theory

Most readers are familiar with the advantages portfolios have in diversifying risk. The principles of portfolio theory were first set out by Harry Markowitz in the early 1950s.[2] Portfolio theory relies on diversification, which in turn relies on the independence of variables. This is another reason why it is important to disaggregate and structure risks: to help make the variables more independent. The theory is that a portfolio of stocks with uncorrelated returns has less variance in outcomes than the underlying individual stocks. This enables ownership of a portfolio of high risk–high reward assets with less risk of loss than would be true of owning any single stock.

Portfolio theory was developed under the assumption that expected returns follow a mathematically normal distribution, an assumption that proves to be largely true—at least in the short term—in financial markets. However, portfolios can be *more* advantageous in taking business and operating risks rather than financial risks because, as we noted above, the asymmetry of ownership of intangible assets gives participants enormous opportunities to take unfair advantage of their own comparative advantages in intangibles.

Think back to our two runners on the path at night, one of whom is familiar with the obstacles. If a runner has the choice of only running races where he or she has such familiarity advantages, he or she is likely to win much more than a "fair share" of races. While an unforeseen accident (such as running into a tree) can always cause the runner to lose a single race, the more times such races are run the greater the odds that the runner with the knowledge and advantages will win more races than are lost.

This is the "loaded dice" effect. With normal dice your chance of winning at craps is very close to 50-50 (49.6 percent because of house advantage). Playing many games does not improve your odds; in fact, the house advantage means you lose more. But if you use loaded dice that give you a probability of winning five out of six times, the more you play, the more you will win. If you can play two games of craps in a row and bet equal amounts of money, you will lose only one time out of thirty-six, will break even one out of eighteen times, and will win the rest of the times.

Why would anyone want to play against a player using "loaded dice"? Of course, no one should. This is what Volkswagen is trying to do in Brazil at Resende—trying to play only where it enjoys "loaded dice." Dell makes the same decision every time it uses an outside supplier, as does a credit card company whenever it outsources credit card processing. Volkswagen, Dell, and a credit card company are, in effect, seeking portfolios of opportunities that take advantage of where they enjoy loaded-dice effects.

This is the portfolio opportunity for companies in the transition economy. If companies, scanning the extraordinary range of opportunities becoming available, choose to compete only where they have significant intangible advantages and if they can build a portfolio of such businesses, they make it highly probable they will achieve very desirable outcomes.

Using options to increase returns and overcome uncertainty

Option theory identifies the value of being able to acquire, for a known price, the upside benefits of owning an asset without incurring the downside risks of owning it. The more uncertain the environment, the more valuable the option. There are four elements that determine the value of a financial option, as Black, Scholes, and Merton explained in the early 1970s: duration, exercise price, time value of money lost by not exercising the option immediately, and volatility.

It is volatility in particular that drives value, no matter whether the price of the asset on which the option is being taken rises or falls. Because of the asymmetric nature of the option itself, an investor's potential loss is limited to the premium paid, while the potential profit is virtually unlimited.[3] The profits of the rising value of the asset are earned by exercising the option (buying the asset); losses from the decreasing value of the asset are avoided by declining to exercise the option to buy the asset, in which case only the price paid for the option itself is lost. High uncertainty increases the value of options because it increases the volatility of outcomes.

Let's return again to our two night-runners. If, in addition to all other advantages, our favored runner also has the option to stop the race halfway and restart the race, the odds of winning are again increased.

The value of an option is even greater, as is often the case with business options, if you have unfair advantages in the costs of creating options, the costs of exercising options, and your ability to extend the duration of the option. Such unfair advantages are often the case in business options due to intangible asset advantages.

Finally, if the outcomes of business options are *not* normal, due to unfair ownership of intangibles you possess, a portfolio of options will also provide you with greater likelihood of achieving desirable outcomes due to the loaded dice effect described earlier.

The only cost to an option is the premium paid to acquire it. *Business options are highly attractive because they can often be acquired at relatively low cost, particularly if you enjoy valuable intangible assets.* A personal computer manufacturer like Dell or Compaq can negotiate highly attractive options in working with others, so the cost of the premium is low. The volume they can potentially divert toward other companies enables these companies to negotiate options highly advantageous to themselves. If conditions change due to currency movements, or changing technology makes alternative suppliers more attractive, they have options over time to change suppliers by, for example, moving from a Taiwanese supplier to a Korean supplier for a particular component. The key here is that Dell has an intangible advantage in PC assembly, whereas the suppliers are delivering commodities.

On the other hand, Intel's position in PC semiconductors is so strong because of its intangibles that it cannot only maintain high prices but also compel manufacturers to make the public aware that their computers are "Intel inside." Personal computer assemblers do not have many options other than using Intel.

Companies such as Caterpillar, Coca-Cola, or McDonald's all have options with their local distributors or franchises. If the local distributors are behaving badly—for example, by making insufficient local investment—these players have contractual options to acquire the distributor or to transfer the contractual relationship. The local distributor does not have equal options.

SHAPERS

Shapers of the transition economy are effective at risk-reward management. Whether consciously or unconsciously, they apply the four risk-reward management principles. They disaggregate and structure risks sufficiently to understand exactly what risks they are taking. They have often organized themselves around largely self-contained businesses—each business acts as a ship—while gaining "convoy" effects by leveraging their core intangibles throughout the company.

They are adept at taking risks only when they have unfair advantages; in particular, they benefit by being able to overcome unfamiliarity, often by leveraging networks that appear to give them "eyes and ears" everywhere. They are adept at gaining insight into the economic interests of all participants, which gives them enormous power in negotiating counterparty agreements and in creating low-cost options. They view confusion, complexity, and uncertainty as an ally because it buys them time to create options others cannot see. They are highly disciplined in their risk-reward decisions. They don't let habit or emotion drive decisions. They suspend judgment until the time is right, using the time available to resolve uncertainty. When the time *is* right, they can move with breathtaking speed. Because of their capacity to act while others remain transfixed by the risks, they can seize the high ground. Consider the following examples.

GE Capital

GE Capital[4] comprises over thirty self-contained businesses ranging from reinsurance to railcar finance.[5] This self-containment serves to structure the risks to which each business is exposed. For example, in the late 1980s and early 1990s, when the commercial real estate markets in the United States were experiencing a collapse in values, the challenges of dealing with those problems were confined to a single unit—other businesses were not distracted or affected.[6]

Intriguingly, GE Capital is still able to get "convoy effects" from its portfolio of businesses despite this self-containment. When GE Capital made a major push into Europe between 1994 and 1996, it created an in-house European acquisition group of thirty merchant bankers who worked as a temporary utility to surface attractive candidates for all of GE Capital's business units. No single business would have been able to mobilize such an effort. In 1995 this group alone closed twenty-one deals. The companies, once acquired, were integrated into its thirty or so self-contained businesses.

In this effort, GE Capital was always searching to gain unfair advantages based on intangibles before it made these investments. The starting point for gaining such advantages was sending over, for each business, talented managers who understood the U.S. core business. Simultaneously, GE Capital relied on the worldwide network of "national executives" maintained by its parent, General Electric. These national executives are senior managers without line responsibility charged with local networking and sourcing opportunities. Many of these executives are highly influential in their communities. GE Capital also drew on GE subsidiaries in Europe, which provided local market contacts with their customers and suppliers. In turn, the small teams of individuals made up from the in-house merchant bankers and the respective business managers from the core businesses explored individual transactions and used these networks and contacts to gain more knowledge from interviews. (Some of the people who have been interviewed by these GE teams use terms such as "sucked dry" in describing the experience.)

Finally, GE Capital is always exploring options. For example, in order to close on the twenty-one European deals in 1995, the in-house acquisition group examined at least 100 and bid on 40. This effort was just a part of a broader effort by GE Capital to globalize its businesses, either by acquiring niche providers in business segments where GE has distinctive expertise or by introducing businesses in underpenetrated markets by leveraging GE Capital's best practices from its U.S. operations. For example, in Europe, GE Capital focused particularly on leasing finance and consumer finance—arenas traditionally neglected by European bankers, leaving a wide-open field for GE Capital to acquire high-margin providers such as the Pallas Group (U.K.) or SOVAC (France).

GE Capital's ultimate objective appears to be to create global, specialized finance microindustries in a series of businesses (e.g., its auto finance business already has a presence in approximately twenty countries worldwide). In the process, it is carefully disaggregating and structuring risk, taking risks only where it has familiarity advantages, relying on portfolios to ensure overall results, and always creating options to increase its returns relative to the risks it is taking.

Enron

Enron is another company attempting to create businesses in a number of new global microindustries.[7] In Enron's case, risk-reward management principles do not merely apply to the way in which it approaches the creation of these businesses; they lie at the heart of its value proposition.

Historically, Enron was principally engaged in the transportation of natural gas through pipelines. After deregulation of the U.S. natural gas industry in the late 1970s and early 1980s, Enron faced the prospect of competing in a commodity market where everyone sold an identical product—molecules of methane. Natural gas prices were highly volatile, however, and by 1990, the majority of gas sales were on either a short-term contract or spot (market) basis. Due to the shortness (or absence) of price guarantees, margins and price forecasting became impossible. This unstable environment placed both buyers and sellers at extraordinary risk.

To remedy this instability, Enron formed a special purpose company, Enron Capital & Trade Resources (ECT), which acted as an in-house "gas bank." This special purpose company served to disaggregate and structure the risks and rewards of this new venture from the rest of Enron. Effectively, ECT was able to reshape the U.S. natural gas market by leveraging its insight into the natural gas exchanges, as well as its production, transport, and financing abilities. ECT's innovation was its ability to bundle natural gas with reliable delivery and predictable prices into a product line under the Enron brand name. This new product was called an Enfolio Gas Resource Agreement. These agreements were contracts, in effect derivative instruments similar to those used in the global capital markets, which provided guaranteed prices for natural gas under a specified set of conditions. Through these contracts, ECT was able to extract a premium from purchases in exchange for assuming some portion of the market risk. ECT was able to hedge itself against market fluctuations and shortages through skillful financial engineering using instruments such as commodity swaps and over-the-counter options to offset the risk assumed for each agreement.

Competitors eventually offered similar products to the natural gas industry, but by then ECT had secured a competitive advantage over new entrants by shaping the market to its strengths. Enron remains the manager of the world's largest portfolio of natural gas–related risk management contracts and the largest supplier of natural gas to the U.S. electrical power generation industry. Enron is now expanding this risk management–based strategy to shape the electrical power generation industry on a global level by attacking markets as they deregulate, locking up long-term contracts with agreed-on pricing with financially stable local power purchasers. Enron is also attacking in the United States, promoting deregulation on a state-by-state level, and is now the largest unregulated power supplier in North America.

Another Enron special purpose subsidiary, Enron Development Corporation (EDC), has been successful in developing over a dozen gas-fired power production facilities in the United Kingdom, Asia, and South America. A facility in Dabhol, India, after several delays, is now on-line. Other plants are planned or in progress in Turkey, Indonesia, the Dominican Republic, and Croatia.

Enron is also using its intellectual property and talent in other industries. Pulp and paper, for instance, are also subject to volatile price fluctuations. By applying the same price-risk management tools as used in the natural gas industry, and actually tying energy pricing for pulp and paper clients to the price of pulp and paper products, Enron protects mills from fluctuating market prices for their products— 30 percent of whose production costs are energy-related. Enron has even deployed its understanding of financial probabilities to "weather derivatives," in order to offer a risk management facility to clients whose fortunes are highly dependent on swings in the weather!

THE CHALLENGES OF IMPLEMENTING RISK-REWARD THINKING

For integrated players

Not everyone is a shaper—though many potentially could be. Presently, most of the world's large, integrated companies find it quite difficult to manage risk-reward relationships using the four principles outlined earlier because of the way in which they and the industries in which they operate are structured.

Most large companies' business operations are heavily interdependent. Historically, these companies succeeded through their ability to integrate internally across geography, functions, and customer classes. But this internal integration makes attempts to undertake new initiatives within existing businesses subject to confusing and complex risks, because of organizing and shared-cost structures that create hard-wired linkages and commingle risks across businesses. Rather than having individual businesses (ships) that can both operate independently and work together as a company (convoy), businesses in these companies are often chained together in ways that make *both* independent and collective action in response to changing conditions difficult. For example, these companies often have extraordinary difficulty taking advantage of increasing opportunities to specialize.

Moreover, most of these companies also find it difficult to place risks with outsiders because there is often a shortage of reliable counterparties. This in turn reflects a lack of global standards and protocols and industry structures, as well as the heavy internal integration of most existing participants. Without reliable counterparties, it is impossible to apply fully the risk-reward management principles outlined earlier. If you must remain internally integrated to deliver output, you cannot effectively shed risks you do not want to take. Nor can you be as effective at arbitrage, as we argued earlier.

As the transition economy gathers pace, and as confusion, complexity, and uncertainty continue to increase, it will become progressively riskier for companies to continue to operate in integrated businesses with interdependent risk-reward relationships. Interdependent risk-reward relationships reduce flexibility. If poorly performing parts of the business cannot be divested, the investment companies have in those operations is illiquid. Illiquidity is itself a major risk because it reduces options and makes it difficult to sell an asset as unfamiliarity and uncertainty are resolved. In an uncertain environment, options are valuable; a lack of options is a great liability.

Moreover, hard-wired business interdependencies expose the entire firm to risks in a single part of the firm. At the extreme, this kind of "systemic" risk across businesses can destroy an entire firm—just as a hole in part of a ship that cannot be sealed off from other parts can sink the whole ship. Systemic risk can even hurt a firm where there is no risk of enterprise-wide failure. For example, if a company overcontrols expense budgets centrally because it does not understand the opportunity costs of such spending in each business, it can create a systemic risk across all its businesses.

The greatest challenge, however, facing large, integrated firms that are not skillful in risk-reward management is that they will be exposed to adverse selection. The skilled players will capture the best risk-reward relationships, leaving unattractive risk-reward propositions to less effective managers. As the transition economy continues to integrate, all existing businesses will be faced with competitors exploiting their own intangible asset advantages and gaining access, specialization, and scale advantages as a result. When competitors do so, and capture volume, the shared cost structures of integrators based on former geographic advantages—shared overhead, shared physical distribution, and shared production—become a disadvantage. National or global value chain integration that formerly provided competitive advantage becomes disadvantageous as participants find they have to cross-subsidize weak parts of the chain.

Large, integrated companies will want to take two key steps if they want to use risk-reward principles to manage business risks: (1) migrate toward more self-containment of individual businesses and new business initiatives and (2) work to create reliable counterparties.

Migrate toward self-containment of businesses and new business initiatives. For a large, integrated producer, self-containing businesses essentially means reconfiguring and restructuring how it is organized and how operations and costs are structured. This will be a challenging multiyear undertaking; it may represent the biggest single challenge for integrators wanting to move from the midgame to the endgame. But it's worth it.

By defining more clearly the microindustry in which each business is competing and self-containing the functions needed to pursue each business, a company not only benefits from focus and specialization effects but also reduces its exposure to systemic risk. Self-containment makes it easier to disaggregate and structure the risks to which the corporation is exposed and to identify any places where it is experiencing adverse selection.[8]

The advantages of integration across businesses will not necessarily be lost, for interaction costs are falling as well. Just as it is increasingly easy to work with outsiders across a global value chain because of falling interaction costs, it should also be easier to work with insiders across a global value chain, even if each unit is self-contained.

Work to create reliable counterparties.   There is enormous potential power in creating counterparties with complementary skills. Unfortunately, in many industries such counterparties do not yet exist. Companies such as Coca-Cola, McDonald's, and Caterpillar have solved this problem through captives. Others have achieved the same effect through spin-offs, while maintaining contractual relationships.

The harder problem is to create counterparties when you need to work with players that are neither captives nor spin-offs. Enron, Compaq, and Dell have solved this problem in their respective industries through innovation. Volkswagen is attempting to solve it in Brazil. The reward for succeeding in the creation of reliable counterparties can be the opportunity to shape a broad-based industry.

For single business companies

Single business, specialized companies have a different set of risk-reward challenges than do large, fully integrated companies. In single business companies, the business and the corporation are the same. There is no convoy, only a single ship.

Many academics have pointed out the virtues of single business companies to shareholders. Essentially, single business companies permit investors to eliminate confusion and complexity and invest in companies where the risks and rewards are easily recognized. By constructing a portfolio of investments with independent risk-reward relationships, the investor is effectively utilizing the risk-reward principles outlined earlier. Putting multiple businesses together under a single shareholder structure only makes sense to the extent that the benefits exceed the extra overhead and interaction costs incurred and the extra confusion and complexity costs to the investor. To the extent that companies do not create more value from owning multiple businesses than the extra costs incurred, they are exposed to conglomerate discounts by the stock market—that is, the whole is less than the sum of the parts.

Indeed, many conglomerates perform poorly because overhead and interaction costs exceed the value captured by being in multiple businesses. They often own businesses exposed to undesirable outcomes because they are at fundamental access, specialization, and scale disadvantages and lack the skills or the will to restructure them. They often overcontrol expense budgets because they lack familiarity with each business's opportunities, thus negating the potential inherent in each business they own. When a conglomerate *is* well run, however, the stock market provides a premium to multiple business companies, recognizing that the whole is worth more than the sum of the parts.

In the transition economy, we believe there is increasing value to well-run companies skilled in risk-reward management to owning multiple businesses. Multibusiness companies can exercise strategic control to gain "convoy effects" not available to passive investors who cannot exercise strategic control over their investments. Multibusiness companies skilled in risk-reward management can construct portfolios of loaded-dice opportunities. They can do this by integrating intangibles from diverse existing businesses to shape new global microindustries. Multibusiness companies have, because of their diversity, greater capacity to overcome unfamiliarity than do less diverse companies. Multibusiness companies also can have greater alternatives, and enhanced bargaining power, to create and negotiate low-cost options with outside partners. Finally, successful multibusiness companies with superior market capitalizations can acquire other companies with relative ease.

Single-business, specialized companies do not have any of these luxuries. They lack the potential to work together and the mass to compete against shapers who redefine how business is done—potentially eliminating the value of their specialty. The challenge for specialists is to become shapers of multiple global businesses in global microindustries built off their special strength without becoming "conglomerates." This will happen naturally as their existing specialized business disaggregates into ever more specialized "micro" and "nano" industries.

MOVING FORWARD: CLASSES OF IDEAS

Most companies are not going to become shapers overnight. How do you begin?

Throughout this book we have advocated an inside-out approach that rests on leveraging your company's intangible assets. We have found it helpful in this regard to distinguish between four types of business operating risk: (1) risks that can be taken with certainty, (2) risks that provide you with unfair familiarity advantages, (3) risks that provide you with unfamiliarity disadvantages, and (4) risks filled with uncertainty. By *certainty*, we mean investments in which the projections of risk and reward can be made with a high degree of confidence. By *familiarity*, we mean you possess intangible assets that give you an unfair advantage over other participants in taking a particular risk. By *unfamiliarity*, we mean that you lack knowledge or intangibles possessed by others. By *uncertainty*, we mean outcomes that cannot be predicted or affected either by you or, in all likelihood, by anyone else.

As firms make investment decisions, they gravitate naturally toward certain investments. Unfortunately, in today's world, most certain investments based on tangible capital investment are equally apparent to others, and therefore have low returns. Most real global opportunities are either founded on leveraging proprietary intangible asset advantages or overcoming unfamiliarity and uncertainty. But most companies have little ability to distinguish unfamiliarity from uncertainty—that is, what is knowable versus what is unknowable. Moreover, they often do not think about where they have familiarity advantages. These distinctions are important because of what they imply about the ability to estimate risk-reward relationships. Where you have both certainty and familiarity advantages, unattractive risk can be shed for an explicit price and attractive risks can be taken. Where you have unfamiliarity, risk can be shed or managed by overcoming the unfamiliarity. Where you have uncertainty, risk must either be taken or decisions must be delayed until the uncertainty is resolved.

We have found it helpful, therefore, to put risk-reward ideas in one of three classes: (1) ideas founded on a high degree of certainty and familiarity that offer high returns relative to investment; (2) ideas that appear to promise high returns relative to investment, but will require overcoming unfamiliarity to determine whether or not an investment should be made; and (3) ideas that offer very high potential returns relative to the costs, but are likely to have unpredictable cash flows and risks given current levels of uncertainty (Exhibit 11-1).

Class 1 ideas

Class 1 ideas have high returns relative to investment because they leverage a company's existing familiarity advantage. They often comprise operations improvement measures that capture "easy" profits lying unrealized throughout the organization; for example, transferring best practices globally or by rolling out

worldwide a product or a customer segment marketing approach
for which the company has developed a compelling value proposition. These ideas typically involve realizing profits from leveraging existing capabilities, often through cross-geographic
arbitrage. Class 1 ideas include decreasing taxes worldwide by
being creative about how business is done in different countries;
increasing worldwide sales through investing in best practice
training; increasing the roll-out speed of products; leveraging
neglected patents; leveraging brands in new markets; and increasing capital productivity. They often involve investments to acquire global scale in an area of specialty.

EXHIBIT 11-1   Three classes of risk-reward ideas

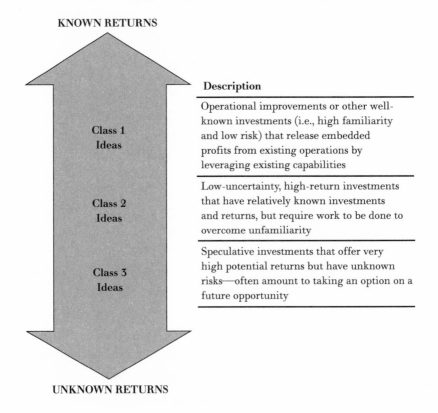

	Description
Class 1 Ideas	Operational improvements or other well-known investments (i.e., high familiarity and low risk) that release embedded profits from existing operations by leveraging existing capabilities
Class 2 Ideas	Low-uncertainty, high-return investments that have relatively known investments and returns, but require work to be done to overcome unfamiliarity
Class 3 Ideas	Speculative investments that offer very high potential returns but have unknown risks—often amount to taking an option on a future opportunity

Many of these opportunities are straightforward operations improvements. German automotive manufacturers have benchmarked their core functions against world-class standards and, by redesigning how they work, have greatly increased their labor and capital productivity in just a few years. Many companies have found high-quality, low-cost labor markets such as Ireland and Scotland that offer subsidies in return for locating plants there. In other instances, companies attack the profitable pieces of a business that other players use to cross-subsidize other less profitable pieces; for example, Virgin Atlantic cherry-picked the highly profitable transatlantic flights that British Airways, American, United, and others use to cross-subsidize their less profitable or loss-making routes elsewhere in the system (such as within continental Europe). There are many Class 1 actions companies can take. And they will increase as the world economy continues to integrate, global structures evolve, protocols and standards are created, and factor costs change.

The range of expected outcomes of Class 1 ideas is a relatively tight distribution (i.e., they are "certain"). But converting these ideas often creates real, new intangible capital such as trade secrets, proprietary best practices, operating talent, and capabilities providing significant ongoing advantages in competing against local and multinational companies or against other global companies that lack the intangibles or the focus to capture them.

If these Class 1 opportunities are so abundant, why not simply pursue them and leave it at that? The reason is that they are essentially ideas about specializing rather than shaping. Companies that focus exclusively on such ideas are vulnerable over time as shapers emerge.

Class 2 ideas

Class 2 ideas have the potential to offer attractive returns, but require that unfamiliarity be overcome before risks and returns can be reasonably estimated. Overcoming unfamiliarity often requires that significant investments be made just to acquire the intellectual property and talent needed to establish whether the idea is attractive. Many companies avoid spending money on these ideas simply because they hurt current earnings. But these ideas often have the highest return on spending in the medium term.

Large companies can easily spend $10 to $20 million or more in expenses simply to determine if a Class 2 idea is worthy of significant investment. Few down-the-line business managers can create room for such spending on their budgets. Invariably, therefore, top management judgment is required to get such funding. This leads to the problem described earlier in the book, that investment in the expenses required to pursue these kinds of opportunities are often never made under the pressure of achieving current earnings.

Of course, if the opportunity is the right global sliver, the potential business profits being forgone may be literally in the billions of dollars, as well as the loss of an increasing returns cycle and the opportunity to dominate a global microindustry. This is why it is essential to have a corporate strategy as described in Chapter 6 and why the inside-out approach is so important. The approach starts out by providing the company some familiarity advantages and therefore increases the odds that overcoming unfamiliarity is likely to have high returns.

Most of the ideas described in Chapters 7 through 10 are Class 2 ideas, whether they involve investing in intangibles, creating global slivers, or capturing cross-geographic arbitrage. Most acquisitions and partnering approaches are Class 2 ideas. That is, investments in overcoming unfamiliarity, and in finding ways of disaggregating and structuring risks given the degrees of freedom in the world economy, are likely to have high returns relative to the risks if the company can leverage its familiarity advantages. In our experience, it is unfamiliarity barriers, rather than true uncertainty, that blocks most people from capturing global opportunities.

The end product of pursuing Class 2 ideas is a Class 1 idea—a relatively unfamiliar potential opportunity gets converted into a relatively certain, familiar idea with high expected returns relative to the risks taken. In the GE Capital case described earlier in this chapter, the small teams exploring acquisition opportunities were, in effect, pursuing Class 2 ideas by overcoming unfamiliarity.

Class 3 ideas

Class 3 ideas involve real uncertainty. Many of the risks cannot even be identified. The ultimate source of many of these risks is the unknown behavior of different competitors, and the interactions of competitors in the evolution of markets and industry structures. Political events, the unknown evolution of technology, and the unknown evolution of standards and protocols are just a few of the causes of uncertainty. No matter how much you invest in knowledge or other intangibles, you are still involved in the vagaries of chance.

Unless you can shape these outcomes by your own actions, any investments you make involve real risk taking. This is why the future belongs to those who can best shape it or are, at least, better prepared to act once the uncertainty is resolved. You can begin to define the structure of a market and industry, the way competitors compete with you, and standards and protocols.

When you start to pursue a Class 3 idea, you have no idea whether you will succeed. Many Class 3 ideas involve innovation. As a drug company, you may see the opportunity to create a cure for AIDS, but be without any knowledge as to whether you will succeed. As a retailer, you may see the need to create logistics and distribution approaches that will be the key to unlocking China, but have no idea whether you will be able to do so. As a mutual fund, you may see the opportunity to create an electronic distribution channel for continental Europe, but lack knowledge of what technological platform will be widely available, when, and at what cost.

Like it or not, many of the future's great fortunes will go to companies that master the challenge of pursuing Class 3 ideas. The trick is always to be making as much progress as possible, so that you can capture the opportunity when the moment is right.

Johnson & Johnson or SAP or AIG always have pipelines of Class 3 ideas under development. The result is a steady flow of drugs and medical devices for J&J, new applications for SAP, and new risks to underwrite for AIG. Enron's development of the Enfolio Gas Agreement cited earlier in the chapter is an example of the successful conversion of a Class 3 idea into a sliver opportunity.

ORGANIZING TO CREATE OPTIONS THROUGH GLOBAL TALENT TEAMS

How can companies make progress in capturing Class 1, Class 2, and Class 3 ideas? How can they shape their own futures? We believe the critical element in capturing all three classes of new opportunities, which are all explorations of opportunities to create options, is the use of special purpose organizational units: the global talent teams we described in Chapter 10.

From a risk-reward management perspective, a global talent team has three generic purposes: (1) it is the vehicle for mobilizing the firm's existing knowledge and other intangibles to gain familiarity advantages against specific, focused opportunities; (2) it creates the new intangible assets needed to overcome unfamiliarity and to take advantage of the resolution of uncertainty; and (3) it enables the company to structure the risks and rewards from investment in creating new options.

Talent teams thus also function as a special purpose vehicle to limit risk. If a decision is made to close down the talent team, the cost of the project is easily brought back down to zero.

The charter of the talent team should be tailored to what the company wants to accomplish. In general, we see three kinds of charters based on the three types of classes of ideas, and therefore three types of talent teams (Exhibit 11-2).

Global SWAT teams. Global SWAT teams pursuing operational improvement, or Class 1 ideas, will usually be made up of temporarily assigned line and management staff drawn together across country and other organizational boundaries. Talent team efforts will usually have a discrete life; once the problem they are addressing is solved, the team will be disbanded, and ongoing

EXHIBIT 11-2   Three types of talent teams

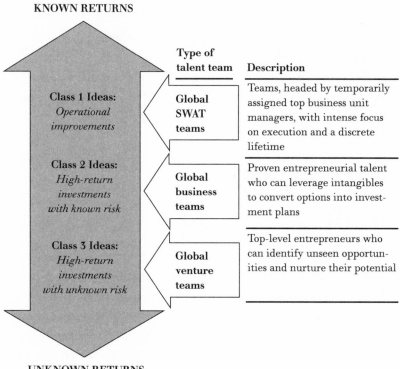

	Type of talent team	Description
Class 1 Ideas: *Operational improvements*	**Global SWAT teams**	Teams, headed by temporarily assigned top business unit managers, with intense focus on execution and a discrete lifetime
Class 2 Ideas: *High-return investments with known risk*	**Global business teams**	Proven entrepreneurial talent who can leverage intangibles to convert options into investment plans
Class 3 Ideas: *High-return investments with unknown risk*	**Global venture teams**	Top-level entrepreneurs who can identify unseen opportunities and nurture their potential

KNOWN RETURNS

UNKNOWN RETURNS

accountabilities for implementation will be "hard-wired" into the day-to-day management of the firm.

Global business teams. Global business teams can serve as the primary vehicles for shaping the company's immediate opportunities, or Class 2 ideas, through overcoming unfamiliarity. Not only do they lead to the deployment of the firm's existing tangible and intangible capital against specific opportunities, they are also the primary means of growing the immediate stock of intangible capital available to the corporation as a whole. The principles behind an effective global business team are straightforward. An accountable manager is assigned responsibility for assembling a team that operates across geographic and organizational boundaries to convert an investment hypothesis into a specific investment proposal. Failure to find a compellingly attractive investment opportunity is a recommendation not to invest. It is up to these teams to specify both the financial and intangible capital investments required and the returns expected.

The success or failure of these teams often depends on the creativity and problem-solving skills they bring to finding ways to make money while minimizing the need for major investment financial capital and high risk. They often discover "foothold" acquisition opportunities and major alliance opportunities. However, they are encouraged to find ways to invest capital, even very large amounts of capital involving major acquisitions, if they can build a compelling case that the returns will be high relative to the risks taken (i.e., to build very large, very successful businesses).

Global venture teams. Finally, there are global venture teams that pursue ideas both unfamiliar and uncertain—Class 3 ideas. Global venture teams nurture ideas by gaining knowledge to overcome unfamiliarity challenges so that, as time resolves uncertainty, the firm is able to see whether the opportunity will generate a high-return, low-risk investment. Even when an option fails to materialize into an investment opportunity, intellectual property has often been created by the global venture team, and this can be redeployed in the organization against other opportunities. These global venture teams create not only a rich pipeline of new opportunities but an equally rich portfolio of talent—genuine global entrepreneurs.

SHAPING THE FIRM

Throughout this book we have argued that the transition economy demands new ways to compete. Classic approaches built on a world of reasonably durable, geographically bounded market and industry structures have relied on heavy capital investment and internal integration to overcome those barriers. Those approaches were appropriate in a world where geographic market boundaries were high. Today, however, as geographic boundaries come down, these approaches make less sense.

We have also argued that intangible-heavy, capital-light approaches are superior today because in a transition economy intangibles are the key to building superior value propositions. Moreover, the trade-off between internal integration and specialization is increasingly tilting toward specialization. Indeed, this intangible-heavy, more specialized approach is the key to the shaping model because it provides the ability to get virtuous cycles of geographic expansion and increasing returns without risking heavy capital investments. In other words, it provides the means to grow earnings rapidly while earning high returns on financial capital.

It is not that shapers do not deploy capital—they are quite willing to commit capital if they can earn high-risk–adjusted returns. For example, if the only way to create a virtuous cycle of geographic expansion is through capital investment and internal integration, because the economy is not sufficiently integrated to permit using a more specialized approach, then a shaper will commit capital and will operate as an integrated player. The difference, though, is that a shaper will be continually looking to shed unneeded capital as the economy integrates—by spinning off captives, by divesting businesses in which it has chosen not to compete, and by outsourcing business functions in which it is less than world class—while continuing to invest in building superior intangibles in areas of specialty. In a transition economy, these opportunities become continuously available because the more the economy integrates, the more it becomes possible to specialize and to shed businesses and business functions, while retaining most of the value added.

As the world economy integrates, a capital-heavy, full business system model makes the firm highly vulnerable to competitors deploying a more intangible-heavy, specialized, and therefore flexible model. A capital-heavy, more integrated approach will also increasingly expose the firm to large financial risks. Heavy financial investment, particularly across borders, exposes the firm to political, currency, and interest rate risks. In a world of turbulent global financial markets, where the equity markets are quick to reward the strong and punish the weak, it is critical to use financial capital sparingly and wisely.

In contrast, an intangible-heavy, more specialized model enables financial capital to be used with high productivity. This approach is based on a willingness to take risks in spending expense dollars but an outright refusal to commit large amounts of financial capital to low-return projects or to projects with large uncertainties. By spending money to build intangibles to overcome unfamiliarity, such an approach enables a company to make progress in a turbulent world without taking large financial risks. This in turn liberates the firm from the risk constraints, highlighted in Chapter 5, that are the root causes of the failure of firms to capture the opportunities of the transition economy. Learning is by trial and error, but in a manner in which the costs of failure are low and the benefits of success can be spectacular.

Companies pursuing such an approach should expect plenty of failures. They are inevitable, given the unfamiliarity and uncertainty inherent in the transition economy. Companies should not be alarmed, provided that all that is lost are expense dollars.

There really isn't any choice except to learn by doing. Some talent teams *will* fail. But it is only by going after a range of opportunities that a company can build the new intangibles it needs to be an industry shaper. When teams succeed, the company can put its energy and resources behind them to build a reinforcing cycle of amassing and leveraging intangible capital. When talent team initiatives turn out to be "dry holes," they can be stopped. If, at the same time, a company divests businesses to their more natural owners, it can steadily upgrade the quality of its entire portfolio of options and businesses.

Over time, the company adapts to an evolving external industry structure while it changes internally to accommodate new, different kinds of talent. Its management model evolves to match its new portfolio of options and more self-contained businesses. It develops capacity to overcome unfamiliarity and manage uncertainty on a regular basis so that it takes risks only where it enjoys loaded-dice advantages.

The hard part is getting started. Top management must exercise leadership through tough decisions on resource-allocation strategy. The best opportunities must be supported—and that support includes committing up-and-coming leaders to them. Every step should be taken to give these first opportunities the highest probability for success, because success will breed success, creating a reinforcing cycle of talent development, intellectual property generation, and opportunity creation that strengthens the companies' unfair advantages, providing momentum for the next cycle.

Today, there are only a handful of global firms that understand this game. They are rapidly growing their earnings and improving their returns on capital. Their understanding of risk and reward and their willingness to configure their company to take risks allow them to attract people with outstanding abilities and to apply those abilities to opportunities where they have a good chance to succeed. Opportunities for early responsibility and a knowledge-rich environment motivate people to create and capture the opportunities where the corporation has natural ownership—opportunities that leverage structurally advantaged intangible assets.

These companies are the natural partners for any new project sponsor, and their involvement lowers the cost of project financing for all other participants. Other, strong players gravitate to them because of their success, and so their projects succeed. More success breeds more talent; more talent, more opportunity; more opportunity, more knowledge, in an upward spiral. The race for the world is on for those willing to accept the challenge.

NOTES

Preface

1. New York: W. W. Norton & Co., 1997.
2. San Francisco: Berrett-Koehler, 1997.
3. New York: John Wiley & Sons, 1996.
4. Princeton, N.J.: Princeton University Press, 1996.
5. July–August 1996, 100–109.
6. New York: Free Press, 1987.
7. Boston: Harvard Business School Press, 1989.
8. Boston: Harvard Business School Press, 1994.

Chapter 1: The Transition Economy

1. McKinsey estimate based on analysis of DRI data and DRI estimates of worldwide GDP.
2. Countries may, of course, exclude their citizens from global markets through policy decisions—and indeed keep the structure of their national industries separate.

3. Assuming a 4% overall real growth rate (a blended rate of slow growth in the developed world and more rapid growth in the emerging world).

4. *Guns, Germs, and Steel: The Fates of Human Societies*, by Jared Diamond (New York: W. W. Norton & Co., 1997).

5. A wealth of literature has been written on the role of the determinants of an individual's or a nation's success. While we do not attempt to synthesize it here, we certainly acknowledge its existence.

6. For a more detailed discussion of the era, see *A History of Rome*, by Marcel Le Glay, Jean-Louis Voisin, and Yann Le Bohec (Oxford: Blackwell, 1991).

7. By *active agent* we mean the party that, through its actions, shaped the evolution of economic integration in its sphere of influence.

8. *Titan: The Life of John D. Rockefeller, Sr.*, by Ron Chernow (New York: Random House, 1998), 150.

9. Rockefeller's empire was broken up by the U.S. government in 1911 because of its stranglehold on all parts of the oil business, but that hardly makes his achievement less extraordinary.

10. *The Wealth and Poverty of Nations: Why Some Are So Rich and Others Are So Poor*, by David Landes (New York: W. W. Norton & Co., 1998), 206–207.

11. There are still, in fact, some states that have prohibitions on interstate banking. Similarly, U.S. regulations drove a difference between the structure of the investment banking versus retail banking industry. The Glass Steagall Act prevented banks from owning a securities business, precipitating the emergence of specialist investment banking houses that now play such a dominant role in the world's capital markets. In comparison, in continental Europe, the majority of these activities occurred within the local universal banks and as a result a less specialized and arguably less competitive capability emerged. This is an example of how the peculiarities of one nation's market trigger a very different structure from another's.

12. We are going to avoid the use of the word *multinational* in this book. We have found that to some people multinational means any company that operates outside its home country, while to

others it means a particular kind of company that has learned how to become an "insider" in multiple national economies. Moreover, *multilocal* includes companies such as banks and health care providers that have proved adept at penetrating local geographic markets across a nation as well as companies that have proved adept at crossing national borders.

13. By *intangible assets* we refer to people, knowledge, reputation, and relationships. See Chapter 7 for a more detailed definition and discussion.

14. Stopford and Wells first examined the stages of moving from a local company to a global company [see John M. Stopford and Louis T. Wells, Jr., *Managing the Multinational Enterprise: Organization of the Firm and Ownership of the Subsidiaries* (New York: Basic Books, 1972)]. They were followed by a rich history of literature covering the challenges of gaining sufficient local responsiveness balanced against the advantages of global scale, including most notably C. K. Prahalad and Yves L. Doz's *The Multinational Mission: Balancing Local Demands and Global Vision* (New York: Free Press, 1987) and C. Bartlett and S. Ghoshal's *Managing Across Borders: The Transnational Solution* (Boston: Harvard Business School Press, 1989).

15. For another discussion on forces in the new world economy, see Pam Woodall, "A survey of the world economy: The hitchhiker's guide to cybernomics," *The Economist*, September 28, 1996, insert. Also "The heart of the new world economy," *The Financial Times* series on "The Global Company," October 1, 1997. Several publications—including *The Economist* and *The Financial Times*—have referred to the fact that, if measured by trade flows, the world economy was more integrated in the years leading up to World War I than it is today. However, this fails to measure integration in terms of intangible assets—the flow of ideas, people, brands, knowledge, and so forth—that is so markedly different from the globalization experienced at the turn of the century.

16. We do not wish to imply that these benefits are instantaneous. When governments open up a particular market, it can take many years for the full benefits to be realized by both local consumers and new competitors. Often deregulation fails to remove all the privileges of the local monopoly—as has occurred in most of the

telecom markets, for example—or it simply takes many years for new entrants to gain sufficient mass and presence vis-à-vis the local incumbents. Moreover, existing local and national industry structures must radically reconfigure, leading to layoffs, business failures, et cetera.

17. The latecomers to the party are a number of African countries, much of the Middle East, and a few Latin American and Asian regimes. Many of the benefits of deregulation have been new local companies that have sprung up to capture the opportunities in their local markets. Indeed, as we will discuss in Chapter 4, many of the major beneficiaries of a more open global economy and a global capital market are the local entrepreneurs.

18. For an interesting discussion of the role of overseas Chinese entrepreneurs, see *Overseas Chinese Business Networks in Asia*, published by the Department of Foreign Affairs and Trade of Australia (1995), and *Lords of the Rim: The Invisible Empire of the Overseas Chinese*, by Sterling Seagrave (New York: G. P. Putnam's Sons, 1995).

19. There is an enormous amount of material on this topic. The theoretical foundation on the relationship between personal freedom and economic prosperity was laid by Adam Smith's *The Wealth of Nations* in 1776 and, more recently, by Frederich A. von Hayek in *The Road to Serfdom* (first published in 1944) and Milton Friedman in *Capitalism and Freedom* (University of Chicago Press, 1963). Empirical evidence is available in studies by the Harvard Institute for International Development (*Emerging Asia*, Asian Development Bank, 1997) and regular reports on the openness of the world's economies produced by the Fraser Institute (*Economic Freedom of the World*), the Heritage Foundation (*Index of Economic Freedom*), and Freedom House (*World Survey of Economic Freedom*).

20. DRI/McGraw-Hill International Model Bank, November 1997.

21. See, for example, "Can 11 Eurostates find harmony? Does it matter?" by George Melloan, *Wall Street Journal*, October 21, 1997. *The Economist*'s "Survey of the future of the state," September 20, 1997, offers a more general discussion of the problem Europe faces in this regard.

22. In *Market Unbound: Unleashing Global Capitalism* (New York:

John Wiley & Sons 1996), Lowell Bryan and Diana Farrell describe how and why the power to allocate financial resources is being transferred from governments to the global capital market.

23. Family-owned and private companies are not immune to these dictates. They too tap into the debt capital markets to fund their operations and expansion and so are also subject to the terms and conditions placed on the access to that capital.

24. Today, trillions of dollars of trades are undertaken every day as participants seek to capture microscopic pricing anomalies between markets through cross-currency arbitrage.

25. Some foreign exchange controls remained until the late 1980s in countries such as Spain and Italy.

26. In many respects, the emergence of global capital markets is actually a good example of how globalization takes place in the market for goods and services generally.

27. United Nations, *World Investment Report 1997* (New York and Geneva).

28. See Chapter 4 for a more detailed account of the demand and supply factors creating this glut of liquid financial capital. See also *Market Unbound: Unleashing Global Capitalism*, by Lowell Bryan and Diana Farrell.

29. McKinsey Automotive Practice.

30. Our colleague, Ted Hall, coined this phrase, referring to a whole set of activities related to searching, coordinating, and monitoring among economic agents. This is often referred to in the academic literature as *transaction costs*. We like this term better because transaction costs are the costs to exchange items of value. Transaction costs are a subset of interaction costs. *Interaction costs* embraces not just these costs but all of the costs of searching, coordinating, and monitoring the work of different parties (including internal integration within a single firm).

31. These figures come from work done by the McKinsey Global Forces Initiative team, a summary of whose work can be found in "A revolution in interaction," by Patrick Butler, Ted Hall, Alistair Hanna, Lenny Mendonca, Byron Auguste, James Manyika, and Anupam Sahay (*The McKinsey Quarterly*, 1997, No. 1, 4–23). The relevant figure at industry level is 50% in service industries and 35% in manufacturing environments. At

the individual level, figures ranged from 80% for managers down to 15% for laborers. Much has been written on the topic, from earlier works by Ronald Coase (e.g., "The nature of the firm," *Economica*, Vol. 4, No. 16 [1937], 386–405) to more recent works by Oliver Williamson (e.g., *The Economic Institutions of Capitalism: Firms, Markets, Relational Contracting*, New York: Free Press, 1985); Paul Milgrom and John Roberts (*Economics, Organization, and Management*, Englewood Cliffs, N.J.: Prentice-Hall, 1992); and Frances Cairncross (*The Death of Distance: How the Communications Revolution Will Change Our Lives*, Boston: Harvard Business School Press, 1997). Also see two recent journalistic series, *The Economist*'s "Schools brief" on globalisation (October 18–December 6, 1997) and the *Financial Times'* "The global company" (October 1–November 7, 1997), in which the fall in interaction costs and related advances in technology and telecommunications are broadly noted as drivers of the growing integration of the world economy.

32. This will be made possible by such technological improvements as the deployment of fiber optic cables offering several million times higher capacity than copper, as well as new technologies for traditional copper that promise to offer up to 16 megabits per second for downstream transmission and 3 Mbps for upstream transmission. In addition, cheaper digital cellular and satellite links are becoming increasingly available, while improved compression will reduce the need for bandwidth (MPEG technology for sound and video delivers compression levels of up to 80 times).

33. We are indebted to McKinsey's Global Forces Initiatives team for the summary that follows.

34. See *Net Worth* by our colleagues John Hagel and Marc Singer (Boston: Harvard Business School Press, 1999) for the discussion of the role of "infomediaries."

35. "Schools brief 'one world?'"*The Economist*, October 18, 1997. For a more detailed discussion of the future roles of telephones, television, and the Internet and the implications for companies, customers, and governments, see *The Death of Distance: How the Communications Revolution Will Change Our Lives*, by Frances Cairncross (Boston: Harvard Business School Press, 1997).

36. *International Telecommunications Development Report 1995,* McKinsey Global Forces Initiative.

37. *Trade* involves the production of goods and services in one geography and the delivery of those goods and services in another through incurring the necessary transport and transaction costs. *Transplants* involve the transfer by trade of only the essential capital goods and techniques of production from one geography to another and then producing goods and services primarily by using local inputs of production. For example, aircraft engines are usually traded but fast food delivery is usually transplanted. For the most part, economic discussion is around cross-border trade and transplants even though goods and services are traded and transplanted within national borders as well. Goods can be delivered through trade and transplants—they cannot be electronically delivered. Services are hard to trade, but are often relatively easy to transplant and deliver electronically.

38. As we will see later in the book, one of the critical issues in determining whether a company performs work within its corporate structure as opposed to outsourcing it is whether or not the resulting total interaction costs incurred are higher or lower. As computing and communications costs decline, and protocols and standards are adopted worldwide, the total interactions costs of coordinating work between specialists will decline. As companies simplify, the need to incur overhead costs will decline. This will decrease the fixed-cost leverage currently enjoyed by large companies because most of the overhead costs will be made redundant.

39. "A revolution in interaction," by Patrick Butler et al., *The McKinsey Quarterly* (1997 No. 1, 4–23).

40. We frequently refer to Citicorp, Citibank, and Citigroup in this book. Citicorp refers to the holding company and Citibank refers to the bank. Citigroup refers to the merger between Citicorp and Travelers, announced in 1998. Therefore any references to Citicorp will be to the strategy of the company prior to the merger with Travelers.

41. Intuit, Inc., 1997 Annual Report.

42. *Value* is often defined as benefits minus cost. We define *value*

proposition broadly as a clear articulation of what value customers get, what value you provide, what value your partners (if any) provide, why the resulting offering provides more value than competitive offerings, and how the economics work.

43. We are far from alone in noting the increasing value of intangibles. A host of others, including Itami (1991), Sveiby (1997), Edvinsson and Malone (1997), and Stewart (1997) have discussed it (see note 1, Chapter 7). Chapter 7 will cover this area in greater detail.

44. Specialization advantages also replace geographic access as the critical determinant of advantage in the new world economy because of the increase in customer choice noted earlier. As customers gain bargaining power they can demand more of whatever they value the most, and since customer needs are diverse, and what they value is different, this drives increased specialization.

45. DRI International Model Bank, U.S. Census Bureau's International Population Center (IPC).

46. IMF, *Direction of Trade Yearbook*, 1983, 1992, and 1997 editions. Conversion to 1986 dollars based on CPI-U data.

47. Dataquest Focus Report, "An Overview of India's Electronics Industry," September 1997; Gartner Group Report, "Offshore programming: Does India have any real competition?" August 5, 1998.

48. That is, the same amount of money buys more of a standard "basket" of goods in one place than in the other.

49. McKinsey Global Forces Initiative estimates, based on data from the World Bank Development Report 1995, *Workers in an Integrating World* (Oxford and New York: Oxford University Press); UN world demographics estimates and projections 1950–2025 (1988); DRI/McGraw-Hill World Markets Executive Overview (4th quarter 1995); *Euromonitor* International and European Marketing Data and Statistics (1996).

50. For a discussion of the risks associated with investment in emerging markets, we particularly recommend "Is foreign infrastructure investment still risky?" by Louis T. Wells and Eric S. Gleason (*Harvard Business Review*, September–October 1995, 44–55) and "Troubles ahead in emerging markets," by Jeffrey E. Garten (*Harvard Business Review*, May–June 1997, 38–50).

51. Donald Schon, quoting Russell Ackoff, in *The Reflective*

Practitioner: How Professionals Think in Action (New York: Basic Books, 1983), 16.

Chapter 2: Running the Race

1. McKinsey Consumer Practice.
2. While we estimate that one-third of the world's industries (as measured by GDP) have formed significant global industry structures, not all of those industries have globalized. That is, part of their structures are still local. For example, in automotives, assembly is quite global, but repairs, maintenance, and distribution remain local or national at best. Therefore, of the total GDP represented by so-called global industries, well less than two-thirds of their output is generated by the global components of the industry structure.
3. The McKinsey Automotive Practice estimates that auto assembly accounts for only 23 percent of the auto industry revenues, and even less of the profits.
4. Concrete is the world's most widely used building material, with annual global production levels of nearly 1.25 billion tons, and yet the industry is incredibly local with thousands and thousands of suppliers. The vast majority of cement—the "glue" in concrete—is produced and shipped within a 300-mile radius.
5. Compustat; AES 1997 Annual Report.
6. Analyst reports used include Donaldson, Lufkin & Jenrette (July 22, 1994; May 18, 1995) and Morgan Stanley (November 21, 1996; May 1, 1997).
7. Guinness is now a division of Diageo plc, the holding company formed by the merger of Guinness and Grand Metropolitan. Guinness Annual Report 1997; ERC 1996 World Beer Market Survey; Canadian 1996 World Beer Report.
8. Annual reports 1990–1997, The Coca-Cola Company and PepsiCo.
9. *The Cola Wars*, by J. C. Louis and Harvey Z. Yazijian (New York: Everest House, 1980) and *For God, Country, and Coca-Cola: The Unauthorized History of the Great American Soft Drink and the Company That Makes It*, by Mark Pendergast (New York: Collier Books, 1994).

10. For a more detailed discussion, see W. Brian Arthur's *Increasing Returns and Path Dependence in the Economy* (Ann Arbor: University of Michigan Press, 1994) and his "Increasing returns and the new world of business" (*Harvard Business Review*, July–August 1996, 100–109).
11. *Market Unbound: Unleashing Global Capitalism*, by Lowell Bryan and Diana Farrell (New York: John Wiley & Sons, 1996).
12. McKinsey German Automotive Practice.
13. McKinsey Global Automotive Practice.

Chapter 3: Midgame Strategies

1. "No regrets" investments are those that make sense regardless of future outcomes. "Big bet" investments could have either high or low returns, depending on what happens in the future. See "Strategy under uncertainty," by Hugh Courtney, Jane Kirkland, and Patrick Viguerie (*Harvard Business Review*, November–December 1997, 66–79).
2. Securities Data Corporation.
3. We use the term "microindustry" to refer to an industry that has come into existence to serve a new cross-geographic market. We use the prefix *micro-* because one of the distinguishing characteristics of these new industries is that they are more specialized than old industries. Please note that the word *micro-* does not mean the industry is small. The product offering may be highly specialized but the market for the product can be huge. For example, the global micromarket for contract catering is $1.7 trillion, of which $160 billion is in the United States (Lehman Brothers report on Compass Group, August 4, 1997; International Foodservice Manufacturers Association Report, 1996; ERC Statistics, 1996).
4. *Automotive News Europe, Global Data Market Book,* 1997.
5. Note that not all newcomers into an industry are specialists. Integrators too, can become specialists if they are willing to spin off those businesses or pieces of the business they choose not to specialize in (preferably finding a better owner to source them from, at a lower price). Specialists need not specialize in only one

area—many companies such as the pharmaceutical giants are global specialists in multiple products.

6. Once midgame conditions are in place, the industry is already "in play," so moving quickly ahead of the competition becomes of far greater importance. Obviously in the faster-moving industries the need for speed increases.

7. Based on 1981 year-end results as reported by Compustat.

8. Hugh McColl's remarks at the BankAmerica–NationsBank merger press conference in New York City, April 13, 1998.

9. "Four opportunities in India's pharmaceutical market," by Rajesh Garg, Gautam Kunra, Asutosh Padhi, and Anupam Puri (*The McKinsey Quarterly,* 1996 No. 4, 132–145).

10. *Carry balances* are the amounts owed by credit card owners on which they pay interest monthly. They are paid off over time under the terms of a revolving credit agreement offered by the issuer.

11. See *Net Gain: Expanding Markets through Virtual Communities,* by John Hagel and Arthur Armstrong (Boston: Harvard Business School Press, 1997), for a complete discussion of webs and "virtual communities."

12. A *counterparty* is an arm's-length relationship of mutual benefit between two suppliers, defined by an enforceable contract.

Chapter 4: Keeping Control of Your Destiny

1. Comparing 1980 to 1992 versus 1992 to 1997, the French equity market grew by a compound annual growth rate of 10.5% and 14.1%, respectively, the U.K. by 10.6% and 16.5%, Germany by 8.1% and 18.9%, the U.S. by 5.6% and 19.0%, and Japan by 14.5% and −1.4% (International Finance Corporation; FIBV. Data is adjusted for inflation).

2. MSCI World Index 1992 to 1997 as reported by Morningstar. Refers to worldwide stock markets.

3. For a discussion of this point, see "Crash, dammit," *The Economist,* October 18, 1997, 13–14.

4. The most serious correction of the world's stock market of the last five years occurred in the summer of 1998, as investors came to

realize how difficult it would be for Asia and then Russia to overcome their economic malaise, and how interconnected the world's economy had become. However, for the reasons laid out in this chapter, we expect that future corrections of this sort will be of relatively short duration, barring an economic collapse so severe that it threatens the world's financial system. Readers interested in these issues are referred to *Market Unbound: Unleashing Global Capitalism*, by Lowell Bryan and Diana Farrell (New York: John Wiley & Sons, 1996), especially Chapters 5 and 7.

5. The description offered by Alan Greenspan, the Chairman of the U.S. Federal Reserve, December 5, 1996.

6. It should be noted that accounting changes that took effect in the early 1990s may have, to a limited extent, magnified the surge in market-to-book ratios. For example, Statement of Financial Accounting Standards No. 106, which was adopted around 1993, required companies to accrue post-retirement benefits during an employee's years of active service, rather than using "pay-as-you-go" methods after retirement. This change caused a slight reduction of book equity in the short term.

7. Data as of June 30, 1998, Global Vantage.

8. See McKinsey Global Institute report, "The Global Capital Market: Supply, Demand, Pricing, and Allocation" (November 1994). See also, for instance, *World Economic Outlook*, the quarterly issuance of DRI/McGraw-Hill, or the international database maintained by the U.S. Census Bureau.

9. Investment Company Institute (based on net new cash flow defined as new sales minus redemptions plus net exchanges).

10. It remains to be seen how much consumer fondness for equities, particularly in Europe, will be affected by major market corrections.

11. McKinsey Global Institute report, "The Global Capital Market: Supply, Demand, Pricing, and Allocation" (November 1994); Salomon Brothers report by Rosario Benavides, "How Big Is the World Debt Bond Market" (September 1997); McKinsey update of research in 1998.

12. Internal Revenue Service, *Statistics of Income Bulletin*, Vol. 17, No. 3 (Winter 1997–1998), Table 13 (Corporation Income Tax Returns, Balance Sheet, Income Statement, and Tax Items).

13. Internal Revenue Service, Corporation Source Book.

14. McKinsey Financial Institutions Group estimates.

15. McKinsey Global Institute, "The Global Capital Market" (1994).

16. McKinsey Global Institute, *Service Sector Productivity in Latin America.*

17. McKinsey Electronics Practice analysis based on annual revenues of the software industry and average life of software within each segment of the industry.

18. Skandia AFS has been a pioneer in intangible capital accounting, adding an *Intellectual Capital Annual Report* as a supplement to its annual financial report, starting in 1994. Its measurement and valuation methodologies are presented in *Intellectual Capital: Realizing Your Company's True Value by Finding Its Hidden Brainpower*, by Leif Edvinsson and Michael S. Malone (New York: HarperBusiness, 1997).

19. *LNA/Media Watch Advertising Summary*, January–December 1997 (New York: Competitive Media Reporting); National Science Foundation, National Patterns of R&D Resources, www.nsf.gov/sbe/srs/natpat97/start.htm#tables.

20. U.S. Bureau of Economic Analysis, *Survey of Current Business* (August 1998), NIPA Table 6.16C: Corporate Profits by Industry.

21. This has been an oft-echoed sentiment in recent years. For examples, see "Rest in Peace, Book Value," by Rich Karlgaard (*Forbes ASAP*, October 25, 1993, 9); or, more recently, "The Coins in the Knowledge Bank," by Thomas A. Stewart (*Fortune*, February 19, 1996, 101–102); "Challenges to the Current Accounting Model," by Robert Swieringa (*CPA Journal*, Vol. 67, No. 1, January 1997, 26–32); "The Old Rules No Longer Apply," by Baruch Lev (*Forbes ASAP*, April 7, 1997, 34–35).

22. A restructuring charge in 1993 was eliminated.

23. Capitalized R&D and advertising were depreciated over five years for this analysis.

24. The Hay Group, 1996.

25. The significance of the difference between the market and book value was observed many years ago by James Tobin, who noted that the ratio of the market value of a company's assets to their replacement cost, denoted q, offers a measure of their intangible

value. See "A general equilibrium approach to monetary theory," *Journal of Money, Credit and Banking*, Vol. 1 (February 1969): 15–29.

26. Karl Erik Sveiby, *The New Organizational Wealth: Managing and Measuring Knowledge-Based Assets* (San Francisco: Berrett-Koehler, 1997).

27. A number of authors have discussed the shortcomings of NPV in moderate- or high-uncertainty environments. A useful discussion of this issue can be found in Avinash K. Dixit and Robert S. Pindyck, "The options approach to capital investment" (*Harvard Business Review*, May–June 1995, 105–115) and in "How much is flexibility worth?" by Thomas E. Copeland and Philip T. Keenan (*The McKinsey Quarterly*, 1998 No. 2, 38–49).

28. "What is strategy?" by Michael Porter (*Harvard Business Review*, November–December 1996, 61–78).

29. Vijay D'Silva, Asheet Mehta, and Bill Fallon of McKinsey first developed this framework.

30. Each isoquant therefore represents a particular market capitalization and any point along an individual isoquant represents the same market capitalization.

31. GECC is part of GE and therefore does not appear on the strategic control map as a publicly quoted, independent entity.

32. All of these, except for C&S, were undertaken in just two years, 1997 and 1998, in one of the most spectacular series of mergers seen in any industry.

33. The capital markets, investment banking, and reinsurance businesses in financial services have developed significant global structures.

34. In Europe, continental-wide cross-border regional structures are being created; in the United States, these structures are also being created across the continent, but in this case within a single nation. Soon these issues will migrate to a global stage.

35. If a strategic control map for all of the telecom service providers in the world were shown, all players would be considered geographic incumbents since the service-providing industry is only now beginning to go beyond national borders. As we were completing this manuscript, there have been no major cross-border mergers of service providers, although AT&T and British Telecom

had formed a major joint venture to provide global service to large companies. Only a few players have begun to expand internationally—notably in Latin America.

5: The Nature of the Challenge

1. We undertook the interviews in 1996 before the enormous waves of mergers and acquisitions in 1997 and 1998. In informal discussions with some of the same companies in early 1998, strategic control issues, both offensive moves and defensive moves, were on everyone's mind.
2. Our findings were supported by a subsequent research effort by McKinsey into the talent constraint facing companies throughout the world. A summary of this work is found in "The war for talent," by Elizabeth Chambers, Mark Foulon, Helen Handfield-Jones, Steven Hankin, and Edward Michaels III (*The McKinsey Quarterly*, 1998 No. 3, 44–57).
3. *Against the Gods*, by Peter Bernstein (New York: John Wiley & Sons, 1996), p. 197. Peter Bernstein is an economic consultant to institutional investors. Bernstein's book pulls together, very effectively, the history of how our modern approaches to risk management evolved from the Greeks, through the invention of Arabic numbers, through Pascal, Fermat, Bernoulli, deMoivre, Bayes, Gauss, Galton, Keynes, and von Neumann.
4. Telefónica also acquired Telesp Celular, the largest cellular company in South America, in partnership with Iberdrola, and Tele Leste Celular, the cellular company in Bahía in northern Brazil, in partnership with Portugal Telecom.

6: A Strategy for the Transition Economy

1. "What is strategy?" by Michael Porter (*Harvard Business Review*, November–December 1996, 61–78).
2. A *global microindustry*, which will be elaborated on in Chapter 8, is a narrowly defined competitive arena (i.e., a value chain role, a product, or customer segment) dominated by a few competitors.

A global microindustry is usually part of a much larger broad-based industry (e.g., personal financial services, pharmaceuticals, electronics).

3. First MidStates is a fictional entity—a composite of nearly a dozen similar large superregional bank holding companies based in the United States. Banks such as Barnett and CoreStates, before they were acquired by NationsBank and First Union, respectively, faced a situation similar to First MidStates' except that they did not have nonbank businesses of equivalent size to that assumed for First MidStates. The strategies developed in this chapter do not reflect any actual client work by McKinsey. We developed the strategies described in this chapter by drawing on the knowledge of McKinsey's Financial Institutions Group.

4. In other words, just as disaggregation is one economic response to intense competition and overcapacity—by eliminating redundant capacity through specialization—consolidation is another response. Through consolidation, overcapacity is eliminated by taking out redundant capacity across the entire business system.

5. FDIC data for 1988 to 1998. As of second quarter 1998, over $25 trillion in assets were already held by the largest 200 commercial banks worldwide. However, trillions and trillions more are held by insurance companies, securities firms, and finance companies. The worldwide financial services industry remains extraordinarily fragmented with even very large players holding less than 2 percent share of the total.

6. Since 1989, HSBC has acquired seventeen banking subsidiaries at a cost of $10.7 billion. Subsequently, HSBC's market capitalization has grown from $13.8 billion in 1989 to $74.5 billion in 1998, some $50 billion in excess of acquired assets.

7. In just the first six months of 1998, Bank One agreed to acquire First Chicago NBD for $30 billion, Norwest agreed to acquire Wells Fargo for $34 billion, NationsBank agreed to acquire BankAmerica for $62 billion, and Travelers agreed to acquire Citicorp for $73 billion.

8. In 1997, the average market capitalization of the top 10 global institutions was $71 billion. Further, by extrapolation we estimate that by 2001, the average market capitalization of this group will be over $230 billion with pretax profits of $15 billion.

9. This assumes that the old First MidStates' shareholders would have

been issued sufficient stock at the time of the sale to make these numbers a fair exchange of value.

10. Securities Data Corporation Mergers & Acquisitions Database. The dollar figures reported reflect the value of disclosed transactions. Overall, there were 16,205 worldwide and 3,414 cross-border transactions recorded.

7: Building Intangible Capital

1. A number of books discuss the importance of intangibles in creating and sustaining a successful business endeavor. Besides those mentioned in Chapter 2 (*Mobilizing Invisible Assets*, by Hiroyuki Itami and Thomas W. Roehl [Cambridge, Mass.: Harvard University Press, 1987]); *Intellectual Capital: The New Wealth of Organizations*, by Thomas A. Stewart [New York: Doubleday/Currency, 1997]; *The New Organizational Wealth: Managing and Measuring Knowledge-Based Assets*, by Karl Erik Sveiby [San Francisco: Barrett-Koehler, 1997]; *Intellectual Capital: Realizing Your Company's True Value by Finding Its Hidden Brainpower*, by Leif Edvinsson and Michael S. Malone [New York: HarperBusiness, 1997]), see also *Intellectual Capital: Core Asset for the Third Millennium*, by Annie Brooking (London: International Thomson Business Press, 1996); *The Balanced Scorecard: Translating Strategy into Action*, by Robert S. Kaplan and David P. Norton (Boston: Harvard Business School Press, 1996); and *Intelligent Enterprise: A Knowledge and Service Based Paradigm for Industry*, by James Brian Quinn (New York: Free Press, 1992).

2. While we distinguish four classes of intangibles, the forms of intangible capital are often grouped in three basic categories, which roughly equate to (1) the skills and knowledge of a company's employees, (2) the internal structures that enhance efficiency and make knowledge internally available, and (3) the leverage that a company has with customers and suppliers. Sveiby, in *The New Organizational Wealth*, refers to these groups as employee competence, internal structure, and external structures; Edvinsson and Malone, in *Intellectual Capital*, talk in terms of human capital, structural capital, and customer capital.

3. Some, such as *The Fifth Discipline: The Art and Practice of the Learning Organization*, by Peter M. Senge (New York: Doubleday/Currency, 1994) discuss the mindset required to harvest a company's accumulated knowledge. Others, such as *Innovation Strategy for the Knowledge Economy*, by Debra Amidon (Boston: Butterworth-Heinemann, 1997) and *Wellsprings of Knowledge: Building and Sustaining the Sources of Innovation*, by Dorothy Leonard-Barton (Boston: Harvard Business School Press, 1997) discuss the ability of knowledge-flow to generate innovation. *Fifth-Generation Management: Co-Creating Through Virtual Enterprising, Dynamic Teaming, and Knowledge Networking*, by Charles M. Savage (Boston: Butterworth-Heinemann, 1996) and *The Virtual Corporation: Structuring and Revitalizing the Corporation for the 21st Century*, by William H. Davidow and Michael S. Malone (New York: HarperBusiness, 1992) discuss the use of technology to translate knowledge into operational efficiency. *The Knowledge Evolution: Expanding Organizational Intelligence*, by Verna Allee (Boston: Butterworth-Heinemann, 1997) warns against thinking of knowledge as a tangible object because it leads to an overly strong focus on databases and storage techniques.

4. A widely recognized concept in the literature on entrepreneurship. See *Intrapreneuring: Why You Don't Have to Leave the Corporation to Become an Entrepreneur*, by Gifford Pinchot (New York: HarperCollins, 1984).

5. *Networks and Organizations: Structure, Form, and Action*, edited by Nitin Nohria and Robert Eccles (Boston: Harvard Business School Press, 1992) provides a good overview of network theory for readers interested in the topic at the generic business level. For an in-depth discussion of how global corporations can themselves be organized as a network, we recommend *The Differentiated Network: Organizing Multinational Corporates for Value Creation*, by Nitin Nohria and Sumantra Ghoshal (San Francisco: Jossey-Bass Web, 1997). They demonstrate that the differentiated network model is the most effective approach to generating and exploiting innovations within a global company.

6. The increasing importance of strategic alliances between potential competitors has been discussed by a number of writers. *Co-opetition*, by Adam M. Brandenburger and Barry J. Nalebuff (New York:

Doubleday, 1996) discusses the use of competitive alliances to shape industries for mutual benefit. *Collaborating to Compete: Using Strategic Alliances and Acquisitions in the Global Marketplace,* edited by Joel Bleeke and David Ernst (New York: John Wiley & Sons, 1993), offers a compilation of essays on the potential benefits of cross-border alliances. *Strategic Alliances: Formation, Implementation and Evolution,* by Peter Lorange and Johan Roos (Oxford: Blackwell, 1992) offers a good overview of the various aspects of forming and managing strategic alliances, as does *Strategic Alliances: An Entrepreneurial Approach to Globalization,* by Michael Yoshino and U. Srinivasa Rangan (Boston: Harvard Business School Press, 1995).

7. In Chapter 8 we discuss customer-based relationships in more detail.

8. In June 1996, the Sabre Group became an independent legal entity. An IPO was conducted in October 1996, in which 18% of Sabre Group equity was sold with AMR retaining the remaining 82%.

9. Later in the chapter, we discuss three different kinds of alliances companies establish in order to operate "control, not own" strategies. The reader will note some overlap, but the differences come from the focus here on relationships and networks, and there on asset-light strategies.

10. See *Net Gain,* by Hagel and Armstrong (Boston: Harvard Business School Press, 1997) for a complete discussion of webs and "virtual communities."

11. For example, *Reputation: Realizing Value from the Corporate Image,* by Charles J. Fombrun (Boston: Harvard Business School Press, 1996) discusses the importance of shaping a unique identity and projecting a consistent positive image.

12. See "If Nike can 'just do it,' why can't we?" by David C. Court, Anthony Freeling, Mark G. Leiter, and Andrew J. Parsons (*The McKinsey Quarterly,* 1997 No. 3, 24–34).

13. "What's in a name? What the world's top brands are worth," by Alexandra Ourusoff, Michael Ozanian, Paul B. Brown, and Jason Starr (*Financial World,* September 1, 1992, 32–40, 45–49).

14. Nevertheless, most industries today remain largely underbranded as a result of their local, regulated status. Outside the United States and United Kingdom, there is almost no meaningful branding of

communication services because there has been no need to build brand loyalty in uncompetitive marketplaces. Utilities everywhere are unbranded commodity services. The brands in most personal financial services outside the United States are very weak. In most countries, the whole retail sector remains fragmented. In addition, the vast chunks of the economy represented by education and health care remain relatively anonymous because they reside largely in public sector hands. Over 80% of the world economy still awaits branding.

15. "Nestlé: The vision of local managers. An interview with Peter Brabeck-Metlathe," by Andrew J. Parsons (*The McKinsey Quarterly*, 1996 No. 2, 4–29).

16. See "Intel's Amazing Profit Machine" by David Kirkpatrick (*Fortune*, February 17, 1997, 60–72).

17. This way of thinking relates directly to the general idea discussed above and set out in detail in Chapter 8 on slivers—that companies should reconstruct themselves around the intangibles in their business system.

18. See Chapter 5.

19. At the end of this chapter, we follow the steps taken by Caterpillar to pass on the local, capital-intensive pieces of the business to their natural owners: well-connected local insiders. In this way, by acting in concert with the best owners of different pieces of the business system, a company can increase the size of the overall "profit pie," such that their share of the profits far exceeds those possible if they owned the entire business.

20. This work has been developed by our colleague David Ernst. "Coffee and one way to Boston," by Ernst and Thomas D. French (*The McKinsey Quarterly*, 1996 No. 1, 164–175) and "Alliances in upstream oil and gas," by Ernst and Andrew M. J. Steinhubl (*The McKinsey Quarterly*, 1997 No. 2, 144–155), discuss the benefits and dangers of strategic alliances in the context of service and energy industries, respectively.

21. IBM has long re-emphasized the value of its patent portfolio as a bargaining tool. "The IBM patent portfolio gains us the freedom to do what we need to do through cross-licensing—it gives us access to the inventions of others that are key to rapid innovation," explained Roger Smith, IBM assistant general counsel for

intellectual property, in a recent article directed at IBM researchers in the company's internal magazine, *Think*. As reported in the November 13, 1990, *Financial Times*.

22. Under twenty-three years of John Bryan's leadership, Sara Lee has operated almost under the cult of decentralization. Each year it challenges its business unit heads to achieve 12% growth in earnings and 15% ROIC. The manager is then essentially left alone to meet the numbers. Those that fail to hit the target for two years running typically leave the company. This approach proved successful in the 1980s in both the United States and Europe in integrating acquisitions into the company and enhancing their performance without making any major changes to the management team.

8: Winning the World Through Slivers

1. "The atomization of big oil," by Timothy Bleakley, David S. Gee, and Ron Hulme (*The McKinsey Quarterly*, 1997 No. 2, 122–142).
2. Microsoft's success in bundling office productivity tools to the corporate market is widely seen as a masterstroke that established its dominance of the PC software market beyond operating systems.
3. In the early 1980s and even before, Ken Olsen (DEC's founder) is said to have dismissed the business need for and usefulness of a PC—a misstep from which DEC never fully recovered. In a similar situation, Microsoft, which had been slow to catch the Internet wave, achieved a remarkable strategic and organizational refocus in record time once convinced of its value.
4. In terms of its implicit market capitalization.

9: Cross-Geographic Arbitrage

1. A *counterparty* is an arm's-length relationship of mutual benefit between two suppliers, defined by an enforceable contract.
2. It is difficult to put a precise number on this cost due to the lack of an equivalent industry structure in the United States. Estimates range from 15% to 30% higher. Even at the lower end of the

scale, the difference would be enough in a relatively low-margin business to be a significant competitive disadvantage.

3. In 1992, the capital productivity of the telecommunications industries in Brazil, Columbia, and Venezuela were 13%, 32%, and 21%, respectively, higher than that of the United States, excluding quality adjustments (McKinsey Global Institute). This was largely due to the advantages of being able to purchase all new equipment; in contrast to the United States, where there was a large installed base of old equipment.

4. The labor costs only 10% of what it would cost in Germany per hour. But it takes two hours to do in India what would take one hour in Germany, so you end up spending 20% of what you would have spent in Germany. $80\% = 1 - (10\%/50\%)$.

5. Daimler-Benz has also focused on particular niches such as the U.S. luxury car market. For example, the Mercedes M class sports utility vehicle, which is produced entirely in Tuscaloosa, Alabama, and is designed to compete against offerings such as Range Rover, has a base price of $34,000 and had a six-month-long backlog of orders at the end of 1997.

6. In reality, a friendly acquisition of Chrysler at a modest premium.

7. In the wake of the financial crisis in Southeast Asia, Japanese auto makers are boosting exports from their Southeast Asian plants, both through the addition of new capacity and the reallocation of existing capacity previously used to supply the local market. Toyota's Thailand plants have begun exporting trucks to Australia and New Zealand, which used to come from Japan; Nissan plans a plant in Indonesia from which it will export engines and parts; and Mitsubishi is increasing exports from all of its Asian plants.

10: Strategy Once More

1. See Chapter 11, "Shaping the Future."

2. In other words, since the opportunity being pursued has the potential to generate huge returns and profit streams, the talent team faces relatively few limits to growth, provided it can successfully convert the potential opportunity into a real business and profit stream. Were the team in a business unit, its ability to

grow would most likely be restricted by the other demands placed on the unit.

3. *Well compensated* here refers to a reward for success along the lines of a small equity holder in the business. The nonpecuniary reward would entail the chance to continue to grow the opportunity into a core business (and the prospect of leading a core business unit, if successful).

4. Many competitive entrepreneurs are simply playing copycat. They combine their local knowledge with someone else's business concept. In Spain, many branded spirits—Gordon's, Baileys, Smirnoff—appear in slight variation, and always at a slight discount, on the shelves of the local supermarket. Louis Vuitton–lookalike bags are dotted around Beijing. It is not only products that are copied, legally or illegally, but also service concepts, cultures, manufacturing processes, and operating systems. In Brazil, a domestic airline, TAM, has copied the service principles of Southwest Airlines. Many U.S. and German auto manufacturers copied Japanese production techniques. There is a lesson here. If you do not globalize your product or concept globally, someone else will. They will take their assets, find investors, and use your ideas to make money.

5. While Monsanto did not use an approach exactly like the one we have described, it is close enough to illustrate the power of talent teams.

6. Skandia has tried something similar to this, as we discussed in Chapter 7.

7. All the First Global Credit global value propositions were developed through internal McKinsey analysis and do not reflect any actual work undertaken for any client.

8. We would like to give credit to our colleagues, Brad Fried and Jim Rosenthal, who originally developed the First Global Credit case and the data mining example.

9. Chapter 6.

10. Chapter 7.

11: Shaping the Future

1. The strategist Russell Ackoff once wrote that there are no such

things as business problems. Consultants, he said, invented problems. Managers face "messes." Risk management attempts to disentangle these "messes." ("The future of operational research is past," *Journal of Operational Research Society*, Vol. 30, No. 2 [1979]: 90–100.)

2. Harry Markowitz first laid out the principles and benefits of diversified portfolios in the article "Portfolio selection" (*Journal of Finance* Vol. 7 [1952]: pp. 77–91).

3. A call option has unlimited potential returns, but the returns on a put option are limited because prices cannot usually fall below zero.

4. This discussion of GE Capital is based on the work of the McKinsey Growth Initiative and interviews and also draws from "If Europe's dead, why is GE investing billions there?" (*Fortune*, September 9, 1996, 114–118).

5. By "self-contained" we mean with individual P&Ls, organizational structures, resources, and management. This self-containment enables GE to ensure its businesses are transparent and highly focused—with the resultant specialization effects—on a stand-alone basis. It is therefore much easier to ensure competitiveness and to manage the various businesses differently through, for example, tailored performance measures or compensation structures linked directly to the performance of each management team. The trick that GE appears to have mastered is to generate much of the necessary sharing of intangibles between businesses—access to relationships, knowledge of markets—without losing the benefits of self-containment.

6. For example, many of the companies we surveyed (see Chapter 5) talked of the difficulties in balancing the focus on future, potential markets versus today's core markets. Other challenges included managing different paybacks and timeframes and differentiating compensation for growth versus steady-state businesses. Self-containment enables far greater tailoring of compensation, budgets, and performance measures.

7. This discussion is based on McKinsey interviews supplemented by information from public sources.

8. By *adverse selection* we refer to the circumstance in which a company ends up with the least attractive set of customers,

employees, or suppliers because the most attractive ones select competitors who offer a more appealing value proposition. This typically occurs when a company "sticks to its knitting" and fails to adapt to rising standards in its particular market (be it for attracting talent, customers, etc.).

INDEX

ABB, 8, 13

ABN-AMRO, 160

Accounting industry, global markets in, 4, 45, 48, 52–53

Accounting practices
using market-to-book ratio in, 112–113, 323–324n. 25
using net present value in, 113–116, 234n. 27
in valuing company assets, 108–112

Acer, 189

Ackoff, Russell, 37, 333–334n. 1

Acquisitions
for becoming shapers, 173–175
in growing market capitalization, 118

in financial services industry, 121, 122, 124, 126, 160, 162, 166
of integrators, 70–71, 74–75, 76
midgame strategies in, 67–69, 90
of specialists, 71–72, 74–75, 76
virtuous cycles of geographic expansion in, 77–80
See also Mergers; Partnerships

Active agent, 9, 312n. 7

ADP, 72

Adverse selection, 296, 334–335n. 8

Aerospace industry, midgame strategies in, 90. *See also* Aircraft industry

ABOUT THE AUTHORS

Lowell Bryan joined McKinsey in 1975. He leads the Global Financial Institutions practice. He has written several books on the banking industry, including *Bankrupt: Restoring the Health and Profitability of Our Banking System* (1991) and *Market Unbound: Unleashing Global Capitalism* (1996). Lowell earned a B.A. from Davidson College in 1968 and an M.B.A., with distinction, from the Harvard Business School in 1970.

Jane Fraser has worked with the company since 1994, focusing on serving financial institutions in North America, Europe, Latin America, and Asia on their global strategic issues. Born and raised in Scotland, she holds an MA in Economics from Girton College, Cambridge, and an M.B.A., with distinction, from the Harvard Business School. Prior to joining McKinsey, Jane worked for Goldman, Sachs in the United Kingdom and for Asesores Bursatiles in Spain.

Jeremy Oppenheim works in McKinsey's London Office and is a European leader of McKinsey's globalization practice. His work focuses on how corporations are reorganizing to capture the next wave of global opportunities. Jeremy holds an MA in Law and Economics from Trinity College, Cambridge, and an M.P.A. from the Kennedy School of Government. He worked as a senior economist for five years with the World Bank prior to joining McKinsey.

Wilhelm Rall joined McKinsey in Düsseldorf in 1977 and has worked in Europe, the United States, Mexico, and Japan. He is the head of the Stuttgart office and leads much of McKinsey's strategic, organizational, and operational work in the life sciences, chemicals, electronics, and automotive industries. Prior to joining McKinsey, Wilhelm was an Assistant Professor in Economics at the University of Tübingen.